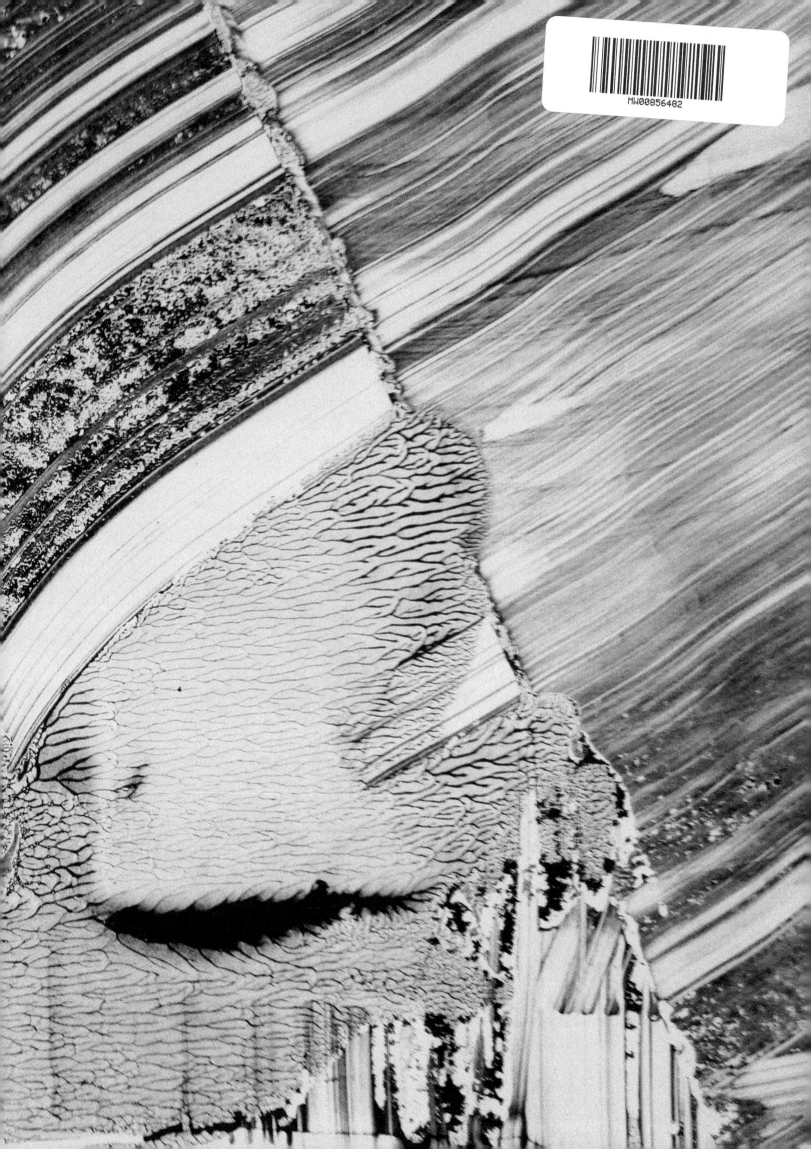

W

K

W

W
K
W

THE CINEMA OF
WONG KAR WAI

WONG KAR WAI   JOHN POWERS

RIZZOLI
NEW YORK

New York Paris London Milan

CONTENTS

PERHAPS
PER

37 VIEWS OF

JOHN

PERHAPS,

IAPS

ONG KAR WAI

WERS

1 When Wong Kar Wai and I first meet to discuss this book at the Four Seasons Hotel in Beverly Hills, the contemporary movie world's equivalent of the Café de Flor, I suggest that its style needs to be a reflection of him, not of me. After all, his millions of fans are fascinated by the man behind, and within, the movies they love. They want to know who he is—and how he thinks.

He gives the tiniest of winces. Unwaveringly polite and usually affable, Wong is not a man eager to reveal himself outside his art. Baring his soul is not his bag.

"But you," he replies, "are the writer."

"And you are the famous director who readers want to get close to. So it's your decision. What kind of book should it be?"

"It can't be boring," he says emphatically. Nor should it be aimed at film experts. He dreads the idea of endless lines of text marching across page after page like ranks of army ants.

I can only agree, but I still need more direction. Although we know what we *don't* want the book to be, what kind of book *do* we want?

"How are we going to structure this damn thing," I say, "so it will reveal the mind of Wong Kar Wai?"

"That's the wrong question," he says. "What you need to ask yourself is this. Should the book be like a menu, a GPS, or a jukebox?"

2 There are many good filmmakers in the world but only a handful—including Jean-Luc Godard, David Lynch, Abbas Kiarostami, and Hou Hsiao-hsien possess a sensibility so strong that their name immediately conjures up a whole way of seeing. Wong Kar Wai belongs to that rarefied company. One can instantly recognize his films by their rootless heroes grappling with love and loneliness, their ticking clocks and restless bodies, their refracted, fashion-shoot surfaces and deep-seated melancholy, their warping of genres and blurring of the line between reality and dream. All this led *Time*'s estimable Richard Corliss to anoint Wong "the most romantic filmmaker in the world." Seemingly incapable of shooting an ugly frame—and as interested in female characters as he is in men—he may be the living filmmaker who best understands glamour.

He's also one of the most consistently rewarding. Beginning with his 1988 debut, *As Tears Go By*, Wong has made ten features, a body of work that ranks among the defining cinematic achievements of the last quarter century. His best films (*Days of Being Wild, Chungking Express, Ashes of Time, Happy Together, In the Mood for Love*, and *2046*) are triumphs, while three more (*As Tears Go By, Fallen Angels*, and *The Grandmaster*) are uncommonly fine films with dazzling sections. They're also a pleasure to watch. Not dauntingly grave like such film festival confreres as Bela Tarr, Nuri Bilge Ceylan, or the Austrian buzzkill Michael Haneke, Wong is a serious director who's hard to catch in the act of being serious.

Over the years, he has won scads of accolades, including Best Director at the 1997 Cannes Film Festival where he later became the first Chinese person ever to head the jury, and the Commander of the Order of Arts and Letters from the French Minister of Culture; his awards from Asia are legion. Yet his true importance is revealed less by official honors and critical hosannas than by the way his work affects those who watch it. People don't merely like his movies. They get a mad crush on them. (In Japan, they buy special chapbooks celebrating their arrival.) Wong's work doesn't simply exhilarate his fans—I vividly remember my own shivers of delight the first time I saw *Chungking Express*—it excites other filmmakers as well. He's the director countless young directors want to be. Boasting a style so strong that it sometimes flirts with self-parody, his work has been echoed, copied, strip-mined. You can spot his influence in everything from movies like Sofia Coppola's *Lost in Translation* to TV shows like *Mad Men* (whose creator, Matthew Weiner, is an aficionado) to innumerable commercials around the world. His work has shifted the visual terrain.

As if this weren't enough, Wong is one of those artists who comes wreathed in mythology. It's not simply that, like Haruki Murakami (whom he admires), he bridges East and West or that he's reckoned to be one of cinema's great avatars of Cool, whose omnipresent sunglasses are at once a trademark and key signature. His methods themselves have become the stuff of legend, rumor, and gossip. The topics are legion: How Wong reinvents his style from movie to movie. How he announces projects then never does them. How he casts huge stars who then barely appear in the final cut. How he shoots for months, sometimes years, attempting to "find" a story. How he's been known to make a second movie while still finishing an earlier one. How his financial backers keep pulling their hair out. How his movies never get completed on time—notoriously, Cannes had to postpone the premiere screening of *2046* because the print wasn't ready—and even when done aren't actually complete. They exist in many different versions, only a few of them definitive, and some of those subject to conspiracy theories worthy of Thomas Pynchon. All of this has made Wong famous—and mysterious.

3 Wong Kar Wai stands a bit over six feet, four inches above the Hong Kong average, with firm skin and close-cropped black hair that make him look younger than a man in his mid-fifties. His nose is wide, as is his mouth, though the latter has lost the moist hint of sensuality you find in photos of him as a youth. When he smiles, which is often, there's something ever so slightly askew about his front teeth that makes him seem friendly. His eyes are intent behind the clear, horn-rim-topped spectacles that he wears in his daily life—at home, at work, out with friends. When he dons his trademark sunglasses, it's like a cop strapping on his holster. He is On Duty.

Although his work is renowned, and sometimes assailed, for being fashionable—why else would the Metropolitan Museum ask him to be artistic director of the Costume Institute's hit 2015 show, *China: Through the Looking Glass*?—Wong Kar Wai is himself no dandy. Unlike, say, David Lynch or Wes Anderson, he has no *look*. He favors white Gap shirts with blue pinstripes (he owns several) and long-sleeve polo-shirts, both of which he wears outside his jeans; for a photo shoot, he may switch to a navy blue shirt, or put on a black Moncler jacket, but this owes less to his need to be stylish than his awareness that white shirts are hard to photograph. He will wear black tie if decorum requires it, as at Cannes—to do otherwise would be a rude and fatuous gesture—but his preferred mode is casual.

Even his humor is tossed off. Neither a born raconteur nor a Wildean epigram machine, he engages in genial joshing and makes odd, whimsical remarks. I was visiting the office of his company, Jet Tone, a few weeks before it moved across town from the 21st floor of the Park Commercial Building in Causeway Bay where it had been for the last ten years. When his friend and "little brother" Norman Wang came to tell us that nobody could get their WiFi to work, Wong shrugged.

"The office can tell we're leaving," he said. "It's unhappy."

It's not for nothing that in *Chungking Express* a policeman talks to his bar of soap about its romantic sadness.

At work, Wong cultivates a reassuring air of centered calm, one slightly misleading in a man whose habit of putting things off—he's the Usain Bolt of delay—suggests that something inside him craves the intensity of on-rushing deadlines. He feels the pressure sharpens him, brings out his best. "I like drama," he says with the matter-of-fact air of one who doesn't actually like things to be matter of fact. Although he's neither nasty nor angry like so many famous directors, his amused benevolence is often at war with a keen impatience. He is, in fact, a striking blend of the coiled and the slack, the focused and inattentive, the control-freak and the connoisseur of chaos. When headed to a specific destination—to a Cannes press conference, for example, or up Tung Lo Wan Road for lunch at Classified restaurant—he takes long purposeful strides. But in the Jet Tone offices, his rhythm is slow, almost shambling. He often appears to be drifting from room to room. Yet it would be a mistake to think he's idling. Like his films, Wong drifts with intent.

A night owl by inclination and habit—there's a reason so many of his films are shot after dark—Wong keeps late hours but nearly always stays at home. Nobody is quite sure what he does there; perhaps his wife, Esther, knows. Intensely private, he carouses far less than when I first met him. No smoking, less drinking. Still, when a visitor's in town, he plays the host, often unwinding with his informal posse of friends and colleagues at Juliette's Wine Bar, a local filmmakers' hangout near his old Causeway Bay office, where he presides over the corner table in a role halfway between boss and big brother. Lounging back in the corner banquette, long legs stretched under the table, he'll tease Wang about his outfit (unlike Wong, Norman *does* adopt a weekly look), talk about what's going on in Hollywood—year in, year out, he asks me about Scorsese—or pass on a little gossip about some director in the People's Republic. Henry James described a novelist as one on whom nothing is lost, and Wong has that quality—he's always taking things in. Even when he's among pals or with a writer like me who's registering his every word, you nearly always sense distance; some important corner of his head is somewhere else. Perhaps he would rather be reading. The walls of his office are lined with books that have worn, in-curving spines. I once mentioned that I was fond of Stephen Frears's neglected film *Gumshoe*. "I like it too," he said, and walking to the shelf, pulled out his obviously-read copy of the novel it was based on.

In the summer of 2014, we met in New York where he'd come to discuss the China show at the Met. I asked how he'd been spending his time.

"In the office," he said.

"Doing what?" I asked.

"Doing nothing."

At the time he was working on a 3D version of *The Grandmaster*, preparing to produce a film in Shanghai, collaborating on a TV series with a Hollywood screenwriter, meeting with the Costume Institute about the China show, and trying to put together a deal for his own next film. To him, all this amounted to doing nothing. Wong only becomes the man he wants to be when making a movie.

4 If any first shot ever revealed a filmmaker's sensibility, it would be the beginning of Wong Kar Wai's 1988 debut, *As Tears Go By*. The screen is divided in half. To the left and beneath, we see a city street with people walking along sidewalks, cars and buses gliding by; to the right is a bank of aqua-blue TV monitors that, atop broadcast images of moving clouds, reflect the streets down below. With this single shot, wholly unnecessary to the action—and serving as a kind of cosmic reference point—Wong alerts us that his work is neither simple nor naïve: He's consciously dealing with *images*. Casually post-modern, this shot puts us, and the movie, at the porous intersection of life and its myriad media-saturated and memory-laced reflections. His work has remained at this intersection ever since, erecting increasingly large and fascinating constructions around it.

5 *As Tears Go By* is Wong Kar Wai's purest foray into Hong Kong filmmaking, yet it is no less distinctive for that. Based on the second of a trilogy of crime movies Wong conceived with his filmmaking comrade, Patrick Tam, the movie was designed to capitalize on the zeitgesty success of John Woo's great gangster picture *A Better Tomorrow*, one of the cinematic touchstones of '80s Hong Kong. Yet, tellingly, its deeper inspiration came from abroad. The relationship between two small-time hoods, Wah and Fly, bears the fingerprints of its most obvious influence, Harvey Keitel and Robert DeNiro in Martin Scorsese's seminal *Mean Streets*.

Andy Lau stars as Wah, a respected small-time Triad (gang) member, who secretly yearns to get out of the life. But he's constantly forced to bail out his crazy-ass friend Fly (Jacky Cheung), whose volatile blend of braggadocio and ressentiment are worthy of Dostoevsky's Underground Man. Meanwhile, Wah is falling for his sweet cousin, Ngor (Maggie Cheung), a waitress from Lantau Island who embodies the clean life he craves but is doomed never to have. His brotherly feelings for Fly will inexorably take him down. And why is this inexorable? Partly because Wah's character is his fate—his capacity for fraternal feeling is, in Triad terms, a weakness—but also because his story lies at the crossroads of character and pop myth hinted at in the film's opening shot. We've all seen enough movies to understand that it's not only Wah's choices that get him killed but also the ruthless logic of pulp fiction.

In the genre's terms, *As Tears Go By* is a clear success, a judgment certified by no less a maven than Quentin Tarantino who once told me that he admired it so much he told Harvey Weinstein that he ought to distribute it. (He didn't). No matter. The movie rightly became a Hong Kong hit, remaining Wong's biggest success in his hometown until *The Grandmaster* 25 years later. It's easy to understand its popularity. Wong gets the emotions right. We feel their vividness, from Fly's passionate and foolish desire to be reckoned a big man to the devoured look

in Lau's eyes as Wah dies. From the beginning, Wong knew how to get the best from actors, and here he neatly plays Lau's familiar knife-edge blankness against the soulful sweetness of Maggie Cheung, in whom he finds a depth and talent no other director had previously noticed—this is the film that got her taken seriously as an actress. The whole movie is energized by the almost hysterical volatility of Cheung's Fly, who, channeling DeNiro with startling prowess and passion, gives the most histrionic, most Method performance in the entire Wong oeuvre.

Mean Streets was Scorsese's fantasy about the life he witnessed as a small, asthmatic kid looking out of his apartment window in Little Italy—the scary, dangerous, and exciting life down below. *As Tears Go By* takes place not far from the mean streets of Kowloon where as a boy, Wong says, he saw ladies of the evening bring home American sailors. I ask him if, like Scorsese, he had watched—and maybe daydreamed about—the tough guys on the streets. Was this one of his inspirations for *As Tears Go By*?

"No," he says with a look of startled amusement. *Where do you critics get your silly ideas?*

6 The Western title, *As Tears Go By,* comes, of course, from the song of the same name by the Rolling Stones. Although evocative enough, it lacks the layered, East-meets-West specificity of the original Cantonese title, *Wang jiao kamen*, or *Mongkok Carmen*, which both places the story in a particular district of Kowloon, and, by alluding to Bizet's opera (itself drawn from the novella by Mérimée), points to what makes the film different from other gangster yarns. Finding his story's true center in Wah's ill-fated passion for Ngor, Wong bends the crime genre to make room for a romantic tale.

At the time, it may have looked as if Wong was simply trying to find a way of sprucing up a gangster story in a decade stuffed with them. In fact, he was already pursuing the great, even inescapable, theme to which he returns in every single film: romantic longing, and more profoundly, romantic loss. Wong's is a universe of missed chances, failed connections, subway cars passing in the night. Young or old, married or single, straight or gay, his characters all discover what Leonard Cohen sang—there ain't no cure for love. It could be a title of this book.

Given Wong's obsessive return to this theme, one might think him an artist who's suffered from romantic woe—you know, Edgar Allan Poe mourning the death of his child bride, Virginia, F. Scott Fitzgerald riding the stormy emotional seas with Zelda, or Woody Allen feeling whatever it is he feels with women. In reality, Wong is the exception that proves the rule of his films. He has long been happily married to his wife, Esther, and has a son, Qing, currently a science student at the University of California in Berkeley. They've been together since they met selling jeans at a Kowloon shop. He was 19. She was 17. That was almost 40 years ago.

"I'm curious," I once asked him. "How come you never stop making unhappy love stories? Yours is happy."

He pauses to think.

"Maybe *because* mine is happy," he eventually says. "It's always more interesting to think about the life you *aren't* living. It excites your imagination.

7 You can't fully understand Wong Kar Wai without seeing him with his wife, Esther, born Chan Ye-chang, a small, attractive Shanghainese woman who possesses an admirable forthrightness and, like her husband, a keen awareness of those around her. We had met many times before, but the first time I saw her in Hong Kong to begin the interviews for this book, she immediately said, "It's good to see you smiling. The last time we met you looked so unhappy, I thought you were going to tell us bad news." In fact, I had been annoyed because that night I'd driven an hour to Wong's hotel in Beverly Hills only to have him turn up 40 minutes late for a meeting for which he'd chosen the time. I wondered what time-devouring vortex I was getting sucked into writing a book with a fabled procrastinator. I suspect Esther might know the answer to that better than anyone.

The two have been together nearly four decades, and when Wong's not shooting or at the office, he's most likely at home with Esther whom he feels he's neglected while off making movies. Watching them in action, you sense that each finds a sense of stability in the other. They share a lovely rapport, Wong attending to her needs with almost chivalric attention, Esther teasingly bickering with him about little things nobody else cares about. Still, such is her loyalty that when I asked her to name her favorite Wong Kar Wai film, she promptly replied, "*The Grandmaster*," which any filmmaker would tell you is the correct answer. You're always supposed to love their last one most.

The way they got together sounds like a scene from an imaginary Wong Kar Wai film set in 1970s Kowloon. They had summer jobs at the same jeans store. After working side by side for 10 hours every day, both realized they were drawn to the other, yet nothing happened. Esther kept hoping he would ask for her phone number—she was too proud to offer it—but Wong kept frustrating her hopes. Even then, he was a delayer. Then on the last day of working together, he finally asked.

"You can have the number," she told him, "but it's six digits and I'm only giving you five. If you want to call me you need to try." She badly wanted him to call but he made her wait three full days. When she asked, he told her that he'd had to try three different numbers to get her.

"At least he made some effort," she says with a laugh. "And he used that idea for the scene in *As Tears Go By* when Maggie Cheung hides one of Andy Lau's glasses."

Although a couple, they wouldn't get married until more than a decade later, once he'd finished that first film. "We decided to get married after it," he says. "We registered to get married even before the shooting and had the wedding in New York after the film was done. She went on to New York to prep the wedding while I worked on post-production. After the film was released, I flew to the States and the next day we had the wedding at her dad's house in New Jersey. We had the party by the water next to the house. It was truly a wonderful moment in my life."

By then Esther had finally seen the film that she'd spent all those years waiting for Wong to make. She caught it at the Rosemary Theater in Chinatown, the same cinema where, a few years later, Quentin Tarantino would take Harvey Weinstein and Uma Thurman to watch *Chungking Express*. "I guess that place gave its blessing to the film," Wong says. "I was sad when the owner finally decided to close it down."

For her part, Esther tells me that Wong has barely changed over the years. He's still kind and preternaturally calm. And through it all—the protracted film shoots, the scary flops and exhilarating hits, the work raising their son, Qing—she has been at once his anchor and his buoy. In the summer of 2013, Wong told me that he was thinking of quitting filmmaking, in part because, with Qing far away at college, he wanted to spend more time with Esther. He knew she wanted it. When I mentioned this to her a year later, she smiled. "That was *then*," she said. "Every minute is changing."

8   *As Tears Go By* was accomplished enough that, had he chosen to continue in this highly commercial vein, we might now know a very different Wong Kar Wai. One can picture him in '90s Hollywood alongside such Hong Kong compatriots as John Woo, Jackie Chan, and Peter Ho-sun Chan, making bigger, more expensive, and vastly duller work—*Tribeca Express*! *In the Mood for Guns*!—with the likes of Keanu Reeves and Winona Ryder (he's always liked pretty actors), and then returning to a post-handover Hong Kong whose film industry, like the rest of the city and soon the world, would have its eyes turned toward the Chinese mainland.

But of course he didn't do that. *As Tears Go By* shows him already seeking to transcend the formulaic constraints of the gangster movie. Not only did he make it in the unconventional way that would become his norm and perhaps his curse, writing the script each day as he went along, but he flaunted a striking level of stylistic invention. Although committed to a certain level of gritty verisimilitude in its portrait of this milieu—these are the least stylishly dressed stars in any of Wong's films—he keeps pushing away from realism. He floods scenes with blues and reds, a visual play of cool and warm, the screen growing redder during moments of violent feelings. He plays out Wah's visit to Ngor on Lantau Island as a long, frankly kitschy but still compelling music-video scene to a Canto-pop version of "Take My Breath Away," the song Tony Scott had used as the love theme in *Top Gun* two years earlier. Most originally, he filmed his action sequences in a manner far different to the fast, visceral, hyper-explicit work of Woo. Shooting at 12 frames per second and then stretching things out by double-printing, he turned routine brawls into street-fight Impressionism. With each punch and leap leaving the kind of luminous trails you see while on LSD, the action became a poetic blur. "Kar Wai *loves* blurry," laughs William Chang, Wong's longstanding designer, costumer, and editor.

Wong's ambition was as clear as his fight scenes were blurred. Although he couldn't slip the bonds of the gangster film any more than Wah could escape the gangster life, you could already sense that he wanted to take genre material and explode it like fireworks. From that opening shot of the monitors to its unsettlingly stylized vision of Wah's death, you can feel him pushing beyond the givens of Hong Kong commercial cinema and starting to transform himself into his true artistic self, the filmmaker who signs himself WKW.

"How ambitious were you back then?" I once asked him.

"I wanted," he said, "to be one of the greatest filmmakers in the world."

9 In the years following the heyday of the late '50s and '60s New Waves—which saw the rise of filmmakers such as Antonioni, Resnais, Godard, and Oshima, all of whom played with our ideas of narrative—both filmmakers and their audience lost much of their ambition. Movies returned to what they'd been before—basically, a delivery system for stories. But telling stories as such has never particularly interested Wong Kar Wai, which is clear from both his filmmaking process and his finished work.

On the very first day of shooting *As Tears Go By*, Wong discovered an important truth about himself: He isn't one of those directors who can work with a finished script and a clearly planned out shooting agenda. Instead, he adopted the practice that he's followed ever since. Beginning with the framework of a story—quite detailed in the case of *As Tears Go By*, virtually nonexistent in, say, *Happy Together*—he writes each film's script as he goes along, day by day, often changing the storyline as he spots potential narrative developments, discovers unexpected qualities in the actors, or simply compensates for earlier problems. "I want you to watch all the extras," he once told me about the excised scenes included on the DVDs of his work, "so you can see all the possibilities, all the different ways a film could go." You can imagine Alfred Hitchcock or Robert Bresson tearing out their hair at Wong's deliberate lack of planning, his willingness to make things up as he goes along.

In fact, Wong's approach matches his sensibility. His movies aren't about tackling social themes, exploring intellectual ideas, analyzing characters' psyches, or doing the other straightforward, easily explainable things that most films do. He seems to have taken to heart Godard's epigram that every film has a beginning, middle, and end, but not necessarily in that order. His movies are not so much plotted as *patterned*; they're organized poetically. They're about moods and images, about seeing things on the angle. His mind runs to episodes, fractured time-frames, teasing coincidences, shifting viewpoints, and a reflexive binarism. His work is a parade of romantic couples, characters with double identities (most baldly, Brigitte Lin's split personality in *Ashes of Time*), or actors playing characters who seem like a version of an earlier role they've played. *Chungking Express* and *Fallen Angels* aren't merely narrative diptychs, but together they also form a larger diptych.

Wong's films aren't "difficult," as people used to say of Godard or Antonioni, but they can be elusive. While they often appear to be telling a simple story, their meaning resides less in so-called drama than in resonant images, aureoles of emotion, privileged moments—a woman bumping into a stranger on the street, the spray from a waterfall falling on a man's face, a martial arts master catching a young woman falling from a staircase. Like Virginia Woolf, Wong rides the waves of time, forever hoping to capture revelations, however seemingly small, that are rich enough to push beyond the stuff of daily life and strong enough to linger in the memory.

Not that his work is precious. As a boy, Wong Kar Wai went to the movies every day with his mother, a cinematic omnivore who favored the larger-than-life stories made by Hollywood and the Shaw Brothers—seeing *Dr. Zhivago* still resonates in his memory. This experience formed his taste, showing him the kind of films that he would eventually want to make, films that conjure a world grander and more enchanted than the one outside the theater doors. He rebels against the suggestion that he makes art films, a phrase redolent of film festival marginality and dusty art-houses frequented by geriatrics who wish the world was still making *Jules and Jim*. It's not that Wong doesn't want his work to be artful, of course, but he never sets out to make something difficult, highfalutin, or aimed at the cinephile audience. He thinks movies should be *glamorous*.

10

Wong Kar Wai is known as a Hong Kong director, which is at once accurate and misleading. Although he grew up in that city, he's not fully of its culture. He was born in Shanghai, where he spoke Shanghainese, only moving to Cantonese-speaking Hong Kong with his parents in 1963 at the age of five (his elder siblings were left behind), an early dislocation that helps explain his characters' air of solitude and rootlessness. Except for working trips, Wong has lived in Hong Kong ever since, but his sensibility is rooted in that city's Shanghainese subculture, known for its obliqueness, refinement, showiness, *shushy*-sounding dialect, and general sense of superiority to southern Chinese vulgarity. To this day, he's a member of the Kiangsu Chekiang and Shanghai Residents (HK) Association, which primarily caters to those whose roots are in Shanghai. He feels those roots intensely. When he talks about his '60s childhood in this community, he gets happily excited. Memories of a boyhood that he describes as Fellini-esque stir something deep in him, which accounts for the care and passion with which he evokes that milieu in his loose trilogy of films: *Days of Being Wild*, *In the Mood for Love*, and *2046*.

At the same time, it's impossible to imagine Wong without the noise, brashness, and full-throttle vibrancy that is Hong Kong. While his calm, carefully modulated personal style seems less an expression of Hong Kong than a carapace against it—not for him bustling mannerisms or loud, honking Cantonese—Wong's work is infused with the city's jittery rhythms, sleepless energy, and air of infinite transcience. This isn't to say that if you go to Hong Kong you'll find the city depicted in his films. You can still find some of the locations—and even ride the marvelous outdoor escalator in Central—but the Midnight Express snack bar in *Chungking Express* is now a 7-Eleven and *In the Mood for Love*'s Goldfinch Restaurant seems on the verge of shutting down. Yet even if these cinematic landmarks remained, you could not visit the city in Wong's films. His Hong Kong is not a documentary record but what you might expect of a man who came upon the city as a child—a brilliantly-wrought dreamscape, a luminous city of the mind that transfigures its dinky apartments, noodle shops, crowded markets, and roaring metro cars. These places are only magical when Wong puts them on screen. Calvino once wrote that the things he finds most real are the ones he invented. The same is true of Wong Kar Wai's Hong Kong.

11

Wong Kar Wai's first truly personal work, *Days of Being Wild* (1990) is a story of aimless, disaffected youth—its Chinese title was the same one given to *Rebel Without a Cause*. Evoking the Shanghainese community of Wong's own childhood (it's not for nothing that the score includes music from *Amarcord*), the film conjures up the past as a gorgeous, somewhat decadent hallucination that often feels as elusive as a ghost story. Set in an earily depopulated early '60s Hong Kong, the action centers on Yuddy, a narcissistic playboy played by Leslie Cheung, an actor whose alluring beauty always carries with it a hint of weakness, even treachery; he's like a perfect fruit in which one can always sense the imminence of spoilage. Yuddy uses his good looks to conquer, then shatter, women's hearts. He starts with Su Li-zhen (Maggie Cheung), a sweet snack bar counter-girl whom he asks to look at his watch for one minute. When she does, he tells her, "I'll always remember that one minute because of you." From that moment on, she's toast. He toys with her then moves on to Lulu, *aka* Mimi (Carina Lau), a cabaret dancer as emotionally flamboyant as Li-zhen is quiet. Even as Yuddy throws away women's love with casual cruelty, others around him pine for it. His lifelong buddy Zeb (Jacky Cheung) is hopelessly mad for Lulu, while a cop (Andy Lau) aids Li-zhen in a moment of her distress then longs for a romantic encounter with her that never comes.

None of this matters to Yuddy, whose life appears to confirm Robert Musil's oracular line that most of us spend the greatest part of our lives in the shadow of an event that hasn't yet taken place. In Yuddy's case, that event is a reunion with the birth mother who abandoned him. Drowning in photogenic angst worthy of James Dean, he spends his non-womanizing hours fighting with his scarily manipulative auntie, Rebecca, played by the indelible Shanghainese singer and actress Rebecca Pan. She's a one-time courtesan who mothers him, smothers him, and withholds the whereabouts of his real mom. Yuddy's quest for his biological mother leads him to the Philippines—a potential home where he does not feel at home—and to his doom.

Although *Days of Being Wild* owes something to the so-called *ah fei* genre of films about troubled and troublemaking youth, it moves in a new, more audacious direction, offering no easy moral points about "kids today." It's the work of a cosmopolitan filmmaker who's been fruitfully influenced by everyone from directors such as Antonioni and Bertolucci, to the Argentine novelist Manuel Puig, who taught him the possibilities of telling fragmented stories from multiple points of view. Indeed, as critic Stephen Teo definitively shows in his valuable book, *Wong Kar-Wai*, Puig's *Heartbreak Tango*—a novel about a handsome but ill-starred ladykiller and the women who love him—clearly sets the template for Yuddy's tale. But Wong does more than merely transpose his characters to Hong Kong and the Phillippines. He makes the story his own, turning the action into (among other things) a meditation on youthful ardor and frustration, the search for personal and cultural identity—it's his first look at the Chinese diaspora and the

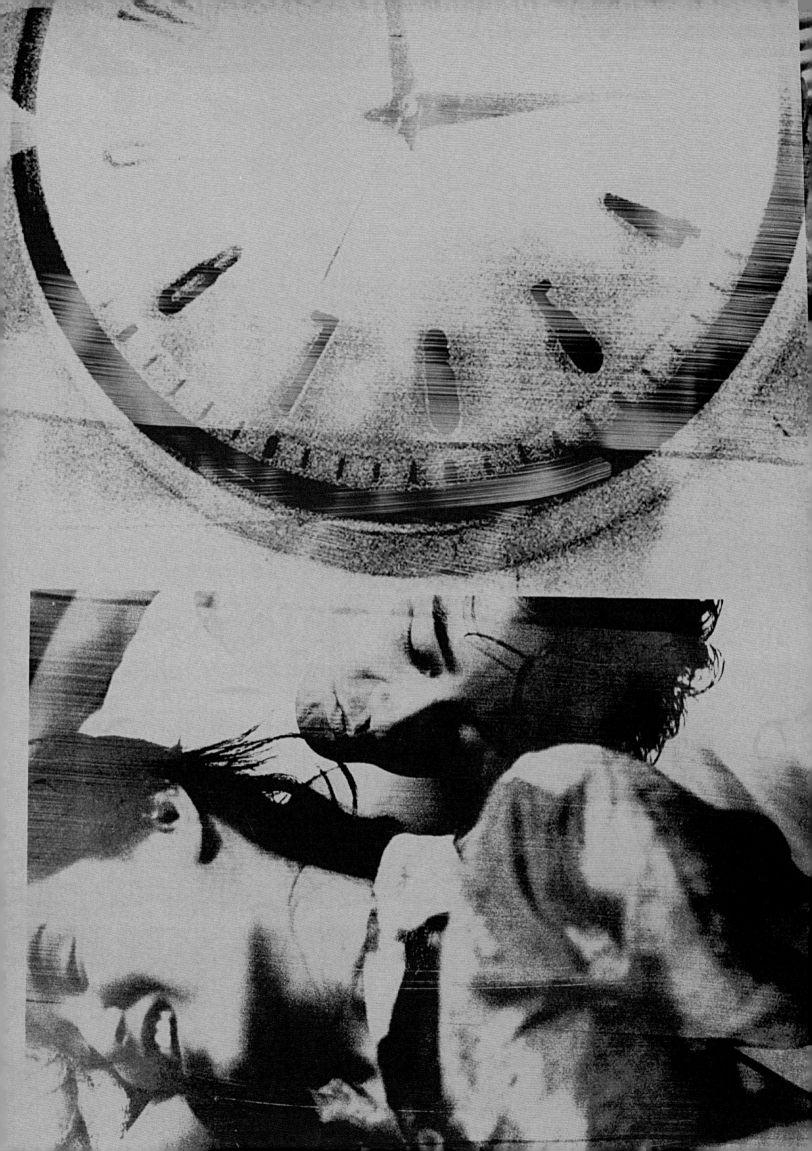

wide-open ways of '60s Southeast Asia—and the inescapable presence of Time. This last element is captured in the interplay of two of the film's governing images. There's the clock we see when Yuddy first meets Li-zhen—which plunges them into the world of passing time—and there's the swooning tropical-paradise tracking shot of twilit Philippine palm and banana trees (accompanied by the dreamily beguiling guitar music of Los Indios Tabajaras), a vision in blue and green that conjures an entrancing yet unobtainable world outside time. Free-falling between the ticking of the clock and the timelessness of nature, Yuddy starts off killing time and winds up killing eternity.

12

Filled with terrific scenes, *Days of Being Wild* is a work of rapturous loveliness and narrative elision that heralded the arrival of the WKW adumbrated in *As Tears Go By.* It marked his first collaboration with the man who would become his defining cinematographer, Christopher Doyle, an Australian Boudu who would become as fabled for his drinking and womanizing as his dazzling camerawork. In its exquisite look, it also marked the first sign that Wong's friend William Chang Suk Ping would become a production and costume designer of such surpassing brilliance that he'd be indispensible; I've never talked to Wong about a film without him praising Chang. Together, Wong, Doyle, and Chang turn the Hong Kong of *Days of Being Wild* into a green-tinted world of moody streets and gorgeously claustrophobic interiors that stay in your mind long after the details of the story have faded away.

　　With its unlikable hero and unresolved relationships, the film was already wildly unconventional by most standards, not only Hong Kong's; the ending provided the *coup de grâce.* Rather than offer us closure, the final scene introduces a character we haven't yet met, a man played with a diamond-cutter's precision by Tony Leung, who slowly and carefully dresses in preparation for—what? We never learn. The movie just ends. Originally this scene was designed to lay the groundwork for a sequel, but its effect has always been deeply disorientating. Who is this guy and what's he getting ready for? Is everything that came before a mere prologue to a film we don't get to see? Even today, watching it feels like stepping onto a trapdoor.

　　It would be an understatement to say that most viewers found this perplexing, especially in what they expected to be a romantic, action-packed film featuring Hong Kong's most popular and attractive stars. Critic and screenwriter Jimmy Ngai was at the Hong Kong premiere and started laughing when he told me about the audience's reaction, which ranged from gobsmacked bewilderment to flat-out fury. Elsewhere the response was the same. In Singapore, viewers began slashing the seats; in Korea, there was nearly a riot. The movie became a hugely expensive box-office flop. It also became an enormous *succès d'estime. Days of Being Wild* won five Hong Kong Film awards, including Best Film, Best Director, and Best Actor, and became the cornerstone of Wong's legend.

　　It would, of course, be invidious to suggest that Wong was the first true artist that Hong Kong cinema produced—King Hu's *A Touch of Zen* won a prize at Cannes as early as 1971, after all—and only a snob would deny the extraordinary skill and inventiveness of directors like Woo, Jackie Chan, and Sammo Hung (whom Wong would later have choreograph the action sequences in *Ashes of Time*). Trained in the wide-open creative ferment of Hong Kong television—

he studied production at TVB, becoming a screenwriter—Wong rode a cinematic wave begun by the likes of Tsui Hark, Yim Ho, Ann Hui, Stanley Kwan, and worldly, iconoclastic Patrick Tam, whose bold editing of *Days of Being Wild* underscored his own intelligence and audacity.

Yet having said that, there can be no denying that Wong's second film leaped ahead of both popular taste and the work of his peers. His daring put him on the road to a directorial superstardom that would soon shift the terrain around him. As David Bordwell notes in his fine book *Planet Hong Kong*, "All Hong Kong directors had to come to terms with Wong's prominence." Outside of Hong Kong, *Days of Being Wild* put Wong on the radar of international film festivals; indeed, he was embraced with a tad too much relieved alacrity by certain middlebrow Western critics and programmers pleased to find a young Hong Kong filmmaker who could talk about Bresson and Antonioni and who made undeniable art films rather than commercial fare with vulgar titles like *Project A* or *The Killer* (which were actually, it should be noted, far better than most "serious" movies). Even more important, perhaps, the movie shifted the attitudes of young Chinese and Asian directors and cinephiles. They had finally found a filmmaker who seemed every bit as modern and cutting-edge as the Yanks or Europeans, one who captured the surging energy beginning to be unleashed in the vast human dynamo running from Southeast Asia to Seoul. My wife, Sandi Tan, saw the film as an 18 year-old in Singapore and still remembers being thrilled by its filmmaking and by the vanished world it evoked. It's still her favorite of Wong's films, and though she knows it almost by heart, when I put on the DVD again while working on this book, she couldn't stop watching.

27

13 *Days of Being Wild* might easily have killed Wong Kar Wai's career, not so much because it earned too little at the box office as because it flouted the whole ethos of Hong Kong cinema. In a single film, he went from being hailed as a hit-maker to being condemned as a self-indulgent auteur. His work was thought to be arty, heedless of the audience, and because it was slow and expensive to produce, irresponsible with other people's money. Faced with this rejection, Wong began seeing himself as an outsider, and despite all the acclaim, does so to this very day.

To save his career, he started his own company, Jet Tone, along with his director friend Jeff Lau. What Wong brought to it, beyond his own talent, was one incontrovertible asset: Star actors wanted to work with him, even though their managers usually didn't want them to. Leslie Cheung was rightly proud of his performance in *Days of Being Wild*, which won him Best Actor at the Hong Kong Film Awards and was easily his finest to that point. Although he had announced his retirement (something Cheung was prone to do), he agreed to be in Wong's next film, a martial arts epic, *Ashes of Time*. He was soon joined by many others including Taiwanese superstar Brigitte Lin, Andy Lau, Maggie Cheung, Carina Lau, Jacky Cheung and the two, often confused Tony Leungs—Tony Leung Ka-fai, best known in the West for his lead role in *The Lover*, and Tony Leung Chiu Wai, who would work with Wong six times, most famously in *In the Mood for Love*. Despite Wong's poison reputation, Jet Tone was able to finance the film through pre-sales because it offered something everyone wanted: the largest and most spectacular cast in Hong Kong history.

What exactly did Wong offer all these actors to attract them? I've talked to many of them over the years and always get versions of the same answer. Doing a Wong Kar Wai film is different from doing a movie in Hong Kong or Hollywood. It isn't industrial, you don't feel you're on a treadmill. Quite the contrary. His way of discovering a film as he goes along—writing each day before they shoot—gives actors the pleasure of doing something fresh and different and a little bit risky. "It's the most fun I've had," Jude Law told me about making *My Blueberry Nights*. "Every day seems new." At the same time, actors feel safe with him. He knows how to be reassuring (as I personally learned from doing this book) and is mindful of what movie stars need and want. No director makes his actors look more attractive than Wong, nor is anyone better at getting natural performances. "I always tell my cast," he says, "I'm your safety net. Don't worry. Jump—and I will catch you." They believe him. Zhang Ziyi has won scads of awards for her work with Wong in *2046* and *The Grandmaster*. She tells me that, even though he sometimes made her do take after take after take, she trusts him absolutely, in part because he makes her do 20, 30, 40 takes until she stops "acting" and becomes her character.

"Kar Wai's the only one who can bring the best out of me," Tony Leung Chiu Wai once told me over champagne. "Other directors may be afraid of me or don't want to push me. They worry that I'll be angry. He doesn't care. He doesn't care about me being a star. With him, even if you're not comfortable with something, you still have to do it. And I like that."

14

Chungking Express (1994), my personal favorite, isn't merely one of Wong Kar Wai's finest films. It's one of the most delightful films of the last half-century, a lyrical valentine to the glories of his home city, the vagaries of romance, and the sheer joy of making movies. Dashed off while *Ashes of Time* was slowly being completed, it is the purest expression of Wong's spontaneous approach, doing for '90s Hong Kong what Godard and Truffaut did for '60s Paris. The movie tells two loosely-related stories about lovelorn cops, one set at night in Kowloon, the other set during daytime across Victoria Harbor in the Central district of Hong Kong Island. In the first story, the very young Taiwanese actor Takeshi Kaneshiro plays Cop 223, whose girlfriend has broken his heart. While chasing a crook on the streets, he bumps into Brigitte Lin's character, a woman wearing a blond wig that makes her look like a Chinese knock-off of Gena Rowlands in *Gloria*. "In 57 hours," 223 tells us over a freeze-frame, "I will fall in love with this woman." And in a sense, he does, but complications ensue—she turns out to be a drug smuggler. In the second story, Wong regular Tony Leung (Chiu Wai) plays Cop 663, who gets dumped by his stewardess girlfriend only to catch the eye of Faye, a counter-girl at the Midnight Express food stand where he eats. Played with otherworldly charm by pop singer Faye Wong, she seems less a normal Hong Kong chick than the world's most charming alien; it's as if an outer space civilization tried to design the cutest young woman imaginable and got it slightly wrong. Faye soon begins breaking into 663's apartment to clean it and bask in his aura.

As with most of Wong's films, describing the storyline of *Chungking Express*'s storyline doesn't do justice to its textures and pleasures. Graced by four wonderful starring performances, this is a movie bursting with delectable moments, from 223's canned-pineapple eating bender to the blonde smuggler's hilarious wrangling of her Indian "mules" in a 7-Eleven, from 633's seduction scene with a toy airplane to perhaps the film's most indelible delight: Faye's extraordinary deadpan dance to The Mamas & the Papas's "California Dreamin'," a song that, before shooting, Wong played for the director of photography Chris Doyle to explain what the film was about. Indulging his taste for whimsy, amorous longing, and thwarted love, Wong whips up more clever conceits—like the great bit when 663 tries to dry a soaked letter on the spinning spikes of a convenience store's rotisserie oven—than a dozen Hollywood romantic comedies. In a shot that would become a trademark, 663 and Faye stand at the snackbar, and while they move at ordinary speed, all the people around them on the street are going so fast they blur—a pure expression of how, for a romantic couple, what's around them is just brightly colored flow lacking all definition. At once organic and fun and dancing with visual brio, *Chungking Express* gives you the feeling that Wong was winging it. Working without permits, the production raced through the city grabbing shots. Even as you marvel at the gorgeousness of the handheld photography by Doyle—this was the film that really launched him as a famous director of photography—it gives you the tantalizing amphetamine rush of urban life.

Never one to do only one thing in a film, Wong turns this knockabout romance into a form of cinematic preservation, offering vivid portraits of two places that for him embody the essence of Hong Kong. Part one centers on Kowloon's Chungking Mansions, a 17-story building known for being a grottily enthralling multicultural swirl of Pakistani café owners, Chinese wage-slaves, and Himalayan hookers. It's "The Ghetto at the Center of the World," as Gordon Mathews titles his illuminating book on the history and sociology of this remarkable structure that Wong knew as a kid in the '60s, back when his father managed a nightclub there, and the address still possessed an air of prosperity. It is a genuinely unforgettable place—brash, hustling, dodgy, and infinitely colorful. I will never forget stumbling across it in the mid-'90s and suddenly feeling different orders of reality collide: It was like walking through Casablanca and somehow finding myself in Rick's Cafe. Its atmosphere is vastly different from that of Lan Kwai Fong, across Victoria Harbor in Central, where Cop 663 meets the young woman dreaming of California. Sort of Hong Kong's version of Soho, this area bristles with the bright energy of markets and food stalls, and boasts one of the world's most pleasing urban wonders—the outdoor escalator that rises block after block through the heart of the city, right past the apartment of 633 that Faye redecorates, and that in real life belonged (and still belongs) to Doyle. Just riding it you feel like you're in a movie.

Shot through with many of Wong's major themes—the manifold configurations of time, the workings of chance, the echoings and doublings of daily life—*Chungking Express* is his sunniest film. Yet even as it captures the bright whoosh of young men and women seeking love in Hong Kong, the city's good cheer is shot through with wistfulness. For all his jokes (and they are very good ones), Wong evokes a Hong Kong full of solitary souls who can't quite bridge the canyon separating their bright public faces from their lonely private dreams. As open to life as its characters, the movie smiles tenderly on those brave enough to keep risking their hearts.

15

Chungking Express turned Wong Kar Wai turned into an international avatar of Cool—especially in the movie world. Film schools urged their students to see it. Filmmakers, both young and not-so-young, copied its style. If it wasn't the most imitated film of the 1990s, this was only because it was surpassed by *Pulp Fiction*. Tellingly, Tarantino wasn't merely one of Wong's big champions—you can find him Quentin-ing on about the movie on YouTube—he distributed it through his Rolling Thunder label. In short, Wong became certified as hip, and this idea of him would last for years, nearly always cutting two ways. On the upside, being seen as a pop icon expanded his fan-base, giving many young Asian kids the liberating sense that someone like them could be the cutting edge of hipness. Wong showed me a funny, touching handmade comic book he'd been sent by a European couple of Chinese origin (Edwin Mak Ho-Yin came from Britain, Sue Man from Sweden) about how much his work and success had opened up the world for them. Less happily, the vogue of Wong Kar Wai fed a perception among detractors that he was a fashion-conscious lightweight who over-identified with, even pandered to, the young. They dismissed him with the then-obligatory sneering references to MTV.

As it happened, I first met Wong around this time, and while I found his films very cool, there was little of the visible bohemian about him; Charles Bukowski or Miles Davis he was not. Yes, he made movies with glamorous young stars and shot in a style that, if you're being lazy, could be written off as superficial and trendy. But Wong has never been addicted to what the larger culture thinks of as the latest thing. He doesn't like to hang out with other artists. Although he knows what's going on, he follows his own instincts, trusts his own taste, and when he lifts someone else's idea, retools it into something uniquely his own. He knows that true cool isn't an attitude or a style, much less a lifestyle. It lies in trusting in your own sensibility.

That said, there is one subject that can't be ignored.

16

"Do you know what really pisses me off?" Wong Kar Wai said to me around the time of *The Grandmaster*. "When I sit down for an interview, and the first question is, 'Why are you wearing sunglasses?'"

I understood his aggravation. Did people ask about Groucho Marx's mustache? Do they ask David Lynch to explain why he closes the top button of his white shirts? Or ask Michael Moore why he doesn't just take off that goddamn ballcap? Such questions usually smack of aggression. They seem to say, "You can't fool *me*." But I also understand why people would raise them. The sunglasses have become so essential to Wong's persona that everyone is genuinely curious about them. Whenever I meet someone who finds out that I know him, the first question is nearly always, "Does he take off his sunglasses?"

Yes, he does. But this wasn't always true. The first time we met, at a restaurant where Tarantino was hosting a dinner for *Chungking Express*, he wore shades the whole night. Although we immediately hit it off, I remember laughing with friends about those dark glasses afterwards—*What is it with this guy?* He wore them again when we met in Toronto in 1995 and two years later when we chatted in Cannes after the premiere of *Happy Together*. But that day we were sitting in the bright sunlight of a terrace outside the Palais des Festivals, so I was wearing shades, too.

Sometimes sunglasses are just sunglasses. They didn't come off until he hosted a dinner for friends and colleagues at one of Cannes' ghastly Chinese restaurants. Ever since then, he takes them off whenever we meet, unless he is somehow on display.

It wasn't until we began this book that I ever considered asking about it. Happily, even before I could raise the issue, we had drinks with Chris Doyle, who erupted into a spontaneous disquisition on this very topic. "People think Wong Kar Wai wears sunglasses because he's a pretentious fucker. Well, he is a pretentious fucker"—he roared happily at his little jape—"but he's also a sensitive man. These idiots don't understand that *all* artists wear sunglasses of one kind or another—they don't have to be real glasses. It's about two different kinds of vision, subjectivity and objectivity. You have your eyes as a man and your eyes as an artist. When Kar Wai puts on his sunglasses he becomes someone different."

A couple of days later, I asked Wong if Doyle had been right. He smiled, and replied, "Chris phrased it beautifully and he believes it, but the truth is, the sunglasses give me the time that I need to react. It's almost like a dark room for me. Some people are very good in public, and they perform nicely. I'm not that person. This was from the beginning. Whenever I was shooting, I had too many things to deal with. I needed the space so that I have a second, or two seconds, to respond. And it eventually became a habit. This is WKW"—he mimed putting on his sunglasses, "and now this"– he mimed taking them off—"is Wong Kar Wai."

I would love to end this section with that lovely evocation of Wong's split identity, which is, after all, a recurring motif in his work. But as any good Freudian would remind us, all of our motives are layered, multiple, overdetermined. Wearing shades may well give Wong time to react in public, but he has other motivations, too. Once sunglasses became part of his cool-director image, almost his logo, it would have been foolish to stop wearing them; he's too canny a marketer to abandon something that helps him stand out in the crowded world of international cinema. Then, too, wearing sunglasses is an assertion of power—just ask any highway patrolman or superannuated member of Papa Doc Duvalier's old Tonton Macoute. If people can't see your eyes, it's hard for them to tell what you're thinking—which doubtless comes in handy on Wong's sets when, for instance, he thinks an actor needs to be put under pressure. While filming *2046*, Zhang Ziyi never saw Wong's eyes. This was hardly accidental. Whether Wong is giving himself time to think or to preventing others from knowing what he's thinking, the sunglasses are all about keeping control.

17 Chris Doyle likes to say,"What came before decides what comes after." With *Chungking Express* proving a desperately-needed success, nobody was suprised that the next film Wong Kar Wai made, *Fallen Angels* (1995), would be another romantic film about young people in Hong Kong. Yet Wong's approach has always been encapsulated by that line from Talking Heads's "Psycho Killer": *Say something once, why say it again?* If Chungking Express gave audiences Hong Kong and romance in all its brightness and warmth, its successor comes steeped in midnight chill. Just as *The Godfather*: Part II deepened and de-sentimentalized *The Godfather,* so *Fallen Angels* harks back to that earlier film, through a lens darkly.

Skipping between multiple characters and multiple voice-overs, the movie is another narrative diptych. This time, however, the heroes aren't cops—they're crooks. The first story (originally intended to be a third part of *Chungking Express*) is about the unrequited love of the Agent (Michele Reis) for her partner, The Killer (Leon Lai). She sets up his jobs, cleans up his place, masturbates (at great cinematic length, if not explicitness) to fantasies of him. She tries to set up a meeting, but the Killer is no good at human emotion; he's a hollow man who barely registers any feeling whether he's gunning people down in restaurants or hanging out with a crazy-fun ex-girlfriend, wittily played by Karen Mok. The Agent lives in the same building as the central figure in the second story. He Zhiwu (Takeshi Kaneshiro again) is a good-humored jailbird—more a juvenile delinquent than a criminal—who spends his nights breaking into businesses and goofing around. He forces men to accept his barbering, makes people eat ice cream from a stolen truck. Mute and lonely, He Zhiwu falls for a young woman he meets (Charlie Yeung) but although it takes him a while to realize it, his most heartfelt relationship is with his father (Chen Man Lei) who manages the place they live.

If you've seen *Chungking Express*, you can't help but notice the many ways *Fallen Angels* mirrors it, from its use of Chungking Mansions to Mok's dyed-blond hair which recalls Brigitte Lin's wig in the earlier film. There are scads of such reflections (Wong loves such things) yet what strikes you first is how different the movies feel. For starters, *Fallen Angels* is an exhaustingly voluptuous piece of style. It is shot almost completely with a wide-angle lens that not only distorts the characters—their features stretch and sprawl—but the physical space in general. In this film about the emotional distance between people, the visual distances between them are also warped. Doyle's photography makes everything a knockout, but it's a curdled beauty that matches the soulless good looks of the Agent and the Killer, whose stylish clothes and dead features make them seem like fashionista zombies. Although Lai and Reis are both pretty, they are lousy actors—he, in particular, could teach a master class on vainglorious preening—and their blankness unintentionally intensifies the film's larger sense of alienation. This is a world in which real human contact has almost disappeared. People don't express themselves face to face. Their communications are mediated electronically, with pagers, jukebox songs like Shirley Kwan's "Forget Him," a Happy Birthday videotape a father sends his young son in Japan.

Fallen Angels was edited by William Chang who as usual also did the production design, costumes, and hair. Putting the footage together he told Wong that the film was problematic—too icy, too unlikable, too bleak. Never one to balk at the need for impromptu invention, Wong went back and added the sequence of He Zhiwu taking videos of his father cooking, lying in bed, washing up in the bathroom. This video diary isn't merely delightful (we watch the dad's comic annoyance at being filmed) but filled with love. It transforms our perception and our memory of the whole film, especially once the father dies and, like a proper Wong hero, the son keeps watching the tape again and again, loving something even more once he's lost it. Indeed, the freeze-frame of the dead father may be the most moving single image in all of Wong's work; perhaps feeling its power himself, he keeps it on screen for an uncharacteristically long time. Its unabashed sentiment prepares us for the film's more muted but more exquisite ending. After a chance meeting, the Agent and He Zhiwu ride his motorcycle through a tunnel, her arms around his body, the Flying Pickets's lovely cover of "Only You" playing on the soundtrack. As they leave the tunnel, the Agent thinks that all she's looking for is what she calls "a moment of warmth," and in a great gesture of transcendence, the camera tilts up to show us the night sky through the buildings. Shot through with the ache of urban melancholy, this is one of the thrilling final shots in contemporary cinema.

18 Christopher Doyle's work is laced with thrilling shots. When Wong Kar Wai first began using him on *Days of Being Wild*, the Australian-born D.P. was a quiet man known for his studious approach. Shooting with Wong liberated something in him. He became more instinctual as a cinematographer. "I learned not to put my fucking intellect between myself and the physical reality of making a film," he tells me. He also began to elaborate a new self-image, an alter ego known as Du Ke Feng ("like the wind") who is as overtly bohemian as Wong is not. Doyle's Catholicism didn't just lapse, it exploded into sin, and the boom it made clearly worked for him. There was a time in the '90s, when he was something unprecedented: a director of photography as celebrated as a famous director. And why not? Beyond being a great D.P., he is the sort of colorful character journalists love, a man known for his pungent garrulity, boundless taste for sexy young women, and a level of boozing impressive even by the standards of his native Australia. "We need more wine," I'd hear him shouting at film festival lunches, where he delighted the beautiful actresses at his table with his happy patter. Far more quotable than the circumspect Wong, Doyle became so celebrated that you even heard it bruited that he might be the true talent behind movies like *Chungking Express* and *Happy Together*, a faintly racist idea (the white guy's the real artist) that went poof the second audiences saw Doyle's gorgeous but exasperating 1999 directorial debut, *Away with Words*.

Doyle and Wong had one of the defining collaborations of modern cinema, a partnership up there with the fabled team of Bernardo Bertolucci and Vittorio Storaro. They did 8 films together over 15 years, finally ending with *2046*. For all the success, their relationship wasn't always easy. Doyle could occasionally go awry shooting a key scene; when Wong took an indeterminate hiatus during filming, Doyle, who didn't want to just sit around waiting, might sign on to shoot something else and have to be replaced for a few days until he got back. So why not fire him? "If he didn't have talent I wouldn't use him," Wong once told me. "But I always knew that Chris has something precious. He always understands what we are doing in a film—I don't have to *tell* him—and he has a very high aesthetic sense all his own." If he sometimes went off the rails, that was just Chris being Chris. "He's a sailor," Wong always says by way of explanation. Indeed, there's something in Doyle's freewheeling energy, so different from his own and William Chang's, that Wong likes, even needs. Besides, he belongs to Wong's "family" and in families you accept people for who they are.

When Doyle agreed to meet me for drinks at Juliette's in August, 2014, Wong said he'd stay for a couple of minutes just to say hello. The two hadn't seen each other in well over a year, since Doyle turned up to see the French present Wong its top honor, Commander of the Order of Arts and Letters. It felt a bit like bringing together an old divorced couple—I didn't know what to expect. But from the moment Doyle arrived, a latter day Rumpelstiltskin with wild hair, baggy shorts, a crazy-loose top, and a young Chinese filmmaker on his arm (she's making a documentary about him), the room was filled with their pleasure at seeing each other again. The two know they are permanently bound by their work—their obituaries will open by citing the films they made together—and by the shared experience behind it. They embraced like warriors who've been though many hard battles together. Tears rolled down the cheeks of the excitable Doyle, and even the more measured Wong was obviously moved. Rather than peel away as planned, he stayed for hours, drinking and laughing with his old comrade. They seemed genuinely happy talking about the past. "It's been a good divorce," Doyle said, "but we remember that the marriage was great."

Like any man possessed of such a sturdy Irish name, Doyle has a joyously freewheeling gift of the gab, and he describes the almost wordless communication between himself, Wong, and William Chang in terms more rude than elegiac: "It's like great sex. We don't have to say 'Hold my hair when you fuck me from behind' because we already know." He's glowingly proud of their work together yet also honest about what it took to get there. More than anyone I've spoken to, he lets you glimpse the ruthless artist behind Wong's soothing manner.

"There's something that happened to me with Kar Wai that I still dream about," he said, looking at Wong rather than at me. "We were shooting something, and he said, 'Is that *all* you can do, Chris? I think that's the most astonishing thing he ever said to me. And he's right. Because either it's, 'Yes, that's all I can do,' or 'No, I wasn't trying hard enough.' That's exactly the thought one should share. 'Is that *all* you can do, Chris?'" He turned to me and laughed. "That should be the title of your book."

19 THE WKW JUKEBOX

Wong Kar Wai loves jukeboxes—they appear frequently in his movies—and this seems only fitting. Perhaps no other director of this era has used pre-existing music more centrally, more skilfully, or with fewer fears of anachronism (nowadays even jukeboxes are anachronistic). Wong is catholic in his tastes—the last time I was in his offices, he had Hans Zimmer's score from *Rush* in his CD player ("It's very good," he insisted)—and in his willingness to borrow, a magpie. He uses music to set a film's rhythms, create its tone, underscore or tweak its characters' emotions, or simply give a synesthetic boost to the observation of his characters' behavior. His work is melodramatic in the classic definition of the term—it mixes music (in Greek, *melos*) with drama. While all of Wong's fans will have their own favorite songs on their mental WKW jukebox—or these days playlist—it's impossible to imagine his career without the following tracks, some old, some original.

"Take My Breath Away," Sandy Lam. Canto-pop hokum, yes, but the song meshes perfectly with Wong's unabashed willingness to appropriate music-video aesthetics for his own purposes in *As Tears Go By*. And it really is kind of catchy.

"Always in My Heart," Los Indios Tabajaras. No song conjures the tropics more brilliantly than this evocative, tingly-good guitar tune playing over the shot of the forest in *Days of Being Wild*.

"Perfidia," Xavier Cugat. This is a song so nice, Wong used it thrice—in *Days of Being Wild*, *In the Mood for Love*, and *2046*—to help bind together his trilogy. Inspiring deep nostalgia for Wong, it taps into the Latin music that surrounded him as a kid growing up the '60s.

"California Dreamin'," The Mamas & the Papas. Played over and over in *Chungking Express*, this song—which Wong terms "innocent and simple, like summer-time in the '70s"—starts out being a joke as Faye Wong dances to it hilariously, yet winds up gesturing at an idea of utopia.

"Forget Him," Shirley Kwan. One of the most famous Cantonese pop songs of all time (it was originally performed by the great Teresa Teng), this isn't merely a message to the Agent in *Fallen Angels*, but an expression of Wong's own obsession with remembering and not-remembering.

"Only You," The Flying Pickets. This cover of The Platters's love song helps give the ending of *Fallen Angels* its air of melancholy transcendence, not least because it's sung *a cappella*, giving us the bare human voice rising amidst the concrete emptiness.

"Milonga for Three," Astor Piazzolla. For *Happy Together*, a hyper-modern film about the tango of love, few musicians could be more apt than the great Argentine composer who modernized tango. His famous "Tango Apasionado" also graces the soundtrack, but this composition has a melancholy that cuts even deeper.

"*Happy Together*," Danny Chung. While The Turtles launched this song in 1967, this Hong Kong version (by the composer who did the music for *As Tears Go By*) gives the friendly tune a rougher edge, befitting *Happy Together*'s underlying ambivalence about the Hong Kong handover to China.

"Yumeji's Theme," Shigeru Umebayashi. Perhaps the best single movie theme of the last 25 years—to hear the opening first notes is to instantly conjure up a whole film, if not a whole vanished world. Wong's knack for cultural bricolage is so deft that Umebayashi's score actually came from an earlier film, Seijun Suzuki's ghostly *Yumeji*, but will be forever associated with *In the Mood for Love*.

"Quizás, Quizás, Quizás," Nat King Cole. Another of Wong's Latin favorite, this 1958 cover of the song by Cuban songwriter Osvaldo Farrés is better known by its English title, "Perhaps, Perhaps, Perhaps," evoking both the state of romantic limbo in *In the Mood for Love* and Wong's own sense of life's many possibilities and uncertainties.

"*2046*," Shigeru Umebayashi. Just as *2046* is a darker and more complex film than *In the Mood for Love*, so Umebayashi's theme (bespoke, this time) surges with a romanticism at once enticing and rather ominous.

"The Christmas Song," Nat King Cole. It's one of those revealing paradoxes that the most potent Christmas songs are suffused with sadness—think of Judy Garland singing "Have Yourself a Merry Little Christmas. Here Cole's still-velvety voice calls up a world of cozy closeness that, paradoxically, make us think of its opposite, the loneliness we see on screen.

"Concerto Alevta," Peer Raben. Wong's work is filled with nods to Fassbinder, and in "The Hand"– which contains echoes of *Lola*, a film attentive to hands—he uses the German director's favorite composer for this haunting piece in which the violin dances and soars with yearning.

"The Story," Norah Jones. Wong was first drawn to Jones through her voice, and in this song she wrote for *My Blueberry Nights*, she not only shows off a voice of surprising lounge-singer bluesiness but her lyrics tap into the film's self-conscious sense of dealing in mythic tropes.

"Stabat Mater," Stefano Lentini. Wong has a fondness for the Italianate and the operatic, and in *The Grandmaster*, he not only uses bits of Ennio Morricone's nostalgia-inducing score to *Once Upon a Time in America*, but this original piece for soprano and orchestra. Playing it against the sexy and balletic kung fu showdown between Tony Leung and Zhang Ziyi, he reminds us that, for him, music is about feeling, not cultural provenance.

20

Among Wong Kar Wai's films, *Ashes of Time* (1994) has always been an outlier. Although begun as a way of salvaging a career nearly wrecked by *Days of Being Wild*, it was anything but a cynically heuristic piece of commercial hackwork. When the first version came out in 1994—not long after *Chungking Express*—it was widely considered a ravishing folly, a parade of pretty pictures. I saw one of the earliest screenings and left feeling both dazzled and baffled (the general public wound up feeling baffled and angry). Marketed as a martial arts tale, or *wuxia*, teeming with big stars, it was as close as a supposed genre film could ever get to avant-garde cinema; it clearly violated Robert Bresson's droll advice, "Hide your ideas but not so that nobody can find them." Although the movie is one of Wong's best loved works among Mandarin-speaking Chinese and hasn't lacked for critical champions (Wimal Dissanayake wrote a brainy book about it, *Wong Kar-Wai's "Ashes of Time,"* it was disliked in Hong Kong and Southeast Asia. Just as bad, it was almost wholly ignored in the West, which was so busy embracing Wong as a chronicler of youthful romanticism that it didn't notice that here was something different. Even Wong himself didn't find the film satisfactory (the music really bugged him) and he kept tinkering with it until 2008 when he brought out the radically reworked version known as *Ashes of Time Redux*. Less challenging than the original, it's also more lucid. In either version it remains one of Wong's strongest and most complex films, a touchstone in the history of martial arts cinema.

The film's starting point was the popular 1958 novel *The Eagle-shooting Heroes* by Jin Yong (the pen name of Hong Kong journalist Louis Cha), whose work was as popular with Chinese audiences as *The Lord of the Rings* or *Game of Thrones* are in the West. In choosing to do it, Wong appeared to be dealing with can't-miss material in an era rediscovering its love of *wuxia*. But Wong isn't a filmmaker who will try to simply put a novel up on the screen. With *Ashes of Time*, he took several brave and audience-alienating steps. He eliminated famous episodes and added new characters of his own. Rather than telling stories of two of its most important characters—the good guy, Huang Yaoshi (who's known as East), and the bad guy, Ouyang Feng (also known as West)—as they appear in the novel, he invented new backstories set during their youth. Even radically, he flipped their essences: The villain, Ouyang, is viewed with sympathy while the hero is undercut. It would be like making a Tolkien adaptation that portrayed the young Gandalf as a hypocritical self-seeker and young Gollum a decent joe who'd had bad luck.

Leslie Cheung plays Ouyang, a master martial artist torn by the loss of his true love (Maggie Cheung) whom he'd given up for fear she'd reject him. He now lives in a rather pleasant shack in the Chinese outback (Wong shot in the Gobi Desert), where he arranges killings for money—he's all about the dough. Over the course of the film's episodic unfolding, he's visited by a series of men and women, who all have a story: his then-friend Huang Yaoshi (Tony Leung Ka Fai), a lady-killer who drinks a bottle of wine that causes forgetting; Murong-Yin / Murong-Yang (Brigitte Lin) a sword-wielding aristocrat with a split personality; a going-blind swordsman (Tony Leung Chiu Wai) bent on suicide because his wife (Carina Lau) loves Huang; a young girl (Charlie Yeung) seeking vengeance for her murdered brother; and Hung Chi (Jackie Cheung), a happy warrior who, to Ouyang's disapproval, will eagerly fight for free. It's a disparate group, yet what they have in common is that they are trapped, and driven by, the obsessions burning in their hearts—passion, rejection, betrayal. Even as Ouyang talks to us sagely in Wong's vividly written voice-overs, we see that he, too, is caught in the self-deception of the obsessed man.

The movie that rises from this proliferation of stories could hardly be less like a typical martial arts picture, let alone a full-fledged epic. This is clear from the movie's extraordinary look: Chris Doyle's ravishingly grainy desert photography that's equal parts acid-trip and Chinese painting; William Chang's striking costumes, which could be pieces from an Issey Miyake collection about the ancient peasantry; the long flowing tresses that often obscure characters' faces, making them hard to distinguish. Rarely have so many stars looked so glamorously unglamorous.

Such stylistic audacity is echoed in the fragmented storyline that offers no real heroes and displays no deep interest in action. Along with Hou Hsiao-hsien's *The Assassin* (2015) this is one of the most internal and abstract *wuxia* ever made, a fact underscored by the use of quotations from Buddhist scripture. When various characters do rouse themselves to do battle, Wong refuses to fetishize the violence. He doesn't try to rev us up or turn us on. (Predictably, most kung-fu movie fans were outraged.) Bored by action for its own sake, he seeks to fill the fights with poetry and emotion, most obviously in the all-but-blind swordsman's suicidal fight against a horde of bandits, in which the slow-motion imagery makes us feel the increasingly heavy weight of both the man's sword and his spirits.

One paradox of Wong's work is that he is at once sensual and abstract. Few films, much less martial arts pictures, are as breathtaking to look at as *Ashes of Time*, never more so than in the images of light through a spinning birdcage in the scenes when Murong Yang visits Ouyang. Their beauty is dazzling, but it would be a mistake not to notice that what we are actually looking at is a bird trapped in a cage. For all their amorous yearning—as ever, Wong is concerned with the romantic couple—the characters are all trapped, too, and not simply by their own obsessions. As the film's Buddhist quotations suggest, they're caught in the essential nature of human reality, the play of time and space. Nearly all martial arts tales are about the hero's triumph, but what triumphs here is the barren, bewitching land that was there before Ouyang and the other characters and that will outlast them for eons—humanity is just passing through. To borrow a phrase of critic David Thompson about Antonioni's *The Passenger*, in *Ashes of Time* the desert is a philosophy.

21 It's ironically apt that one of the films best known for copying Wong Kar Wai should be *Lost in Translation,* because for millions of fans his work has been *found* in translation. For those of us who don't speak Chinese, his movies' nifty English-language titles emphasize his status as an international filmmaker. Even when they don't come directly from well-known American songs, they carry a charge of Westernized pop. But, of course, these English language versions aren't the original titles, or even their proper translation. Think how different—and how much less familiar—Wong's sensibility would feel if one initially encountered his work with literally translated titles, especially the first seven movies that made his reputation.

Mongkok Carmen	AS TEARS GO BY
The Story of an Ah Fei	DAYS OF BEING WILD
Chungking Forest	CHUNGKING EXPRESS
Fallen Angels	FALLEN ANGELS
Evil East, Malicious West	ASHES OF TIME
Spring Light Piercing In	HAPPY TOGETHER
Kind of Like the Most Beautiful Times	IN THE MOOD FOR LOVE
2046	2046
Eros	THE HAND
My Blueberry Nights	MY BLUEBERRY NIGHTS
The Grandmaster	THE GRANDMASTER

And naturally, these are only translations.
Here are the actual Chinese titles—

旺角卡門	Wang jiao kamen
阿飛正傳	A fei zheng zhuan
重慶森林	Chong qing sen lin
墮落天使	Duo luo tian shi
東邪西毒	Dong xie xi du
春光乍洩	Chun guang zha xie
花樣年華	Hua yang nian hua
2046	2046
愛神 – 手	Ai shen – "Shou"
藍莓之夜	Lan mei zhi ye
一代宗師	Yi dai zong shi

22 In his essay on Kafka, Borges remarked that every writer creates his own precursors by virtue of whom he chooses to follow. The same is true of all artists. One of Wong Kar Wai's key precursors is Manuel Puig, the gay Argentine novelist who, like Wong, spent his childhood immersed in movies (and was, as it happens, disdained by Borges for reasons clearly spiked with homophobia). Puig's books didn't merely inspire Wong's approach to telling stories, most overtly in *Days of Being Wild*, but filled the filmmaker's head with daydreams of life beneath the Tropic of Capricorn. Once Wong decided to make *Happy Together*, about a gay couple leaving Hong Kong during the run-up to the 1997 handover to China, it was almost inevitable the film would be shot in Argentina.

When the film premiered in Cannes in May of 1997, much of the conversation predictably centered on its gay theme. Coming out nearly a decade before *Brokeback Mountain* brought gay love stories into the cinematic mainstream, *Happy Together* wasn't merely the first film about Chinese gay people that most Westerners had seen, but its lead actors, Leslie Cheung and Tony Leung Chiu Wai, were two of the biggest stars in Asia. (Imagine the impact in the U.S.

if, in *Interview with the Vampire*, Brad Pitt had mounted Tom Cruise.) Wong was clearly aware of the promotional value of this pairing. To announce the film, he held a press conference at which Cheung and Leung danced the tango. Yet watching the film today, what's striking is how matter-of-fact it is about gayness. Striking from an outsider's perspective, anyway. From the inside, this was predictable. Many of Wong's closest friends and longest-term collaborators are gay, and they'll tell you that they've always felt comfortable working with him because he's completely comfortable with them.

Interested in individuals rather than questions of sexual preference, *Happy Together* is another of Wong's tales of failed romance. It centers on the unhappy relationship between sober, essentially (but not always) decent Lai Yiu-Fai (Tony Leung) and alluring but unreliable Ho Po-Wing (Leslie Cheung), who's forever betraying Lai then saying, "We could start over." Although they clearly have sexual chemistry, they can't work things out. Even their attempt at a touristic visit to Iguazu Falls ends in disaster, an emblem of which is a kitschy lampshade they own bearing an image of the waterfall. Caught in a hopeless cycle, they make love, they argue, they separate. When Lai finds work as the doorman at a tango bar, Ho shows up on another man's arm; when Ho turns up badly beaten at Lai's apartment, Lai secretly confiscates his passport to keep him there. Driven mad by Ho, Lai eventually sinks into depression so deep you wonder whether he can survive it. Then he meets a fresh-faced Taiwanese, Chang (Chang Chen), who plans to visit Ushuaia on the southernmost tip of Argentina where, it is said, all sorrows can be left behind.

Although it has many rivals, *Happy Together* may be Wong's most visually exciting work, from the microcosmic bedroom/battleground of Lai's apartment with its echoes of Nan Goldin's photography to Christopher Doyle's overwhelming helicopter shot of the Iguazu Falls, the payoff of an entire film's exquisite photography. Along the way, the movie transforms Buenos Aires into an enchanted cityscape, where rain glistens on melancholy streets, taxis veer gorgeously around midnight plazas bejewelled with lights, and even the red, yellow and green of the city buses echo the palette that William Chang employs in his production design and costumes. All this is so dazzling that it can take a while to realize that Wong is working at a new, heightened level of intimacy and emotion. Cheung could hardly be better as the mercurial Ho, capturing both the elusive charm that makes him enticing—he's a gifted wheedler and cajoler and seducer—and the reckless impulsiveness that makes him a danger to everyone, himself included. In his first great screen role, Leung is even better as Lai. His performance is an encyclopedia of secret looks and glances that take us deeper than either he or Wong had gone before; it sets the template for his subtle brilliance in In the *Mood for Love* and *2046*. Although as a straight actor, Leung got credit for playing a gay character, what *Happy Together* showed was something more important than such modest courage. From this point on, Leung would be known as an actor of deep and poignant feeling. As for Wong, *Happy Together* was his most mature work to date, less cute and whimsical than the movies that preceded it, sharper-eyed about overblown adolescent passions, rawer and rougher in its vision of erotic connection. Bathed in the strains of Astor Piazzolla's music, Wong traveled to what felt like the end of the earth and created a genuine heartbreak tango.

23 THE WKW GPS

Wong Kar Wai was five years old when he was transplanted from Shanghai to Hong Kong, one of the world's great crossroads cities. He grew up within a Shanghainese community that was trying to create a new life, if not recreate a new Shanghai, in a Cantonese speaking culture that was neither completely familiar nor completely alien. Small wonder that, without ever making an explicit point of it, Wong would become cinema's great chronicler and poet of the Chinese diaspora. His movies speak for, and to, the countless millions of Chinese people who have left their own (or their parents' or their grandparents') native soil and set off searching for a place that might feel like home.

Indeed, Wong's career puts the lie to clichés about the inward-looking, Middle Kingdom provincialism of the Chinese. His work has always brimmed with an openness toward the wider world that you rarely find in, say, American movies. Truly international, it quivers with a sense of possibility global enough that a snackbar girl in *Chungking Express*—played by Faye Wong, herself a real-life migrant from Beijing—can suddenly become a stewardess and fly to California. In his three films about Hong Kong's colonial '60s, Wong evokes an effortless social fluidity that feels all the more magical because, in the days before cell phones and the internet, one approached each new country with a sense of discovery. *In Days of Being Wild*, Leslie Cheung's Yuddy goes to the Philippines in search of his mother and winds up in Manila's Chinatown where he meets Andy Lau's character, a one-time Hong Kong cop who has now become a sailor (Wong's own father worked for years on ships). In *In the Mood for Love*, Tony Leung's Cantonese writer Chow Mo-wan lives in a Hong Kong apartment with Shanghainese neighbors, but moves to Singapore, ground zero for Hong Kong's tropical fantasies about the so-called Nanyang Chinese in what was once known as Malaya and then ends up in Angkor Wat. In *2046*, Chow ends an affair with a Chinese-born, Singapore-based gambler played by Gong Li and moves back to Hong Kong where he becomes close to a young woman (Faye Wong again) who winds up moving to Japan with her fiancée. Of course, given China's tumultuous past, not all such migrations are voluntary. In *The Grandmaster*, the rough beast of history chases Ip Man from both his home city and his homeland, leaving him to land in Hong Kong where he would train Bruce Lee, who, as the roaming nature of Chinese life would have it, was himself born in San Francisco.

All this motion reflects itself in language. One of the striking features, perhaps motifs, of Wong Kar Wai's work is the way people speak different tongues in the same scene without anyone seeming to notice. Sometimes this difference is emphasized, as in *Chungking Express* when Takeshi Kaneshiro's cop tries to pick up Brigitte Lin in Mandarin, Cantonese, English, and Japanese. Most often, though, Wong treats it simply as a given in his part of the world.

Nowhere does the solitude and splendor of wandering reveal itself more movingly than for Tony Leung's Lai in *Happy Together*. Heartbroken and alone in a Buenos Aires that doesn't welcome him, he winds up doing what numberless Chinese exiles, émigrés, and travelers—including Wong himself while making the film—have done before him. He finds emotional shelter in that classic, and ubiquitous, refuge of the diaspora: a Chinese restaurant. He takes a job in the kitchen alongside Chang, and this connection to a familiar culture helps straighten out his head. Lai makes some money, finally visits Iguazu Falls and enjoys a rapturous experience, then flies back around the world to the capital city of the diaspora, Taipei. He doesn't make it all the way back home to Hong Kong, if Hong Kong is indeed still his real home. It's about to become part of China.

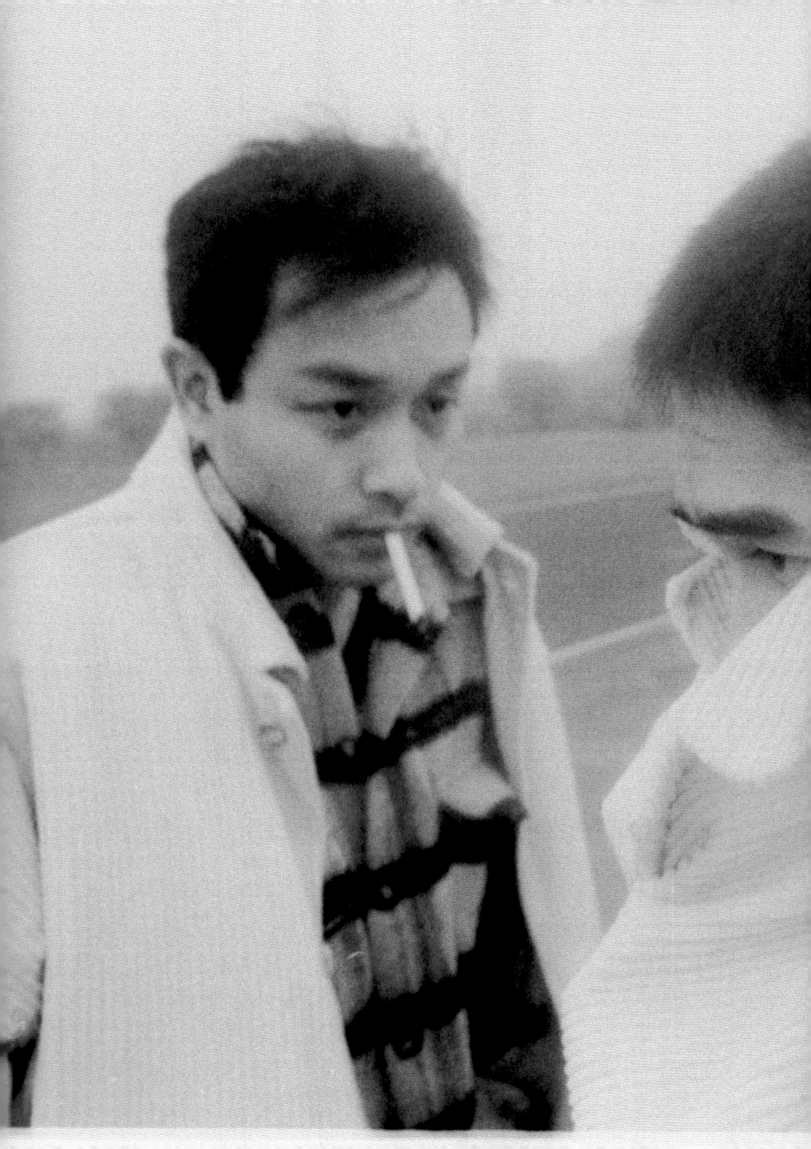

24

"All my films are about Hong Kong," Wong Kar Wai once told me, "even if they're set in Argentina." While many in the West saw *Happy Together* primarily as a love story, his compatriots saw it something more timely and relevant: Wong grappling with the meaning of the handover to China. They knew it wasn't coincidental that the film should open in Hong Kong one month before that historical transfer of power. Nor was it coincidental that it should begin with a shot of Hong Kong passports and end with Tony Leung's Lai on a train in Taipei, not Hong Kong, heading into an indeterminate future as the soundtrack plays Danny Chung's cover of the pop song "Happy Together"—a title that could be read as predicting a successful union, or as a slash of bitter irony. Even the movie's defining image, the aerial shot of water rushing down Iguazu Falls, is layered with political intimations that cut in different directions. At once thrillingly spectacular and patently dangerous—Chris Doyle, who's terrified of heights, shot it while hanging out of a chopper—the roaring waters that combine in these falls are an expression of the inexorably rushing power of reunion that can be seen as both a symbol of great strength or the downward pull of destruction.

Such indirection and ambivalence typify the politics of Wong's work. He's not in any conventional sense an ideological filmmaker. "It's never been my intention," he said at the Cannes press conference for *2046*, "to make films with any political content whatsoever." A cautious man allergic to grand pronouncements, he doesn't make message movies, much less give political speeches or man the barricades. The rise of China has been the biggest story in the world for the last 20 years—no place has felt this more deeply than Hong Kong—yet Wong's work is notable for its apparent lack of interest in post-revolutionary China, either in its Maoist incarnation or today's hyper-capitalist model launched by Deng Xiaoping, whose death appears in a news report Lai watches in *Happy Together*. It's not that he doesn't think about political issues, but he weaves his ideas (and they are intuitions more than ideological stances) into the intricate fabric of his work. This makes him ripe for interpretation, especially by critical admirers who, almost to a one, prefer to think of him as being some sort of social radical whose political ideas bubble beneath the surface of his work. They'll tell you that the scenes centering on the objects in Cop 663's apartment in *Chungking Express* is a commentary on what Marx called the Fetishism of Commodities. They'll tell you that *Fallen Angels*'s dark vision of Hong Kong is about the sinister power of Capital. They'll tell you that the scene where Ip Man breaks the cookie in *The Grandmaster* is actually a metaphorical (and treasonous) suggestion that Hong Kong should be broken off from China. Wong doesn't concur with any of these interpretations—I've asked him—yet such are the complex inner dynamics of his work that an argument can intelligently be made for all of them. After all, the meaning of a text goes far beyond conscious intention. Still, it's probably truer to say that these complex inner dynamics *are* his politics. In their lack of overtness—in their reflections, fractures, contradictions, ambivalences, and submersions in the image—his movies stand outside and against both the inescapable sloganized marketeering of consumer capitalism *and* the enforced dogmas of totalitarianism.

25 The list of Wong Kar Wai's virtues would not include patience. He is devoted to avoiding things that are "boring." It's a word he uses constantly. He finds interviews boring. He finds business meetings boring. He finds most movies boring, especially long ones. He even finds it boring to eat hairy crab, a Shanghai delicacy that requires winkling out the meat from the shell. "He's just too impatient," laughed his wife, Esther, as one night he sat at the table watching us greedily devour them and waiting for something less troublesome to eat. Perhaps Wong's attitude is infectious, for he is joined in his hatred of boredom by his longtime collaborator William Chang, who can barely stand to sit still for anything he thinks dull, and cinematographer Chris Doyle, a man so fidgety he would sometimes leave town during brief lulls in shooting—he always needs to be doing something. In their abject horror of being bored, Wong and his cohort often seem less like hard-charging Hong Kong filmmakers than Oxford toffs in some early novel by Evelyn Waugh.

This attitude has shaped Wong and Co.'s filmmaking. They always want to do something new—film in Argentina or Manchuria, shoot *Fallen Angels* with a wide-angle lens, make a martial arts movie whose stars are better at acting than flying leaps and windmill kicks. Why is there so much green in *Days of Being Wild*? "Because Fuji [film] is blue and Kodak [film] is red and we wanted to do something different," Doyle told me. "Novelty is a generous enough incentive to push you somewhere you haven't been."

The best example of this came in a loosely defined project Wong began in the late 1990s. *A Story about Food* was intended to be a romantic triptych starring Tony Leung and Maggie Cheung, each tale set in a different era. Wong actually shot the first episode, which was set at night in a deli in late-'90s Hong Kong, yet even as he knew it was pretty good, it didn't excite him—the whole thing struck him as too familiar. He realized he'd gotten bored with the filmmaking style that he, Doyle, and Chang had elaborated in their previous films. They had it down so pat there was no thrill of discovery, "When we walked into a room," he says, "we always knew where the camera would go." So he abandoned that footage and decided to shoot in a way unlike anything he'd done before. Chalk one up for boredom. What emerged was his most famous work, *In the Mood for Love*, which in *Sight & Sound*'s 2012 decennial poll of international critics, ranked as the 24th greatest film of all time.

26 While each of Wong Kar Wai's films has its own mental atmosphere, its distinctive emotional tang, none lingers more deeply in the memory than *In the Mood for Love* (2000), the second of his loose trilogy set in '60s Hong Kong. Merely to think of it is to find oneself plunged into a nocturnal world of apartment hallways and shadowy streets, hidden glances and radiant cheongsams, gliding camera moves and music pulsing with exquisite melancholy; the image of Maggie Cheung walking up the stairs has inscribed itself in our cultural memory. One reason for such imaginative density is that it lovingly recreates—and burnishes—a Hong Kong indelibly etched in Wong's own memories of growing up Shanghainese in a building very much like the one he depicts in the film. Although not the most personal of his works in its romantic theme, the Hong Kong it conjures—though much of it was actually filmed in Bangkok—may make it the film closest to his heart.

The story is bracingly simple, yet somehow mysterious. It's the story of two married people, writer Chow Mo-wan (Tony Leung) and an executive secretary, Mrs. Chan, played by Maggie Cheung, whose name here, Su Li-zhen, is teasingly the same as the actress's character in *Days of Being Wild*. On the same day, they become neighbors in a rooming house where the atmosphere is dominated by an energetic, mahjong-playing Shanghainese matron, Mrs. Suen (the pitch-perfect Rebecca Pan). Their first encounters are polite, even formal. But not so long after they meet, Mo-wan and Li-zhen begin to suspect that each of their spouses is having an affair; it gradually dawns on both that they're having it with each other. Unexpectedly bound by these strange circumstances, the two begin to see one another outside their apartment building, where nothing ever goes unnoticed. He takes her to dinner at the Goldfinch restaurant; she helps him write science fiction in a rented hotel room with the talismanic number *2046*; they play out imaginary scenes between their partners. The two start falling in love, yet their relationship remains honorably chaste and self-denying ("We won't be like them"), and it's unclear to them what they should do. Although adultery is far from rare in their world—indeed, Li-zhen must help her boss manage his mistress—these were more restrained and decorous times. Played with luminous restraint by Leung and Cheung, for whom this is her iconic role, they become the highest expression of Wong's fascination with missed romantic connection and the often-bleak workings of fate.

Some critics have grumbled that the film is too simple, and this may be true of its storyline. Yet to focus on the plot is almost to miss the point. Yes, it has the classic tropes of a romantic melodrama or so-called women's picture; yes, it wants us to like and identify with its repressed not-quite-lovers; and no, it doesn't have the complexity and tonal richness of, say, Ophuls's *Madame de . . . .* But this simplicity is deliberate in a film that pushes its style so far that it often feels like a musical or even a dance film. (In 2010, the Shanghai Ballet actually performed an adaptation of *In the Mood for Love*.) Indeed, in a career known for its attention to style—which Wong sees as the substance of cinema, not its window-dressing—*In the Mood for Love* stands out as the most self-consciously mannered of all his works and the most openly nostalgic for bygone splendors. Every inch of every frame has been carefully designed by William Chang, from a green lampshade that deliberately echoes Fassbinder's *Ali: Fear Eats the Soul* to the leafy wallpaper in the Goldfinch restaurant, to Li-zhen's immaculate coiffure (Cheung spent hours every day having her hair painstakingly ironed and set) and her ever-changing array of cheongsams, each seemingly lovelier than the last. Eschewing the hand-held shots for which he and Chris Doyle became known after *Chungking Express*, Wong sets his camera gliding in tracking shots, including a few marvelously choreographed sequences in that tightly confined apartment building. The film turns less on dramatic outbursts than classic images of its stars—Cheung's mask-like beauty bathed in gold, Leung's small, private looks suggesting an inner universe of longing. It's a film of tender epiphanies, as when Mo-wan and Li-zhen's meeting on the street transforms time itself and they start moving in slow motion.

Mad Men's Matthew Weiner told me that he found all this so inspiring that the opening shot of his show's hero, Don Draper—whom we see from behind, drinking—was borrowed straight from a shot of Leung in *In the Mood for Love*. He calls the picture "a benchmark in how to do period and create glamour in a realistic setting filled with peeling wallpaper and dripping walls with trash in the street." He's particularly impressed with Wong's ways of using clothing to tell a story. "The costumes are always rooted in reality—they take into account the economic status of the character—but they also tell you who the person wants to be. He makes you feel the character is dressing up, not that the director is dressing them up to make them into a symbol. It's about how people become transformed when they dress up. But it's also about the relationship between dressing and *un*dressing—how they're transformed when they take off those clothes."

Perhaps the finest use of fashion in contemporary film, Wong's evocation of Hong Kong bathes us in an aching beauty that, at times, seems to suffocate the very passions it adorns; those cheongsams can squeeze the life out of you. In the end, it is no surprise that Mo-wan steps away from what appears to be his hopeless pas de deux with Li-zhen, lighting out for Singapore whose aura of lazy, Nanyang freedom is signified by a palm tree. It's classic Wong that this film of apparent simplicity should end by radically expanding its field of vision. Even as newsreel footage of Charles DeGaulle places what we've been watching in the context of colonialism, Mo-wan's visit to Angkor Wat makes us see how he and Li-zhen, in their story of unrequited love, are part of the grand, mythic sweep of human life depicted on the stone friezes of those enduring ruins.

27

If Wong Kar Wai has unqualified respect—and maybe a smidgen of envy—for anyone, it is his production designer, costumer, hair-and-make-up artist, and film editor William Chang Suk Ping, his closest and most important collaborator since before the beginning. He calls him "the guardian angel of my films." Back when Wong was still a writer, he and Chang used to spend long nights together drinking and talking about cinema—what was good, who they liked, what they dreamed of making themselves. They discovered an affinity so deep that one is reminded of the marriage between Baz Luhrmann and his brilliant production designer wife, Catherine Martin—you can't imagine the one without the other. Trusting Chang's taste completely, he has never done a major project without him. When the Met's Costume Institute asked Wong to be artistic director of its 2015 *China: Through the Looking Glass* show, it was inevitable that a few nights before it opened, I'd see the two of them talking together in the exhibition space. Chang is, after all, an inventive and fastidious artistic mind. It was he who insisted on period underwear in *Days of Being Wild* so the clothes would hang properly, put the blond wig and red shades on Brigitte Lin in *Chungking Express*, designed *In the Mood for Love*'s stylized '60s setting, and had the courage and clout to tell Wong that the original cut of *Fallen Angels* was disastrously cold and unlikable. "He's an even bigger pain in the ass than me," Wong says fondly, recalling how Chang's perfectionism has more than once led to long delays in the shooting schedule.

Easily the shyest member of Wong's inner circle, Chang, who works for other directors as well, doesn't like to be photographed or do interviews. But he has a quiet charisma that makes you come to him. He is one of those people who appears to be in on some secret, which may be why stars are drawn to him and why everyone on Wong's sets seems to confide in him. When we met to talk about his partnership with Wong at Classified, a European style restaurant in Causeway Bay, he was laughingly amiable but also nervous—he kept slipping outside for a smoke. He told me, as Wong had earlier, that the two know each other so well that they never, ever talk about what needs to be done. When Wong settles on his idea for a new film, he tells Chang who, receiving no other instruction, sets off to create its ambience, its costumes, its hair-dos, its look. He's free, aside from budgetary constraints, to dream up what he will.

"When Kar Wai tells me an idea, I don't think anything. I walk around waiting for something to come. I'm like Kar Wai—it's just waiting, waiting all the time." He laughs. "I have to look for a starting point. Maybe a magazine cover, maybe a jacket—I often start with a costume. It depends. But when I finally meet the thing, I instantly know it is exactly the thing for the film. But I don't know why I have this idea. *In Happy Together* the thing was the brown and yellow sweater that Leslie [Cheung] was wearing, and wallpaper I saw in some Brazilian airport—I don't remember which one. I took a picture of that wallpaper and put it in the film." And does Wong always go along with his choices? "Nearly always," he says, then starts laughing. "I remember in *Fallen Angels* I bought a really shocking pair of green shoes for Michele Reis. Kar Wai, said, 'Are you joking?' He didn't shoot them. I can always tell when he doesn't like something. He doesn't say anything. He just won't shoot it."

Normally, Wong does shoot it and what shows up on the screen has won Chang international recognition for being one of the greatest—and given his budgets, perhaps *the* greatest—designer in contemporary movies. If *Chungking Express* made Chris Doyle a star, Chang finally got his full due after *In the Mood for Love*. Fifteen years after its release, my colleagues at *Vogue* still rightly rhapsodize about the more than twenty high-necked cheongsams, also known as *qipaos*, that he designed for Maggie Cheung. When I mention that his work in this film probably inspired the whole Met show, he sighed: "After all these years, it's always *In the Mood for Love*.

It was actually very normal in those days for women to wear a *qipao*. My mother wore one every day, not Western clothes. In those days, everybody had a tailor come to their house. Kar Wai and I didn't think it was going to be a big thing. We didn't think the clothes were very special or anything like that, but after showing it to the public at Cannes, everybody was saying, *It's so beautiful!*" He gave a bemused smile. "It was like the Western audience thought they knew better than us."

Like Wong, Chang puts enormous faith in auspicious coincidence and magical thinking. "Things will come to you if you think really hard," he insists. "They really will. On *Days of Being Wild*, I was looking for an old fridge, in those days very hard to find, and I kept thinking of it and thinking of it, and then my assistant found one. If it's always in your mind, things will come to you eventually. For *Happy Together*, I went with Chris [Doyle] to shoot the waterfall in Argentina, and there was so much water pouring—when we took the shot back, everybody loved it. Later, Kar Wai said he wanted to shoot the waterfall again. But when we went back, there was almost no water. With the first shot, it had been raining for a week. It was pure luck. Kar Wai and I always believe this: Accept and it will come."

28

When I asked Wong Kar Wai about the ending of *In the Mood for Love*, I was shocked by how much his original conception differed from the film he actually released. Audiences adore Tony Leung's Chow Mo-wan for his soulful decency and reticence, but Wong had planned to make him a tad caddish. Rather than pine for Maggie Cheung's Su Li-zhen, he was going to lure her into bed in Singapore as a warped form of revenge against her—how dare she feel superior to his adulterous wife! This would, of course, have soured everyone's perception of Mo-wan and, I suspect, made the film much less beloved. But this cruel seduction never happens in the actual film, and the reason has little do to with what we normally think of as artistic "vision." Wong fully intended to include this scene—which has some of the raw humanity he loves in Fassbinder—but when the production ran out of time to make the Cannes deadline, he improvised a new ending: the metaphysical finale in Angkor Wat.

Although I can't help but find this change disconcertingly arbitrary—Mo-wan's whole character was transformed simply because the film had been promised to a festival?—such changes are not rare in Wong's films. The "bonus features" of his DVDs provide a trove of outtakes that don't mesh with the films we've just seen. On the *Happy Together* disc, there are scenes of Lai getting involved with a Chinese tourist played by Shirley Kwan; *In the Mood for Love*'s extras show us a comically mustachioed Mo-wan's return to Hong Kong in the 1970s, years after the actual movie ends.

"If you are paying attention," Wong explained to me one night, "you realize that every story can go in so many directions. And each of those directions can also go in many more directions." As he said this, I couldn't help thinking of Borges's story "The Garden of Forking Paths," which tells of a legendary Chinese maze-designer and writer whose novelistic magnum opus attempts to create a fictional world in which we see every possible outcome of every event, to follow every fork in every path. Although Wong's sense of possibility is not so insanely ambitious, he does shoot endless hours of footage that may or may not—he never knows in advance—take his film along a new narrative fork. William Chang tells me that he edits it all in case Wong wants to include it.

There is, of course, nothing uncommon about a filmmaker making big changes in a movie. Test audiences have brought many a dead character back to life in time for opening day, and occasionally gotten them killed. What makes Wong's case special is that his filmmaking process isn't an attempt to render a finished idea on the screen—the way Hitchcock shot the whole film in his head before the cameras ever started rolling. Nor is he obsessed with creating a cinematic version of the *pièce bien faite*, as the French once termed the perfectly-tooled drama. Instead, he places enormous faith in serendipity. Closer in spirit to an explorer than to an architect, he sets out to *discover* a film, a long journey that can begin with something as ephemeral

as a concept (gay Hong Kongers in Buenos Aires) or the call of an actress's face (Nicole Kidman's led Wong to dream up his never-made film about a White Russian spy, *Lady from Shanghai*). This approach clearly pays benefits—his works shimmer with life—yet it often leaves his films feeling slightly off kilter. As with Godard and Terrence Malick, there are patches that dip, jostle each other or come out of the blue—the way Tony Leung suddenly turns up at the end of *Days of Being Wild*.

I once suggested to him that his way of making movies reminded me of those mansions built by eccentric millionaires with rooms added onto the back, doors leading to nowhere, and gables rising at weird angles from the roof.

"No," he said, "that's not right. It's like *this*." He took out a piece of paper and quickly drew a tree. "You plant a tree in the garden and you expect it will be a perfect tree. But then something happens, maybe a storm blows off a branch—like when Leslie had to leave early when we were shooting *Happy Together*—and you realize that it no longer looks the way you expected. So to regain balance in your garden, you plant a bush over here"—he scribbled one in to the right of the tree—"but for some reason it doesn't grow as well as you like, so you plant a flower over here and one over there, but only one is really nice, so you dig up the other one. And you keep doing this. Then, at some point you stop, and if you're lucky, what you have will be beautiful. It won't be what you expected, but the garden will still be beautiful."

29 When *2046* first showed in Cannes in 2004, it had already become notorious as a run amok project, an endlessly-delayed, years-in-the-making film that, so the rumors went, left famous Chinese stars sitting around bored in expensive Bangkok hotel rooms while Wong Kar Wai, like the target of a clumsy satire about pretentious artists, drifted about trying to find "inspiration." As if that wasn't enough, the Cannes screening had to be put back, a rescheduling that left some festival faithful fulminating—how dare this vainglorious Hong Kong huckster make the world's greatest festival wait on him! The only problem with this narrative of directorial hubris and folly was that *2046* turned out to be thrilling. If its splendors are occasionally a tad over-ripe, the film marks a kind of culmination of Wong's work—"a summing up" he told me at the time. Lavish and expansive, this self-reflexive sequel to *In the Mood for Love* is an operatic blend of romantic melodrama, science fiction, and teasing commentary on the future of Hong Kong. If it remains less admired than its predecessor, that's because it's bigger, darker, and messier. What's good in *2046* cuts far deeper.

In a terrific old-school movie star turn, Tony Leung returns as writer Chow Mo-wan, but he's not the same lovelorn cuckold we last saw whispering into a hole in Angkor Wat. Now dashingly mustachioed, he wears the surface cynicism of the romantically wounded hero in a classic Bogart or Gable film. Since losing Li-zhen (Maggie Cheung appears here only in the briefest of flashes), he's become a lady killer. We discover that, back in Singapore, Mo-wan had an affair with a gambler also named Su Li-zhen (another of Wong's doubles) played with great feeling by Gong Li. But he can't forget the original. Returning to Hong Kong, he moves back into the hotel where Li-zhen once helped him write. Unable to rent their old room, 2046, he settles for 2047, beginning a series of encounters with the women who move into 2046. He helps out the doomed Lulu (Carina Lau), Yuddy's old lover from *Days of Being Wild*. He begins a platonic friendship with his landlord's daughter, Wang Jing-Wen (Faye Wong), who's in love with a Japanese man (Takuya Kimura) her father won't let her marry. In the film's finest scenes, he wins and breaks the heart of a lovely, high-class party girl Bai Ling, played with wrenching depth by Zhang Ziyi. Students of screen acting should study Zhang's and Leung's shifting emotions in their final dinner at Goldfinch Restaurant (where, it's worth noting, Wong carefully has them sit on the other side of the room from where Mo-wan dined with Li-zhen in *In the Mood for Love*). It's hard to get better than that.

As if all these love stories weren't enough for one film, Wong interlaces a second level of reality, showing us the imaginary world that Mo-wan invents for his science fiction novel, *2046*, which is based on the actual relationship between Jing-Wen and her Japanese boyfriend. Set in a sparklingly dystopian world of high rises and bottomless loneliness—Wong says his original inspiration here was Godard's *Alphaville*—the action centers on a high-tech train to the magical city, 2046, where nothing ever changes. Only one man has ever gotten there, Tak (also played by Kimura), who lost the love of his life there. Riding this train filled with boundless memories, he meets and falls for one of the android assistants, who in a parallel to the real world, is also played by Faye Wong. Like the Hong Kong in which Mo-wan lives, the future that Mo-wan invents is a place of lost love and inescapable memories. Which is to say that it's about himself (and, glancingly, the '60s vision of the future). This is, in fact, its primary interest. As science fiction, the futuristic scenes are neither especially engaging nor satisfying, despite Carina Lau and Faye Wong making for very fetching androids who can cry actual tears. Not only does Kimura give a drab performance, but Wong actually shot elaborate footage of the city 2046 that we never see in the film but whose absence we somehow feel. It's like looking at a tree with too many missing branches.

Wong Kar Wai did not choose the number 2046 arbitrarily. It marks the final year of the 50-year period following the handover, an interim phase during which China promised to allow "one country, two systems"—meaning Hong King would remain semi-autonomous before being fully integrated. That said, this symbolic date carries no obvious political charge. As Stephen Teo has noted, its male lead, Tony Leung, comes from Hong Kong while all the film's actresses were born on the Mainland, yet it's hard to know how to parse the meaning of this teasing detail. Certainly there's no suggestion that the futuristic city of 2046 is the embodiment of, say, Chinese tyranny. If there is a political theme in the film, it's the same one as in Mo-wan's personal story: the price of being stuck in memories of the past. *2046* is about the need to change. Mo-wan needs to get past Li-zhen and, as Faye Wong's character tells him, move on to 2047. Hong Kong needs to recognize that it can't forever stay the same city it was the day before the handover.

Put in this way, the film may sound schematic and bloodless. In fact, *2046* is positively bursting with juicy material—the usual spectacular production design by William Chang, Chris Doyle's stunning photography (their last collaboration to date) and a luxurious score that ranges from Shigeru Umebayashi's lushly romantic score to Nat King Cole singing quite movingly, during moments of holiday sadness, about chestnuts roasting on an open fire. Not to mention the superb performances by Leung, Gong Li, and Zhang Ziyi. Or the sheer proliferation of love stories and melancholy memories. Or the many carom-shot references and internal

rhymes that point us back to his earlier movies. This is a busy film, yet hidden within its busyness lies one of Wong's recurring ideas. For all the restlessness of his style and his characters, his vision of true happiness seems to lie in quiet moments. It's writing with—not sleeping with—Jing-Wen that Mo-wan calls "the best summer," and this thought recalls Lai's remark in *Happy Together* that he and Ho were never happier than when Ho was ill and they just stayed together in their room. For Wong, the truest bliss seems to come, almost by surprise, in those flickering moments when genuine feeling emerges from the hurly-burly of daily life or the flames of romantic ardor. Is there any more soulful moment in his work than the one in *Fallen Angels* when Takeshi Kaneshiro watches his father watching the videotape his son has made of him and affectionately saying to himself, "Stupid kid"?

30

According to William Chang, you can count on three things turning up in a Wong Kar Wai film: rain, jukeboxes, and clocks. Of this trio, the last are the most inescapable. You find them tick-tocking away from the very beginning of his first personal film, *Days of Being Wild*, when Yuddy tells Su Li-zhen she will always remember a single minute in April of 1960, to the climactic railway station fight in his latest film, *The Grandmaster*, where the platform clock counts the minutes until the showdown. The omnipresent clocks are appropriate because Wong's work is obsessed with time's many permutations—in itself, as a psychological perception, and as a cinematic device. He speeds time up and slows it down; he makes it repeat itself and come back in tiny echoes like a cry bouncing down a canyon; he hopscotches between the past, the present, and the future. Aware of time's unrelenting flow, nearly all his characters spend their lives being carried along by its human consequences—the play of memory and nostalgia, of forgetting and not-forgetting. They are constantly looking backward in hopes of recapturing something impossible to recapture, a hope that Wong suggests defines most of our lives. "Why can't it be like it was before?" Zhang Ziyi asks Tony Leung near the end of *2046*, a line that nearly every Wong hero or heroine could ask. If there's any saving grace, it comes in the moments of piercing truth and evanescent splendor that can redeem, if not stop, the passage of time.

Because of his affection for '60s Hong Kong—its fashion, pop songs, décor—Wong is often reckoned a nostalgist. In some ways, this is obviously true. As we were doing interviews for this book, he never looked happier than when he took me to the retro Goldfinch Restaurant in Causeway Bay or when he rhapsodized about the picturesque world of his childhood, a Hong Kong *Amarcord* that inspired almost all his films. Yet it is one thing to be excited by the style of the era when one grew up and another to want to actually live there. Wong's nostalgia is not naive. For all his love of form-fitting cheongsams and the Latin rhythms of Xavier Cugat, he's under no illusion that life in '60s Hong Kong was better or freer. *In the Mood for Love* shows how imprisoning those days could be, while *2046* is precisely about the danger of being trapped in memories of a past to which one can never return. Wong knows that time moves on, and like it or not, so must we.

This is a truth steeped in sadness, regret, melancholy. What gives Wong's clocks their force is that they pull us back to one of Wong's unwavering themes—the truth of transcience, the inescapability of loss. In a sense, of course, this is the human condition. All things must pass, all men are mortal—we all know *that*. Yet it is difficult knowledge to keep in our heads. In his work, Wong seems never to forget it. Even at their most whimsical, love-struck and radiant, his films are imbued with awareness that the world, and what we love in it, will forever keep slipping away from us.

31

THE WKW MENU

Like a groaning dim sum cart, Wong Kar Wai's work has always been full of food, from canned pineapple in expired cans to the seasonal dumplings that the Shanghainese Mrs. Suen serves in *In the Mood for Love*. Some of his characters sell food like Jacky Cheung's Fly with his fishball stand in *As Tears Go By*. Others serve it, like Faye Wong handing Tony Leung's Cop 663 his chef salad in *Chungking Express*. Sometimes, they wash it off plates, as Leung's Lai does at the Chinese restaurant in *Happy Together*. *In the Mood*'s romance between Tony Leung's Mo-wan and Maggie Cheung's Li-zhen takes some of its flavor from the fact that they meet while buying wonton noodles. *My Blueberry Nights* is actually named for a food.

Wong is so renowned for food scenes that it's assumed he's a gourmand, if not an actual gourmet. When people learn that I've occasionally had dinner with him, they nearly always say something like, "You must've eaten really well." That, alas, isn't true. Although I've had a couple of fantastic meals with him over the years, including a feast of roasted duck, mock goose, and hairy crab at the Kiangsu Chekiang and Shanghai Residents (HK) Association, Wong is not by any stretch what people call a foodie. In Manhattan, he stays in a hotel whose downstairs is occupied by an inventive East-meets-West restaurant run by David Chang, whom you might call the Wong Kar Wai (or perhaps Quentin Tarantino) of American chefs. No matter. He prefers to eat across the street at the Midtown branch of Joe's Shanghai having mediocre *xiao long bao*, rice cakes, and crispy fish in a sauce that is too sweet. This isn't because of timidity on Wong's part—he talks delightedly about being taken to eat pig vulva in Tokyo—but because he doesn't favor that kind of fashionable restaurant.

Although Wong does have a taste for Japanese food, his palate's default setting is Chinese, enough so that we've shared some dire meals at restaurants in Cannes with names like Le Royal Bambou. The first few times we met in Hong Kong, he took mischievous delight in tweaking my comically touristic desire for "authentic" local fare. One night he took me to dinner and insisted on ordering. The first two dishes to arrive were chicken kidneys in broth, and to my blanching dismay, slabs of tofu the size of the monolith in *2001* sitting in what looked like a trough of tepid pig's blood. "I've already eaten," he said with a smile and sat back to watch me choke the corpuscles down. (The kidneys, though, were delicious). Even on my last visit, finishing up the interviews for this book, he took quiet delight in ordering me that Cantonese specialty, pork lung soup.

"Dinner is a very intimate thing," he said over those lungs. "Anyone can go for coffee or a drink, but you agree to have dinner with someone, that's different. It has a meaning. You really *see* people when you watch them eat." As we talked, I grasped something I should have realized much earlier. Wong puts so much food in his films not because he's obsessed by food itself but because the down-to-earth reality of food—and eating—can be so charged with so much meaning, from Proustian nostalgia to seductive brio to lovesick binging. Just as he has little use for movie sex scenes and action scenes, which he finds "boring" and unrevealing, he feels not the remotest attraction to so-called food porn. He'd never show a dish just to make the audience's mouth water. Wong's characters may be constantly eating, but almost without exception, this is only because this helps him express what he actually does care about—emotion.

32

If one had to choose Wong Kar Wai's most perfect work, the winner would probably be "The Hand," his 43-minute contribution to *Eros*, the three-part 2004 omnibus film dragged down by, of all people, the great Michelangelo Antonioni in whose honor Wong had agreed to contribute. Largely shot in a sleepless 72-hour period during a break from making *2046*, this immaculately-turned melodrama has the compressed purity of a Maupassant short story—one idea, nothing extraneous, emotions flawlessly calibrated. Set around the same time as *2046*, it gives the '60s trilogy a gorgeously wrought capstone.

Chang Chen stars as Zhang, an apprentice Hong Kong tailor whose slippery boss sends him on an errand to the apartment of Miss Hua, a gorgeous, high-class courtesan played by the gorgeous, high-class actress Gong Li. While waiting outside for admission, he overhears her having sex with one of her "boyfriends." When she finally deigns to see Zhang, she notices his sexual excitement, and for some reason—whim, manipulation, response to his youthful good looks—she proceeds to satisfy him with her hand. So begins a long relationship between the devoted Zhang who tailors her clothes with doting care– he's fallen for his fantasy of this woman—and the far more practical Miss Hua who feels no qualms about yelling at him or letting him suffer the presence of her lovers. Even as years pass and Miss Hua starts to fade, losing her wealthy clients, moving to cheaper digs, running up clothing bills she can't pay, Zhang remains touchingly faithful to her or, perhaps more accurately, to his dream of her.

While "The Hand" bears clear resemblances to Fassbinder's *Lola*, even featuring music by Peer Raben who scored that earlier film, Wong says his immediate inspiration for "The Hand" came from the 2003 SARS epidemic that hit Hong Kong hard. It was considered risky to touch someone you didn't know—you could get infected. Zhang does get "infected" by Miss Hua's hand—the disease is love—but Wong's handling is almost chaste. The film's most sensual moments come when Zhang is doing his work as a tailor, measuring Miss Hua's body with his hands, testing the cut of the fabric, a process that Christopher Doyle shoots with an almost fetishistic gaze. Such displacement is typical of Wong who dislikes sexual explicitness on film, finding it not just crude but psychologically mistaken. The true source of eroticism, he says, lies not in the flesh but in our dream of the one we love and desire. No actress is better to dream on than Gong Li who, one might say, à la Godard, is an axiom of the cinema. In this, one of her best and most deeply-felt performances, she makes us feel Miss Hua's fall from imperious sexiness to tragic poignancy, yet she never becomes a whit less fascinating—we understand why Zhang is drawn to her. We are also reminded that, in an era when Hollywood has almost forgotten about women characters, Wong revels in showcasing them. He has no superior as a director of actresses. Maggie Cheung, Carina Lau, Faye Wong, Brigitte Lin, Zhang Ziyi, Gong Li—they are never lovelier or more artful than when working with him. He has, one might say, the touch.

33

Wong Kar Wai's key collaborators are all famous except one—his producer, Jacky Pang Yee Wah, an energetic woman who probably spends more time with him than anyone other than his wife, Esther. Always bustling, always laughing, fond of cigarettes and wine, she is not only the member of Wong's team it's most fun to hang out with, but she also serves an invaluable function. She knows how to get done what needs to be done and does it in a spirit that he admires—Pang is a boost, not a drag. "To get things ready for a film is very hard," Wong says, "and many people get depressed. But Jacky's always outgoing and upbeat. That's something unique about her. She knows exactly the complexity of what has to be done, but at the same time, she's always positive about it."

More than a quarter century on, she still remembers the first time Wong entered her consciousness, back when she was starting out as a lowly production assistant. "I went to a midnight show in Mongkok of *As Tears Go By*," she told me one night on the roof of the new Jet Tone offices in Cyberport. "I was so fond of the film I walked from Mongkok to Tsim Sha Tsui and all the way back. There weren't any other Hong Kong filmmakers making a film like that. I thought, 'I want to work for this man.'" She was in luck. When much of the production team quit *Days of Being Wild*—they couldn't live up to Wong's demands—she landed a job as a production assistant helping with locations. She instantly displayed the resourcefulness that would eventually make her Wong's right hand woman. Wong desperately needed to shoot in Queen's Café, a Hong Kong institution, but nobody could make that happen. "What I did," said Pang, "was that my assistant and I went there for lunch and dinner for two months. Soon we knew everybody there, so we talked to the manager and asked if we could meet the owner. Everybody was so helpful—and we got the place!" She laughed and shook her head. "We were so fed up with the food there."

She's been getting what Wong needs ever since. It was Pang who was left behind as human collateral in Manila when *Days of Being Wild* still had bills to pay in the Philippines. It was Pang who paid off the Triads in Buenos Aires during the filming of *Happy Together*—"I was used to doing it here in Hong Kong," she told me, grinning. It was Pang who found the electrified warming boots for cold-hating action choreographer Yuen Woo-ping as they shot *The Grandmaster* in the bitter winter of Manchuria. When Wong needed to secure a last minute permit to shoot at Angkor Wat—where no one had filmed—it was, of course, Pang he sent to Cambodia, and though it was a holiday weekend in the nearby town of Siem Reap, she got the papers and *In the Mood for Love* its finale. "I love being able to know I did it," she said, still pleased 15 years later.

I'd been told that Pang would be a good person to talk to about the frustrations of working for a filmmaker notorious for delaying, improvising, stopping production, and flirting with deadline disaster. But when I brought this up, she was having none of it. By now, she told me, everyone on a Wong Kar Wai film knows the drill. His films have established their own version of normal, and everyone accepts that this is what Wong needs. In case I needed reminding, she added with a firmess born of loyalty, "The rest of us are doing our individual things. Kar Wai is the one who holds everything together."

No doubt that's true, but Wong can't speak highly enough of her ability to pull off things others might find impossible. "Jacky is the only one of us with patience," he told me. "Dealing with Chris, William, and me can be hell. Just imagine, if you need to move from one location to the other and it's *your* job to get the three of us on a bus. William will be slow, and I will be talking, and Chris at the last minute will be, 'I have to make a call' or 'I have to take a pee.' You can never get these three people walking at the same time to the bus. That's what she has to do—get us on the bus. And she *does* it."

34

In the summer of 2014, I talked to a young Chinese-American who'd done some work for Wong Kar Wai in New York and admires him inordinately. He told me that when he first met the director, he'd expected him to seem like a Real Artist, but "he was more like a Chinese businessman."

He wasn't wrong to think this. Wong is a case study in what it takes to thrive as an independent filmmaker in an industry now defined by extremes: Even as a handful of blockbusters make hundreds of millions of dollars, there's a glut of smaller films that struggle to be seen, much less turn a profit. In his dream world Wong would focus exclusively on making labors of love; in the actual existing world, he's had to become a businessman. He is a good one, too—"over-good," a distributor once told me—although whenever I mention this he gets annoyed. It's as if I'm suggesting that he's one of those guys like Takashi Murakami for whom courting commercial success is part of their art. In fact, I say it respectfully. Wong has played the game well enough that, for nearly a quarter century, he has not only been able to pursue his personal vision—making the films he wants, in the way he likes, on the schedule he needs—but he retains ownership of the copyrights to all eight of the films he's made since becoming independent. This is a self-won freedom enjoyed by only a smattering of filmmakers, of whom Godard is surely the doyen. When I asked how he's managed to achieve this, he said, "You have to be tough."

I once asked William Chang why, given all his own enormous gifts, he had never become a director. "I don't want the responsibility," he replied. "I don't want to do what Kar Wai has to do." This means not only starting his own production company, Jet Tone Films, but running his own talent agency, Project House, which manages actors like Chang Chen and Wong's greatest star, Tony Leung. It means chasing money in the markets that have it—in 2014, he signed a deal with the Chinese juggernaut Alibaba. It means being personally involved in selling and marketing his work—he's brilliant at thinking up special edition DVDs and booklets that, for the Japanese in particular, are cinematic catnip. It means making different cuts of a film like *The Grandmaster* for different markets, an enterprise that horrifies many fans and critics—shouldn't there be one definitive version?—but doesn't faze Wong, who keeps tinkering with films he doesn't think quite perfect. It means feeling responsible for his 25 employees, some of whom have been with him for 20 years and count on him for their livelihood. It means maintaining his company's cash flow by shooting music videos such as "Six Days" for DJ Shadow and oodles of much-emulated commercials for brands like Dior, Lancome, and BMW. Some of Wong's ads are so strikingly successful—for instance, the remarkable *www/tk/1996@7'55"hk.net* for designer Takeo Kikuchi—that I find them unnerving. As if to demonstrate his detractors' claims, they show how easily his style can be turned to commercialism.

Of course, now that consumerism is the world's reigning ideology, it is a bit late to get pious about a director making advertisements. Martin Scorsese, David Lynch, David Fincher, Wes Anderson, Clint Eastwood, and Spike Lee have all done ads—not to mention Fellini, Bergman, and even that scourge of capitalism, Godard. Wong uses the comparatively easy money he makes from commercials to keep himself going in order to make films that aren't particularly commercial. For him it's no big deal. "All the brands want is your name," he told me. "As long as you show the car or handbag, they don't care what you do."

The major brand that Wong represents is, naturally, the filmmaker WKW. Although one might think his fame would make it a snap to finance his films, each time is a struggle, not least because the market for so-called art films keeps shrinking and shifting. Over the last decade Wong has been working to expand his reach, making *My Blueberry Nights*, an English-language film shot in the U.S., and *The Grandmaster*, a martial arts film shot in the prosperous China whose audience has made it his biggest commercial hit to date. That film was handled in the U.S. by the Weinstein Company, whose boss, Harvey Weinstein, Wong respects for his perseverance—"Say what you will against Harvey, he is a very hardworking man"—and by Annapurna Pictures, whose founder, Megan Ellison, he admires. "She wants to associate herself with the films she would like to see," he said, and then sighed. If only the rest of the film world could be that way.

35

My Blueberry Nights is an anomaly in Wong Kar Wai's career for several reasons. It is his only film in English, it was shot in the United States, and even his biggest fans don't think it successful. "Why do you dislike it so much?" he asked over drinks one evening in Causeway Bay. I gingerly tried to explain that I didn't hate it but that I'd found it . . . disappointing. Its star, singer Norah Jones, wasn't much of an actress. Its title was, to an American ear, excruciatingly precious. And its love story was a throwback to a kind of youth-drenched film he'd left behind twenty years earlier. As I said all this, Wong sat quietly, occasionally nodding. He is one of the rare directors able to listen to criticism of his movie without feeling the need to answer back—at least, if you're not giving him instructions on how to improve it, as some festival pooh-bahs presumptuously do. "I understand," he said when I finished, then half-jokingly added what he always says whenever I bring up this movie: "But you know that in Russia, it was my most popular film."

I don't doubt it. *My Blueberry Nights* belongs to the long, ill-starred tradition of foreign directors so bedazzled by America that they can't resist making a movie about it. There's an entire sub-genre of such films, many of them fascinating auteur messes like Antonioni's *Zabriskie Point*, Bruno Dumont's *Twentynine Palms*, Péter Gothár's *Just Like America*, Emir Kusturica's *Arizona Dream*, Paolo Sorrentino's *This Must Be the Place* (the world's first Holocaust road comedy, complete with bison) and Wim Wenders' *Paris, Texas*, a film so gaga about the monumental scale of the West that it wowed dinky little Europe, even winning the Palme d'Or at Cannes. What these films have in common is that they're so caught up in mythologizing America that America itself eludes them. The same is true of *My Blueberry Nights*, but in a way all its own.

Harking back to Wong's earlier, not-completed project *A Story of Food*, this episodic film transplants a Hong Kong idea to American soil. Jones plays Elizabeth, a young New Yorker whose favorite diner is run by a British expat, Jeremy (Jude Law) who tells her that her boyfriend is cheating on her. She spends the rest of the night eating blueberry pie, swapping tales with Jeremy and eventually putting her apartment key in a bowl that—in a conceit that's 200-proof Wong—he keeps for customers who are leaving but may one day come back to claim them. Trying to solve the vagaries of love, Elizabeth hits the road, sending postcards to Jeremy as she goes. Her first big stop comes in Memphis, where, working as a bartender, she watches the extravagantly fervent relationship between an alcoholic cop, Arnie (David Strathairn), and his estranged wife, Sue Lynne (Rachel Weisz), who's a cat on a hot tin roof. From there, she heads west to Nevada, where she befriends the poker playing Leslie (Natalie Portman), whose own love issues turn on her complicated relationship to her father. Eventually, Elizabeth returns to Manhattan where, in another quintessential Wongian twist, she realizes that she's traveled the country looking for the man who'd been across the counter all along.

If you didn't know who had made *My Blueberry Nights*, it would probably seem like a talented young American director's charmingly misguided attempt to mimic Wong Kar Wai. It offers a handsome lead actor in Law, an unexpectedly amusing performance from Portman, a passionate turn by Weisz, and gorgeous cinematography by Darius Khondji that is probably a tad too pleased with its gorgeousness. But coming from the man himself three years after *2046*, it goes down like a very weak solution of WKW. Wong's magic touch with actresses didn't work with Jones whose energy is wrong for cinema—singing she's a star, acting she ain't, to retool a famous line from Fanny Brice. Even worse, the English-language script (co-written with novelist Lawrence Block) has a cloying naiveté you don't find in, say, *Chungking Express*, where Wong's dextrous command of Chinese makes his words pitch perfect.

Yet having said all that, it's worth noting that his original conception contains the germ of something interesting. Far from being unaware that he was dealing in the myth of America, Wong intended to have Elizabeth's travels along the American road also be a quasi-mythic journey through American tropes, starting from a Lower East Side café that recalls Hong Kong and gestures (I imagine) toward the early days of Jim Jarmusch. Memphis would embody the delirious emotionalism of Tennessee Williams, Wong's favorite playwright. Vegas would give us the high-stakes milieu of *The Cincinnati Kid*, one of his favorite films. And in the final sequence, which he couldn't afford to shoot, Elizabeth would visit the Los Angeles of Robert Altman. Had this L.A. sequence been included, it would have been easier to appreciate the film's architecture and Wong's play with mythology. Without it, we lose much of his self-conscious awareness that

he is enacting emotional rituals that have been done innumerable times before. As Jones sings in the film's theme,

> The stories have all been told before
> I guess that's just how it goes.

36 Wong Kar Wai has been so successful at establishing himself as a sophisticated international filmmaker that it is sometimes easy to forget how deeply rooted he is in Chinese culture. Never have these roots revealed themselves more clearly than in his 2013 *The Grandmaster*, perhaps the least Westernized of all modern martial arts films. Partly inspired by Wong's own childhood when he used to look into the *kung fu* studios in his Hong Kong neighborhood, it tells the story of Ip Man, the martial arts master of the *Wing Chun* school who became famous for training Bruce Lee. While it received a mixed reception in the West, my Chinese friends think it one of his finest, and most profound, films.

Carrying himself with magisterial calm, Tony Leung stars as Ip, the married scion of a wealthy family from the southern city of Foshan who has devoted his life to the practice and inner discipline of *Wing Chun*. When the Japanese invade Manchuria in northeast China, the retiring northern Grandmaster Gong Baosen (Wang Qingxiang) comes to Foshan for a ceremonial meeting with his southern counterparts at a brothel known as the Gold Pavilion favored by marital arts adepts. Part of this ceremony involves Gong being challenged by a younger southern man—in this case, Ip. Ip prevails, much to the fury of Gong's daughter, Gong Er (Zhang Ziyi), who is her father's natural heir—she alone knows all the secrets of his deadly "64 Hands" technique—but, as a woman, is officially excluded from taking over his mantle. Still, to maintain the family's honor, she challenges Ip to a contest. As anyone who's ever seen a movie knows, they are destined to fall in love. As anyone who's ever seen a Wong movie knows, their love is destined to be filled with loss, regret, and melancholy. They are kept apart by the grand workings of history—in particular, the war and revolution of the 1930s and 1940s—and by the private workings of Er's fiery nature. She has devoted herself to avenging the betrayal of her father by his successor, Ma San (Zhang Jin), an unprincipled *Xingyi* master who easily lives up to his nasty good looks.

On the face of it, *The Grandmaster* sounds like a juicy epic melodrama in the *Dr. Zhivago* vein—it offers the sweep of history, the exotic locations, the separated lovers, even the snowy landscapes. Yet Wong isn't interested in conventional dramatic storytelling. The action skips from era to era with little more than a voice-over to tell us what's happened. Characters turn up, fight with Ip Man, and disappear before they've really registered. The film merely glances at the big emotional moments—for instance, Ip Man losing his family during World War II—that other filmmakers would play out, if not shamelessly milk. In short, much of what would fill a normal epic, kung fu movie, or biopic is deliberately missing from *The Grandmaster*, which like *Ashes of Time*, is a film that, for all its splendors, pares things to the essence. And like *Ashes of Time*, it left many viewers and critics, especially in the West, confused and believing it dramatically inert. You can perhaps forgive such perplexity, for Wong's approach to Ip Man's life is far from obvious. It recalls Borges's remark about art being both algebra and fire.

From the opening frames, the film burns with a sumptuous profusion of wondrous things to look at: an ancient Manchurian temple, William Chang's exquisite Gold Pavilion with its clientele dressed in equally exquisite costumes, the streets of '50s Hong Kong with its émigré cafes and seedily tantalizing neon. (Yes, this is another story of the Chinese diaspora.) Wong's visual panache hits its peak in the three dazzling set-pieces that dominate the action. The movie begins gloriously with Ip, elegant in his sleekly-cut cheongsam and white hat, doing battle at night amidst the silver dance of rain on slate gray pavement. This fight is followed by Ip's encounter with Gong Er in the Gold Pavilion, a fight that begins as a *kung fu* contest that traverses luxurious rooms and leaps atop bannisters yet winds up being filled with romantic emotion. The third great action scene comes near the end when Er has her final showdown with Ma San on a railway station platform swirling with snowflakes as the longest train you've ever imagined just keeps roaring by. Even as Wong makes sure that we register the force of the action in these scenes—feet kicking chests, fists conking chins—he emphasizes the combatants' physical grace. Just as *In the Mood for Love* verged on becoming a musical, *The Grandmaster* can almost be seen as a dance film. Inventively stylized by choreographer Yuen Woo Ping, the martial arts have never looked more balletic than here—they're an art form, not merely a way of beating people up.

While all this visual opulence (superbly shot by Philippe Le Sourd) gives *The Grandmaster* its fire, the algebra lies in Wong's underlying idea: the clash between two different ways of living out a tradition. What makes Ip a hero is that, through everything, he hews to the righteous path of *kung fu*. He not only honors the discipline of *Wing Chun* to become a master of the art but does the thing one must do to be a true grandmaster: He passes the legacy on, even at the cost of his own private life. Despite Leung's eloquently watchful performance, Ip's insistence on giving himself wholly to martial arts makes him nearly impenetrable—his life lacks savor. You see why Wong felt the need to invent the fictional character of Gong Er, who, in Zhang's stinging performance, yields to the fury and mire of human veins. While Ip gives up everything for the transcendent glory of martial arts, she's the film's wildly beating heart. She gives up everything—happiness, martial arts, even love—for family honor and vengeance. As so often happens in Wong, his heroine proves more vivid than his hero.

At the beginning of the film, Ip Man describes the Chinese characters for the term kung fu, saying: "Kung fu—words. A horizontal and a vertical. Make a mistake—horizontal. Be the last one standing, and you win." By the end, Gong Er is horizontal and Ip Man is still standing; her family's martial arts school is lost, while he lives vertically on. Although Wong says he's personally closer in spirit to Gong Er than to Ip Man, *The Grandmaster* nevertheless celebrates Ip Man's victory in holding on to values he thinks important and not letting them be washed away by changing times. Coming in a period when so much of the Chinese past is being erased in the mad rush for prosperity, the film takes on a larger meaning that's at once social and spiritual. What starts out looking like a martial arts saga expands, on reflection, to reveal itself as a much larger story about the preservation (and loss) of cultural tradition in the face of onrushing change.

37

Wong Kar Wai's films interweave many rich and variegated themes—time, memory, exile, heartbreak, the many faces of Hong Kong—yet in trying to explain why I love his work so much, I find myself beginning with beauty and ending with emotion. These qualities once lay at the heart of the cinematic experience, which was designed to pull us out of ourselves and take us into a world richer and more magical than our own. They have largely gone missing in a present-day cinema largely devoted to ugly CGI effects and homely "indie" realism, to acting that prizes wrought-up "honesty" over heartfelt elegance, to impersonal violence over sexual love—"Guns are the jewelry of men," the poet William Matthews wrote of the movies—and to masculine narratives that marginalize women. Wong's work goes against all this, even in a *kung fu* film like *The Grandmaster* whose emotional peak comes when the ravaged, opium-addicted Gong Er (immaculately lit, of course) finally tells Ip Man that she always did love him. Like a director from Hollywood's Golden Age, Wong understands the romantic appeal of movie stars, and knows how to capture their aura on-screen; yet he also has a forward-looking belief that cinema isn't ultimately about plots or dialogue but about capturing evanescent moments of poetry, truth and emotion, about expressing that which can't be reduced to words—spring light piercing through the ordinary and leaving it transfigured.

Wong makes ravishingly lovely films in a world made skeptical, even suspicious, of beauty by too much easy prettiness in advertising and by a long-since-vanished avant-garde's belief that true art should assail bourgeois sensibilities. This has led some detractors to refer to his style as "eye candy," an idea at once puritanical—what precisely is so wicked about a movie being a pleasurable confection?—and wrongheaded, for it suggests that Wong's work lacks the deep-dish substance, the meat and potatoes of art. In fact, he is simply following Valéry's dictum that one should be light like a bird not like a feather. Without belaboring his own seriousness, Wong is forever searching for new styles of beauty—the playful, post-New Wave lyricism of Faye Wong's antics, the tango-lashed melancholy of a grubbily gorgeous Buenos Aires, the elegantly stylized nostalgia for an impossibly glorious Hong Kong—and within this beauty, which is never cold or Olympian but charged with longing, he's searching for something vital, an idea, an emotion, a shimmering flash of transcendence that gets inside you and warms the blood. For him, beauty isn't the denial of feeling but its costume. This is clear in his unwavering attention to his actors; he never lets his style get in the way of their humanity.

One night in L.A. we were talking about the dreamy pleasures of old movies, and I told him I was impressed by the way that, in his own work, everyone is always filmed as if they were beautiful.

"You know, I don't shoot them that way because I like beauty," he told me. "I do it because I love them."

SIX CONVE

JOHN POWERS

RSATIONS

WONG KAR WAI

One torrid summer afternoon, Wong Kar Wai takes me to see the street where he grew up: Knutsford Terrace in Tsim Sha Tsui on the Kowloon side of Hong Kong. It's a relatively quiet, two block long pedestrian street in the southern shadows of the Hong Kong Observatory where he used to play as a boy. In the 1960's and 70's of his youth, the neighborhood was a melting pot of peoples, flavors, cultures, and moods that would later populate his memory and films. Back then it was primarily a residential street that was home to a range of immigrants to Hong Kong. His neighbors included recent Shanghai arrivals, some poor and some well off—movie stars, writers, ladies of the night, tailors, Indian shopkeepers and Filipino musicians. There was even a guest house with a terrace on which White Russian émigrés would sit outside and drink. Nearby and within walking distance were the two cinemas, London and Princess where he saw his first films both with his mother and by himself, and the upscale nightclub, The Bayview, where his father worked. His school was next door to their apartment; the shops his mother frequented, all relatively close by. One's life existed within a circle of a few blocks, so he tells me. It was left to one's mind to fly beyond.

Today Knutsford Terrace is known for its lively nightlife, and like much of Hong Kong, it has been inexorably modernized. Along the street one now finds more than 30 bars and international restaurants with names like Munch, Black Stump, The Salted Pig, and Mama Bahama's Caribbean Bar. Wong's childhood home at #2 Knutsford Terrace has vanished. The spot is now occupied by an Italian restaurant with the cute name Papa Razzi, an unconsciously ironic nod to the world-famous filmmaker who once lived there.

Although the area has changed significantly, Wong vividly remembers his old street. Pointing at the buildings, he walks me by his old school, a sunken concrete patch that used to give him nightmares, and a drainage culvert next to an alley. "We used to shimmy up the building's pipes here. It was one of those kid things you did to be daring—a bit exciting and dangerous."

The sun is blazing and eventually we retire to an upstairs restaurant down the street from #2. Called the Knutsford Steak, Chop & Oyster Bar, it's all glass and glistening wood.

"So what do you think of your old street?" I ask.

"A few years ago, when I first saw it again," he says, "I thought, It's nice. It's energetic. Young people will enjoy it."

"Yeah, but didn't you find the changes kind of depressing?"

He shakes his head. "It's better to see the old neighborhood have a new energy and new form rather than die and become a ghost town."

"And does Knutsford Terrace strike you as an interesting place to shoot these days?"

"No."

And with that we begin talking about things he clearly does find interesting, things I'd never heard him talk about before.

AMARCORD

It's strange. I've known you for twenty years yet I know almost nothing about where you come from. So let me start with something simple: Do you consider yourself a Hong Konger?
— Can we talk about that tomorrow? *Laughs.* It's a bit complicated.

Okay, let's start at the beginning. You were born in Shanghai but you moved to Hong Kong as a kid. In 1963, right?
— Yes, I was five.

Why did your parents leave Shanghai?
— Actually, they left Shanghai twice. The first time was in 1951, after my older brother was born, but my mom went back to Shanghai after my sister was born and my dad returned to his job on the high seas. Later he decided to settle in Hong Kong, because he had an organizational background and could speak English. He had experience from working on a Scandinavian cargo line, in charge of inventory, food, stores, and meals. He got a job in a famous Chinese restaurant as by then there were many tourists in Hong Kong. My mom joined him at the end of 1962. We lived in Tsim Sha Tsui.

Your parents were part of that wave of migrants to Hong Kong?
— There were two big migrations to Hong Kong. The first was after the civil war ended in 1949 and then later when the Great Famine started around 1959.

They brought you, but what about your older brother and sister?
— They only had permission to bring one kid. My parents had intended to go back and to bring my older sister and brother, too, but then the Cultural Revolution started and the border between China and Hong Kong was closed, so my brother and sister couldn't leave and had to stay with relatives. We didn't see each other until almost ten years later.

What do you remember about Shanghai?
— Not much. Mostly our apartment and streets around it. We lived at the top of a five story, western-style walk-up on Huai Hai Road–it used to be called Avenue Joffre. My mother worked at a lightbulb factory. She would walk me to my grandmother's house on the way to work every day. It was a ten to fifteen minute walk. It was a nice area with trees on both sides of the street and you could hear the leaves rustling in the breeze. The Shanghai Philharmonic practiced close by, and sometimes when she picked me up after work, you could hear the music. In the winter, those trees were white-washed with lime at the roots to prevent them from freezing. Later, I read that a Shanghai writer from the 1920s once described how they resembled the legs of cancan girls. I also remember the public showers because nobody had indoor plumbing at the time. You couldn't see anything through the steam, but you could still hear the ladies giggling.

What neighborhood did you live in?
— The former French Concession. We lived close to my mother's father's compound. His family name was Ko and he had actually designed *all* the gardens in the Concession. My grandfather was a very stern man, well respected in his community. He had three sons and three daughters and placed a high value on his children's education. The eldest, my big uncle, was well-educated and spoke fluent French and worked as a translator for the French police, but even so, in that household, it was Grandfather who had final say in everything.

There were also many grandchildren. In my generation I have more than 20 cousins. Everybody lived in the same compound. There was a house with different buildings, in front of them a garden with beautiful wisteria trees. At dinner, the children would occupy one table while the adults took up another. Grandfather would eat alone. He was very aloof. Everyone sat at another table, even his eldest son who was by then in his 40s.

He sounds forbidding.
— I never met him. He passed away before I was born. I came to know him through my mom, who always spoke of him fondly. My mother was born in 1933 and saw China as a 1940s student. Even though she had a traditional upbringing, she was modern by the standards of that time. She enjoyed dancing and had an active social life. She was the only person in her family who was that way, and she influenced her younger brothers to go out at night and have that lifestyle. Though she was rebellious and disregarded many rules of her father, she was his favorite daughter.

When he became older, he was fond of sweets but he was too proud to ask for them. But my mom knew, so she'd go out and buy cookies, and every day when he'd go out walking—he walked like this [*WKW stands and begins walking with his hands together behind his back*]—she would take some of the cookies, put them in a handkerchief, and put them in his hands. Neither of them ever said a word. But that kind of relationship, distant yet with a mutual understanding, was not uncommon in traditional China. That was what I used as the basis for the relationship between Gong Er and her father in *The Grandmaster*.

How did she meet your father?
— My mother told me she never quite understood why she married my father because they basically had different backgrounds. His father had died when he was only 3 years old, so he had to start taking care of himself at a very early age. He was a second steward on that cargo ship when they first met. It was an officer's position. So I guess my dad looked okay when he was young—tall and respectable in his seafaring uniform. And although mom had many admirers, somehow she was attracted to this man who traveled a lot and knew things that the other young men didn't know.

It sounds like she came from a more cultured background.
— I would put it this way—my mother grew up in a large family. With the opportunities she was allowed, she had the freedom to see life beyond immediate practicalities. She had many interests—music, cinema—and thanks to her parents, she was

a good cook and always sensitive to style. My dad was the opposite. He left home at the age of 12 to become an apprentice and
was a self-taught man. He was a man of practical consequences.
I don't mean he had no interests besides making his living, they
were just not his priorities. He was disciplined and tidy. When
he passed away, I picked up all his things and discovered that
he was very neat and organized, keeping diaries of all the years
he traveled, and holding onto the cards or receipts from the
restaurants he went to. He also numbered each of the letters
he sent to my mom from different ports to make sure they were
not lost. He had files of his documents, passes, union cards. I
even found my entry permit to Hong Kong!

He was a sailor. Did that make him hard to know?
— I hardly knew my dad before I was five. He was like a
stranger back then. He was always at sea and only came
home once a year. He'd show up with his beret and pipe, and
would have some small gifts and this large duffel bag of
canned foods and sugar. Since there was rationing in China
at the time, these things were rare. I only got to know him
after we moved to Hong Kong and settled in. Housing in Hong
Kong was expensive back then because there were so many
other immigrants from China. Like other families, we sublet
two of the rooms of our apartment to keep expenses down
and kept only the main room; and we shared the living room
with the tenants. Though he wasn't really a sailor any longer,
my dad did hold on to things from his life at sea, like his big,
stainless steel desk that dominated our room. Home was
like a second office for him and I was his only crew. *Laughs.*
Later he became the manager of the most popular nightclub
in Hong Kong. He'd go to work until 3 in the morning, then
wake back up in the afternoon. I had to polish his shoes every
day before he went back to work.

What was it called?
— Bayside. It was a westernized nightclub, run by a very rich
Filipino family. It was located in the basement of Chungking
Mansions where I shot *Chungking Express* years later. At the
time, it had the best live band in town and was the hottest
nightspot for movie stars and celebrities. When the Beatles
came to Hong Kong, they held their press conference there.

Was it hard for your parents when they first came?
— They were in good shape when we arrived. The only thing
is, we didn't have any relatives here and couldn't speak the
local dialect. In Shanghai we had all those cousins, uncles,
and aunts, so normally after work everyone gathered together
at my grandfather's place. We'd all have dinner there once
mom got off work and then go back home. It was always full
of people. Once we moved here, it was really only the two of
us, as my father worked at night and came home and slept in
the daytime. It was dreadful.

So is this when you started to go to the movies?
— Back then, Tsim Sha Tsui was full of cinemas. I still remember

the cinemas that we often went to—The Princess for Hollywood
pictures, The Sands, which specialized in European cinema, and
The London for the Shaw Brothers productions which were shot
mainly in Mandarin. In those days, cinemas still had curtains.
I always remember the anticipation and the excitement of the
curtain going up and revealing what was behind it.

Do you remember the first movie you ever saw?
— Yes. It was on our second day here. It was a black and white
Cantonese thriller. This was the first time I saw a naked woman
on the screen—not fully naked, but some sexy lady in her lin-
gerie got murdered.

Did you like that?
— It was something new to me. I never went to the cinema in
Shanghai. But in Hong Kong we started going almost every day.
Even when I went to primary school, my mom would pick me
up after class with my lunch and we went right into a movie.
Laughs. Mom followed Hollywood films when she was young.
She was a big fan of Clark Gable, Errol Flynn, and her favorite
star was Robert Taylor in *Waterloo Bridge*. After 1949, China
banned all Western films, so it was natural for her to pick up
her hobby after all these years. Being far away from her family
and her other children, the movies were also an escape for her.
She soon found herself attracted to a new generation of movie
stars, mostly actors: William Holden, Steve McQueen, and Alain
Delon. She liked a leading man with a handsome face. John
Wayne was never her cup of tea.

Not enough sexiness with John Wayne?
— She found him boring.

So she liked romantic things then?
— She had very diverse tastes: comedy, martial arts, even vampire films! She really enjoyed Christopher Lee who always
played *Dracula*. He was my nightmare. *Laughs.* Together we
must have seen hundreds of films. That explains why, whenever
I was asked to name the person that had the biggest influence
on me in filmmaking, the answer would always be my mother.
She was the one who introduced me to cinema. She was my
film school.

We're sitting in a bar overlooking your old street, Knutsford
Terrace in Tsim Sha Tsui. Right near your school.
— Imagine if your school was next door to where you lived.
Laughs. At that time school was for only half a day. After school,
my classmates would go spend time together, but I never joined
in because when school ended, I'd see my mother's face at the
window.

So what would you do?
— Mostly listen to the radio and read. This was way before the
television days in Hong Kong and there was nothing much for
kids to do in Knutsford Terrace. The first thing that my father did
every day when he woke up was read the newspaper. Because

87

he woke up late, I always read the papers before he did. Although my father was not a very traditional man, he kept telling me, "You have to finish all these classics, the Chinese classics." So he brought me the four books.

Forgive my ignorance, but what are they?
— *Journey to the West*, *Dream of the Red Chamber*, *The Water Margin*, and *The Romance of the Three Kingdoms*.

Did you have a favorite?
— *Dream Of the Red Chamber* was too difficult for me at that age. I liked *Three Kingdoms* better back then. I read it over and over. Looking back, I'm glad my dad urged me to read these classics because they are the DNA of our culture. It would be difficult to understand Chinese thinking without knowing these books. Years later, following the path of my dad, I bought the same books for my son, but he preferred reading *Harry Potter*. *Laughs*. A while back, I had a friend who owned a video game based on *Three Kingdoms*, and I thought it was kind of silly when he recommended it to me. But I did try it eventually. From the moment I sat down to the time I stopped, it was 48 hours straight without sleep. Esther [*WKW's wife*] thought I'd lost my mind! *Laughs*. I couldn't stop playing because I didn't know how to save my game and I was so close to taking over all of China!

What else did you read?
— At that time, my brother and sister still lived in Shanghai, and the only way to communicate with them was to write letters. My father always encouraged me to stay in touch with them and they always talked about the books they had read. Most of the Western classics were banned in China then. Books by Dickens, Balzac, and the Russian masters were the few exceptions, so I felt that had I to pick them up, too. No one else I knew read them. For me, it was mostly out of curiosity instead of passion. And I only focused on the chapters that I found interesting and skipped most of the rest. But the pleasure of reading somehow kicked in and it became my habit to read everything that I could get my hands on, whatever it was. I began to discover books that I could identify with, works of contemporary writers such as [Osamu] Dazai, [Raymond] Carver, and the Latin Americans.

What was Tsim Sha Tsui like when you were a kid? Was it exciting?
— Tsim Sha Tsui in the old days was like Soho today. It was alive 24 hours a day because it was filled with nightclubs. And wherever there are nightclubs, there's all sorts of interesting life. I remember the places closed around 3, but the rule was that you couldn't serve alcohol after midnight, only tea. So in the bars, they'd put alcohol inside the teapots. Ask any old U.S.

Navy sailor or Marine who served in Korean or Vietnam. They'll tell you good stories about it.

Did you ever drink alcohol from a teapot?
— I was too young then and the rules didn't last until I was old enough to drink. What a shame. *Laughs*.

You've set three of your movies, *Days of Being Wild*, *In the Mood for Love* and *2046*, in '60s Hong Kong. Did that seem like a glamorous era to you?
— Hong Kong came alive after, I'd say, '58. The wars brought a lot more Navy men to the area. They had their vacations here and brought with them American influence—the music, the drinks, and all the American pop culture. We called it the Seventh Fleet Syndrome, which covered Hong Kong, as well as most of Southeast Asia and even Korea and Japan. You can easily see it in some of Haruki Murakami's earlier novels. Once every month, Tsim Sha Tsui was filled with sailors. You could find them on the streets, in the shops, even at our place! By then, two of our tenants were women who worked at night. I remember once they hosted a Christmas party for their "boyfriends" at our place. They decorated it with a fake Christmas tree covered in tiny little lights. The living room filled up with sailors bringing drinks, turkeys, and balloons. It was quite surreal for a kid at my age.

So growing up you'd see all these Navy guys on the streets. Was it scary or fun?
— No, it was normal. Like a flock of migrating birds, they hit the town regularly. Growing up in the Kowloon version of *The World of Suzie Wong*, I was no stranger to miniskirts, high heels, and mascara. There were always women around who were

like Carina Lau's character in *Days of Being Wild*. That's why I feel very close to films by Fellini—I know that world. My childhood was sort of a *La Dolce Vita: Hong Kong Style*. I've known all these women—rambunctious, sexy, strong but vulnerable, and very friendly.

Did this excite you?
— Not really, I was too young then. And they always treated me like a kid. It wasn't all about the women, though. Neighbors around us were like convenience stores for those guys. They supplied all their needs: nightlife, food, even clothing. Once in a while, I'd find a line of sailors queuing up outside the door of the tailor who lived next to us. The boys wanted to have suits made. Delivery normally took 48 hours. But in case of emergency, the tailor would often offer 24 hour delivery with a 50% extra charge, and magically the suits would always be ready on time. Only later did I find out that if the deadline was too close, sometimes the tailor wouldn't bother to sew—he'd simply put the suits together with glue! *Laughs*. I was amazed that he never got into trouble with his customers. None of the suits was ever returned, and he never got any complaints over the years. Not even once! Isn't that amazing? I always thought that maybe they never washed them or it never rained in Saigon, so the secret of those suits was never found out.

So things weren't boring on Knutsford Terrace.
— Knutsford Terrace had its day and night. Daytime was quiet. When evening approached, the drama began. By then, my dad was working at the nightclub. He usually returned home around 3 a.m. and my mom would cook him late dinner. But sometimes, his friends would invite him to play cards after work. If he was lucky that night, he would show up before the first light of the morning with *dim sum* in hand. If he wasn't back by then, it meant he was probably in trouble. My mom would dress up and go out to find him. It was quite unusual for a regular woman to go to a card game in those days. Most of the time she would come back with my dad in a few hours and there was always *dim sum* in *her* hand. When I became older, she taught me all sorts of games: cards, *Pai Gow*, which is a kind of Chinese dominos, and mahjong, the way her father taught her. And she taught me another piece of wisdom she learned from him–a good gambler knows when to quit.

Was her father a good gambler?

— I'm sure he knew his game well. There was an old saying in China: *The best way to understand a person is to watch the way he gambles*. It was common in those days that people applied this in deciding their business partners, husbands, or son-in-laws. My mom told me about one Chinese New Year after she met my dad. Her father invited him to come to his house for lunch. People were playing *Pai Gow* for fun and the betting wasn't too serious. Her father offered my dad his chips and excused himself from the table. My dad was obviously into the game that day. He stayed until the end of it and lost most of his chips. Afterward, my grandpa pulled my mom aside and said there are two types of gamblers—the ones who gamble to win, and the ones who do it just to gamble. He warned her: "Your new boyfriend is a lousy gambler. You'd better stay away from him." My mom always joked that her dad was probably right. *Laughs*. I guess because of my mom, the life of a gambler has always fascinated me, and that explains why I often have a gambler character in my films.

Your grandfather obviously had a big influence on your mother.

— He basically trained her like a son. He always said my mom would've been a successful man if she was a boy. And she saw him as kind of a role model. Sometimes, she would use him as an example to tell me what to do. She'd say, "If you want to be a man, you *have* to do it like this. That's what a man is supposed to do."

When we were still in Shanghai, food was rationed and what was available was not very nutritious. My mother had come down with hepatitis and had to go to the hospital. The patients needed better food and when we went to visit her, I smelled it, a 2 inch by 2 inch square of braised pork and sauce on top of rice—more meat than I'd ever seen. But instead of eating it herself, she gave it to us. It was the best meal of my life.

That's very generous.

— In Hong Kong, she managed our household and was popular among our tenants because she was always helpful. She was warm and charming, and always paid attention to details. I still remember one of the tenants who was a night lady. This was in the 60s. She was a looker and always dressed her best. When the ships arrived, she would start early and pick up the first drunk kid she found at the bar. Then she would drop him off at the house and take off with his money and passport, looking for her next target. Those poor kids were normally young service-men who'd just joined the Navy. Many were country boys fresh from their hometown and had no idea how to handle women or liquor. They would wake up in the morning with no money, no passport, and no one to turn to. Not much later, the girl would be back and be as charming as possible before she took off again for the night. My mother felt sorry for these boys because they had nothing to eat and had to wait until this woman came back. So she would sometimes feed them noodles she cooked. Later on, when they came back to Hong Kong, some of these guys would pay her a visit. My mom was a very kind woman and treated them like friends. She would say, "If my son was in this kind of situation, I would want someone to take care of him."

Do you think she was happy?

— She was an outgoing, happy person when she was young, but the fact that two of her children were still in China tore at her. She spent hours and hours writing letters to them. During the Cultural Revolution, supplies in China were short. We had to send oil, clothes, books, and many things back–and she had a big family in Shanghai. Besides her own children, her cousins all needed these things and my mother would take care of that. She got extra income from playing mahjong–she was very good at it. In our apartment, it was 24-hours mahjong. I'd wake up in the morning, they're playing; come back from school, they're playing; and when I went to sleep, they were still playing. But more than the money, it was a way for my mom to forget what she couldn't control.

And your father?

— He was the kind of person who always looked forward. What was done was done. He just kept himself busy. On his day off, he would take out his tool box to fix things. He had spent ten years on a boat, so he knew his tools well and had enough skills as a craftsman. My mom and I would be his assistants. *Laughs*. He was very proud of his tool kit and always took good care of it. He liked to show off his tools to me and taught me how to use them, which I hated. He wanted me to be a disciplined man like him; he needed everything in the right spot at the right time. The way Tony's character at the end of *Days of Being Wild* puts everything in just the right place—that was my father. He liked to mock me for being a sloppy sailor for the way I bunched money up into my pockets.

Judging from your working methods, you sound more like your mother.

— I think so, too. And then a year ago, when my son asked me to help him fix up the apartment that he just moved into with his roommate, the first thing that I did was to get him a tool box! *Laughs*. Only then did I realized my dad's influence on me. I never liked the idea of having a big, stainless steel desk in my house, but at my office or anywhere that I work, there's always a large table with books, scripts, and files neatly laid out on it. Other than these things, the influence of my mom was much bigger.

And you were closer to her, I imagine.

— I adored my mother. When I was young, my dad was usually quite distant and very strict, and in some ways like a tyrant. Mom was my only ally. But that was when I was still a kid. When I was in college, studying graphic arts, I started smoking. It was the cool thing to do. I remember the first time he asked me for a cigarette. That was when things changed. I only wish that we'd had that smoke earlier. It was only later, when he retired and I became a writer, that we had some time together.

If he wanted you to read the classics, he must have respected that you became a writer.

— No, he didn't want me to be in this business. He said, "No, no—not practical. You should go to work in a hotel." Back then, I had long hair, tight jeans, so you could understand why. It wasn't until I began working at the TV station that he was relieved. I wasn't a complete write-off and he started to see some value in me. When he passed away, I found an entire script that he'd written on opened-out packs of Camel cigarettes. But he never mentioned it, and never commented on my works. That was my father. He was not very expressive with words or his feelings.

When I was young, he always wanted me to work in his business. One summer, I worked part time in a coffee shop in WanChai where he was the manager. One of the guys who worked there always gave me a hard time for being the manager's son. My dad worked the night shift then and one evening when he came back to work, he led this guy out the back door and picked a fight with him, roughed him up, but still took a punch in the eye. For the next few nights, he put on his sunglasses during work. But he never talked about it.

Your mother must have been pleased with you, anyway. She went to movies with you every day and came from an aesthetic background, with her father designing gardens.

— She didn't live to see any of my films. But I'm sure she would have liked them if she did because I know her taste. The last film that I saw with my mom was *Jaws*. It was at the Ocean cinema by the Star Ferry. Afterward I took her to a coffee shop nearby. She was not in good health by then, but it was an enjoyable afternoon for her. When *Raiders of the Lost Ark* premiered in Hong Kong, I managed to get two tickets and asked my dad to go with her. I had to work that night but I knew she would like it.

Your first movie was about gangsters. Growing up did you meet gangster types or see them around?

— No. I only saw gangsters in films at first, but I came to know real ones later when I began working in the film business. When I was young, the only people I knew were our neighbors: tailors, sailors, women of the night. And we had writers, too. There were two of them in our building. One was an editor of a newspaper, like Tony's character in *In the Mood for Love*. He wrote columns to make extra money. I knew all the martial arts stories from him. He was the model for Tony's character—but not as handsome.

In your childhood I can sense the origins of at least three of your movies.

— Except for the gangsters, they're all there in those different rooms. So in the writer's room I have the martial arts—

So that's *Ashes of Time* and *The Grandmaster*.

— There were the tailors, so that's *Eros*. And I knew lots of Indians because Knutsford Terrace had a huge Indian community. I grew up surrounded by Indians—so that's *Chungking Express*. And when we first moved here, on our street there was a guest house mainly for White Russians. I could see princesses and countesses getting drunk on the terrace. That's *Lady from Shanghai* [a dropped project about a Russian spy set to star Nicole Kidman]. Down on Kimberley Road, there were lines of martial art schools. So that's also *The Grandmaster*. And underneath the martial arts schools, there were barbershops and Shanghainese restaurants. There were also famous writers and retired movie stars around. Really, it was *all* there. My first four films are shot mostly in the neighborhood where I grew up.

Each of these films started off from memories, or many memories I've combined. They are like my memoirs and as such, are subject to errors and distortion. Some people think the best way to decode or understand a filmmaker's work is to study his or her childhood. Sometimes that works, but not always. Looking into your past, you keep lingering between fact and fiction.

Although the world thinks of you as being from Hong Kong, you actually grew up in a specific subculture, the Shanghainese community. Your first language is Shanghainese. Your wife, Esther, is Shanghainese. Your longest and most important collaborator, William Chang, is Shanghainese. You obviously feel a special affinity there, right?
— It's just natural for me because in those days you could easily tell the Shanghainese community from the Cantonese. They're very different. Different food, different tastes, even different cinema. The Shanghainese always think they're more sophisticated, and the Cantonese locals think that the Shanghainese like to show off–they're superficial, slippery, and like to look better than they actually are.

I've heard it said that the Shanghainese are more refined.
— Yes.

And that when the Shanghainese are dishonest, it's in a different way than the Cantonese.
— In the '20s, Shanghai was already the most prosperous and cosmopolitan city in China. After '49, a lot of wealthy business-men came from there to Hong Kong–they were in textiles, real estate, banking and the stock market. They were trying to rebuild Shanghai in Hong Kong, which at that time was still a very small town. And they brought a lot of influence. Local Cantonese then were very solid. If they had ten dollars, they'd spend five, but the Shanghainese were different. If they had ten dollars they'd say, "We have a hundred. And we've *spent* hundreds." *Laughs.* Leverage was around, but the Shanghainese businessmen popularized it, inflating the market until it crashed in 1952. It bankrupted many of them and gave locals the impres-sion that Shanghai people are not reliable, that they talk big but they are not *real*. In those days, the differences were very clear. The Shaw Brothers productions were in Mandarin and were made for immigrants, for the non-Cantonese speaking people here. Their pictures were refined and more upper-class, while the local productions were very low-budget, Cantonese operas or comedies, and that was it. You could sense when I

was growing up that the Shanghainese felt more sophisticated than the locals.

I've heard Chinese people say that it's typical that, of all the Hong Kong filmmakers, it would be you who would make the kinds of films you make.
— You mean all the Shanghainese touches in my films?

They meant something less nice.
— Oh, I see. That my films have the look but not the substance. Well, everyone's a critic. *Laughs.*

Which brings us back for a moment to Shanghai. After you left, were things okay in the family compound?
— Yes, but later on it became very difficult. First came the Cul-tural Revolution in 1966, which shut down colleges and schools, then the "Down to the Countryside Movement" in 1968. The state asked all the students to go out to remote villages because the population was concentrated in the cities and city jobs were scarce. The idea was to make the country more equal. It was something that students were supposed to volunteer for, but you wouldn't say no because in that case you would be con-sidered unpatriotic. Years later, my sister recalled this classic scene at the train station when she saw my brother off: fresh graduates in high spirits, martial music and drums celebrating their contribution, tears of mothers who had never been apart from their children. And when the whistle finally sounded, all of those conflicting emotions came to a point. It was tragedy on an epic scale.

Those kids' excitement must have vanished as soon as they saw Mongolia.
— It was very different from the city, especially for kids from

Beijing and Shanghai. In those places there was nothing. Those villages were separated by decades of development. In those places there was no tissue paper. Just imagine all the girls from the city.

You'll never make a film about this, will you?
— No, I heard about all of this but never witnessed it.

There haven't been a lot of films on the subject, have there?
— Not really. My brother's generation is the same as many of China's leaders today. Their generation had to halt their studies after high school. In 1977, Deng Xiaoping finally ended the policy and started rallying students to return to university. Only a few lucky ones were able to start back up and that really changed their lives.

Isn't that what happened with Zhang Yimou and the other Fifth Generation directors?
— Yes. That's why by the time he got to go to the film academy, he was already thirtysomething. My brother wasn't as lucky, even though he was talented and quite refined. He was very good at soccer and the Shanghai team wanted to take him. But since his parents were living outside of China, he didn't get the chance. The music academy also wanted him because he could sing so well, but he was again denied entrance for the same reason.

At first, he was fortunate enough to be allowed to stay in Shanghai after high school. But that was only for a couple of years. Then, when my sister graduated, they said he could stay but that she was assigned to Mongolia. He said, "My sister won't make it in Mongolia. She should stay in Shanghai." And so he volunteered to go instead. That changed his life completely.

Did he ever talk about it?
— He told me about those days, when he was assigned, first to Anhui, then later to Jiangxi, and showed me a photo from then. He looked almost like Jiang Wen in *Red Sorghum*, bald and big, but wearing shorts. There was nothing to eat, so people ate anything that moved—snakes, rats, whatever. One of his jobs was to carry watermelons to town. To get there, he had to walk almost half a day. He told me about the time he was out on the road and came across a wolf coming the other way. They eyed each other down and just kept walking their own way. My brother had lots of stories like that.

How did your brother and sister feel about you going to Hong Kong? You clearly had an easier life. I know it wasn't your fault, but did they resent you?
— They never felt that way towards me because it wasn't my choice. In the later days of his life, my dad told me that it was a hard decision. Because only one kid was allowed to leave with my mother at that point, he had to decide which should go to Hong Kong first—the eldest son or the youngest? My father never anticipated the Cultural Revolution, so he took the youngest one, me, because he thought my brother, who was 14 then, was old enough to take care of himself and his sister for a while. He

believed that in a few months, he could come back and take both of them to Hong Kong. But that never happened. And I feel very guilty about this.

What do your brother and sister do now?
— My brother passed away peacefully in the summer of 2015. He never got married.

He did something heroic, though, in volunteering to replace your sister. And she?
— My sister got married and had a kid. She came to Hong Kong with her husband in the early '90s. But later on, they decided they preferred Shanghai, so they went back and started a business doing interior design. My brother lived next to my sister and she took really good care of him. I know she always wished that she could do more because of the sacrifice he made for her.

How does this enter your movies? I'm trying to think if there's anything in any of your films that deals with this kind of guilt.
— I never touch on this. It's a past that they preferred to be left alone. I haven't wanted to exploit it. I think it's not right to do anything that might make them feel embarrassed.

Of course, you now have a family of your own—your wife and your son, Qing, who's studying engineering at Berkeley. You were still a student when you met Esther. Meeting her changed your whole life. Did it seem that way at the time?
— I met her when I was 19. I was a graphics student at the polytechnic and had a summer job selling jeans. That's where I met Esther. We got along well, but it wasn't like love at first sight. She was a bit serious at the beginning, but that was not her real nature. It was her first job, so she wanted to be as professional as possible. But I felt she was special. Our shop was at the basement of a huge department store, and every day there were hundreds of people passing by, but she was always the person who stood out to me, the only person that I wanted to get close to. She was better than the world she lived in. Even today, I feel the same about her. She's the sunniest person I ever met and "sunny" is not something anyone would ever call me. So I think we're a good match.

You don't seem particularly dark.
— I would say I'm between dark and sunny. *Laughs*. Most of the time, I'm in the middle.

So when we're talking now, doing this taped conversation, are you having to work at not being gloomy or are you being natural?
— Natural. But honestly, I'd prefer not to answer all these questions. If there was a choice, I would rather be the one observing instead of being observed.

Back to Esther. She told me that she thought you were special, too, but that you didn't ask for her phone number until your very last day working together.
— That's normal. I said, "We should stay in touch." So she gave

me her number. In those days, Hong Kong numbers were six digits, and she only gave me five. I had to guess the other one which was actually quite easy. But I got the message—I had to make an effort.

She claims that this was the origin of the nifty romantic bit in *As Tears Go By* when Maggie Cheung hides one of Andy Lau's drinking glasses and says that if he ever needs it, he should give her a call.
— You can easily see the connection.

She also told me that you say all the women in your films are her.
— That's true. I remember Wim Wenders once said most of his films were personal, but never private. For Esther, watching my films is private. She took her whole family to see *As Tears Go By*, but after ten minutes, she decided to sit somewhere else and watch the rest by herself. Over the years, she would watch my films in quiet concentration, then turn to me and say, "That's *me*, right? You stole that," when she recognized a moment, a motion, or a line that was familiar.

Some say that you go through many women before you find the right one. In that sense, I'm lucky. I have one who can also be many. That doesn't mean all my female characters are based on Esther, but in them, I can see glimpses of her. She seldom comes to the set, but she's always been there with me. That's why her name has always been the first to appear on screen for the films that WKW produced. These are *our* films.

Not to get all Freudian on you, but is Esther like your mother?
— In a sense. Both are amazing women—great wives, and the best moms their kids could possibly have. But in my memory, my mother remains nostalgic and melancholic, while Esther is always positive and optimistic. If my mother was the moon, Esther would be the sun that always shines. Before we got married, she stayed over at my place one night and I remember watching her sleep. When Esther's asleep she always looks like she's having the happiest dream. I remember thinking, "I want to wake up with this person every day."

It's a shame your mother never saw your movies.
— I was still a writer when she passed away. Writing screenplays in those days took teamwork. You had a writers' room with five or six writers there, and if it was a comedy, you had to provide gags. Then someone put it together in a draft. But I preferred to work alone. I would take a draft and disappear for, like, six months. People started calling and my mom got worried. "You're going to get fired," she'd say, and I'd tell her, "I know, but I'm going to get it done tomorrow." And I'd go out every day, just like we're doing now—to a restaurant or a coffee shop—and try to write. It was a time when there were coffee shops that were so quiet that you could spend your whole day there without the waiters or waitresses bothering you. You can't find places like that anymore. I really miss them! But my tomorrow was never-ending. By the time I finished a script, it was no

longer what they wanted. People started calling me the master of delay.

I can attest to the truth of that moniker. How come this didn't ruin you from the start? Because you had a reputation for being a very good writer?
— To be a writer in the film business, you need two skills—pitching and writing. I guess I'm good at pitching and that keeps me hanging on.

You love novels. Did you ever think of writing them?
— No, because I knew it would be endless. Anyway, to read and write are completely different things. Writing is about ideas, techniques and most of all, discipline. The pressure of putting the first word on a blank sheet of paper is agonizing. It's almost like being caught in a corner. It's embarrassing. That's why I always admire good writers. It seems easy for you, at least from my perspective. For me, it's like hell, and you know very well that there's no one to help you except yourself. It's many days, or many months, or even many years of solitude. That's why I prefer filmmaking. At least, you're not the only one who's suffering!

Maybe so, but I've always heard that you were considered a great screenwriter.
— It's hard for people to recognize your writing when you're also the director. So I can hardly say my career as a scriptwriter has been rewarding. Just imagine, after all these years of hard labor–writing like a lunatic before or during or even after shooting–and people call me a director who always shoots without a script!

However, I did learn a lot from the experience of being a writer at the beginning of my career. It helped me to understand the psychology of a director. There were directors who looked at your script and said, "This is a great idea, but I don't think we have time for this. We'll do it next time." Sometimes they meant it, but usually it's just an excuse, and you knew there would never be a next time. There's always a gap between reading a script and how you visualize it. When I was working on a script, I thought it would be very good, but when I looked at the final film, I'd think, "That's not exactly what I imagined. The only exception was with Patrick Tam. We worked together on *Final Victory*. He treated each of his films as his "first rose and last rose"–an idea from a line by Jean-Luc Godard, whom he greatly admired. Patrick never waited for "next time" to do something. He just did it. *Final Victory*'s script was already good and he made it even better.

In these early days, you seem to have found a co-conspirator in William Chang. He's been your most important collaborator from the beginning. Without him, your career would look far different. I sometimes think of him as your other spouse.
— I met William through Patrick, when I was writing for *Final Victory*. William had become known through one of Patrick's films [*Nomad*, or *Lie huo qing chun*] and we got along well. In those days, we spent almost every night together drinking

and talking about films. I'm afraid that we used up our quota of conversation during that period. Since then, we haven't had to talk. He's knows me so well and I know him so well that we don't need to talk—our communication is beyond words.

You were obviously influenced by Patrick Tam. Let me ask you about other Hong Kong directors. As you were starting out, who did you admire?
— I mainly followed genre films when I was a kid, and my attention to directors came much later. There are many filmmakers whose work I like. From the early days, it was King Hu and Li Han-Hsiang—they were in the first generation of filmmakers who emigrated to Hong Kong. Most of their films were inspired by Chinese Opera, in Mandarin, and appealed to audiences of my background. I can't say all their works were perfect, but most of them were unique and more refined than their contemporaries. I also like Sammo Hung and Lau Kar-Leung, who were the finest among the second generation, with a martial arts background that brought a special kind of authenticity. On the contemporary side, there were two directors I particularly liked. Tsui Hark has always surprised me, and the other is Johnny Mak. He only made two films but when you watch his work, they both are original–you don't see any references. Tsui Hark is original, too. Even if he has ideas that come from here and there, the way he treats things is all his.

Largely owing to *A Better Tomorrow*, your first film was a gangster movie. We'll talk about that later. For now, let me ask something else. From our conversations over the years, I've always sensed that you bridle a bit at being labeled a "Hong Kong filmmaker." From the beginning you seemed to think of yourself as something more.
— Basically all my films are about Hong Kong regardless of where I shot them, and I'm proud to be a part of Hong Kong Cinema. But I don't like any label which may or may not be relevant to my works. After all, Cinema is Cinema. What really matters are the films and not about where they come from. When I was young, the idea of "World Cinema" didn't exist. We watched work by Oshima, Ozu, and Kurosawa, films by Satyajit Ray, Antonioni, and Truffaut. Those were the films I really enjoyed. They stood out from the others. They gave me goosebumps. *This* was the world I wanted to be part of.

And speaking of the world you're part of, let me re-ask the question you ducked at the beginning. Do you think of yourself as a Hong Konger?
— If you asked me this question before 1997, I would have said I am Chinese, as my dad always emphasized that we were from China. And it's always been my understanding that Hong Kong is a part of China. Then, after the handover, there were constant reminders everywhere you went of us having a distinctive Hong Kong identity. Even when we went back to the Mainland, we were introduced as Hong Kong directors. *Laughs*. I guess I'm a beneficiary of the one country, two systems policy.

NOT
HITCHCOCK

You started your directing career with a gangster film, *As Tears Go By*. Where someone like Quentin Tarantino loves genre material, I don't think of you as someone naturally drawn to it.

— No, I'm not. But this was after *A Better Tomorrow*. I remember the first time I watched it — we went to the midnight show. We already knew the film was going to be big, but we didn't know how big. That night it was overwhelming. After the screening, most of the audience, most of them guys, walked out like Chow Yun Fat, like they were gangsters. Chow Yun Fat instantly became the icon of the city. In the film, he was wore this raincoat, so then everyone dressed like that, even in China, with the sunglasses and the toothpick. That was Cool. So it was a time to make gangster films.

How did you come up with the story?

— *As Tears Go By* came from working with Patrick Tam, who at the time was called "the Godard of Hong Kong." He was one of the main New Wave filmmakers of Hong Kong who studied abroad and came back with new ideas. They had a fresh cinematic style. Back then, it was a group of writers sitting in a room. But Patrick hates offices. Every day, we spent hours together, but never in the office. We would meet at a coffee shop in Central. He would talk about projects, about life, and about films that he thought were good. And instead of talking about the plot and characters, which directors normally do, it was all about structure and form, which was new to me.

At the time, the company I was contracting with offered him a film and he wanted me to write the script. The producers suggested he make either a comedy or a gangster movie, since that's what was popular. Patrick thought why not both in one film—a black comedy with gangsters! *A Better Tomorrow* had already been a big hit. The critics were saying it was a metaphor for what Hong Kong might face in 1997. But rather than step into John Woo's arena, Patrick wanted to try a different concept. His idea was something simple, like *The Apu Trilogy* meets *Mean Streets*.

Ray and Scorsese—that's a peculiar pairing.

— He thought a story about two small-time gangsters had enough material to be a trilogy. The first one could be about them as teenagers, the second would happen in their twenties, and the last one would be in their late thirties or forties. Heroes had already been done. Instead of big heroes who were winners, these two would be losers. They were heroes who didn't make it and became disillusioned.

Patrick knew nothing about gangsters, so he worked on the structure. He had me fill in the story because, by then, I was no stranger to that world. There was always someone on set connected with that side of society, and I spent a lot of time around them. One of these guys was a stuntman, a good-looking guy, wanting to be an actor. At the end of every night he would say, "This is the last time I'm drinking. Tomorrow will be a new day." Then the next night it was, "This is the last time. Tomorrow will be a new day."

That was his last line *every* night. *Laughs*. I told Patrick that I thought that this guy would make for an interesting character. He agreed. At that point we wanted to call the trilogy *Today Is the Last Day*, but the producers weren't amused. They thought audiences would see the poster and think the new movie was already being marked for a last showing. Instead, they decided on *Final Victory*.

That was the third part of the trilogy. How did you get to make *As Tears Go By*?

— *Final Victory* came out to great reviews, but it wasn't close to *A Better Tomorrow* in terms of box office. The audience obviously preferred heroes to losers and so there was no chance to make the rest of the series. A year later, I joined Alan Tang's new company, In-Gear, as a writer. He had produced successful gangster films before and actually was the biggest on-screen gangster hero before Chow Yun-Fat. After two years, he asked me, "Do you want to be a director?" I said, "Of course." I told him I wanted to make a film about a policeman and a mysterious woman in Mongkok, kind of inspired by Bizet's *Carmen*.

Ah, so that's why I've always found *As Tears Go By*'s Cantonese title so baffling. It means *Mongkok Carmen* but has nothing to do with the story.

— Yes. Alan agreed to the project and we even announced it. Then one night, he told me the good news: He had gotten Andy Lau to sign on. But there was a catch—it had to be a gangster film and not about a cop. He knew about the trilogy that I'd developed with Patrick and suggested I pick up the second episode, about the two gangsters in their twenties. And that became *As Tears Go By*. That's why I asked Patrick to edit the film. He already knew the story.

So after several years of writing, was directing what you expected?
— I'd worked a lot with Patrick and took his way of shooting *Final Victory* as a model. Patrick told me to do a shot list. He would take days to do those and was always well-prepared on set, like Hitchcock. When I started *As Tears Go By*, I thought I would be like that, too, with a finished script and a complete shot list. *Laughs*. But there are so many things to deal with as a director—the sets, the costumes, the lenses, and even the number of extras. So normally, I would write at night because it was quiet, especially after midnight. With *As Tears Go By*, the first day of shooting was going to be the next day at 8 a.m., but that night, I remember thinking, "I'm really tired. Better take a nap and wake up at five to do the shot list." The next thing I knew, it was already eight. When I went to the set, everybody was already there, the actors, the crew. I said to William [Chang], "I haven't made my shot list." He gave me a look and said: "Why don't you set up a wide shot first." He had been in this business longer than me, and he knew it would take hours to set up. So while that was being set up, I snuck out through the back door and sat down to work. So from day one I knew: I'm not Hitchcock.

And how did people react to that?
— Everybody was freaking out. Here's this new director who shows up completely unprepared. But after the first few shots, I was okay. I remember after the lunch break that day, I was already getting used to the process. I thought, "Well, I know how to do this." You see, the way I write my scripts is always very direct and straightforward. I hate having too much detail. It gets in the way of pacing. I keep things simple and relevant to the scene. Action, lines, mood—basically a shot list. I seldom make actual shot lists anymore, nor do I believe in making plans. A film only gets made starting on the first day of shooting. During the actual shooting there is always chaos, confusion, unexpected issues. A perfect day on set is rare, and being able to accept this is essential.

Still, didn't you worry on that first day? You were a new director working without a script.
— The thing is, I'm a writer. So *I'm* the script. I could tell the actors what to do, what to say, and even how to say it because I knew the story by heart. I made changes when we needed them. If a line was too long for the actors, if the scene didn't work, or the set wasn't ready—anything. I kept changing the script, and ended up writing like crazy every night during shooting. And the stress *was* terrible. Two weeks into the film, I was a complete wreck. My eyes were too tired. I needed space to think. This was an adventure and I had to be fearless. I began to wear sunglasses.

You had a really strong cast. Andy Lau's the doomed hero, Wah. Jacky Cheung is his crazy-ass friend, Fly, and Maggie Cheung is Ngor, the innocent girl Wah falls for. How did you choose Jackie and Maggie?
— Maggie was pretty new then. She'd grown up in England and was discovered through beauty pageants for her looks. She did some modeling, commercials, and some TV, but didn't have any real training. People liked her, but few thought of her as a serious actress. Jacky Cheung and I had worked together on a comedy I'd written and I thought he was the right person to play Fly.

He was. He's probably the best person in the film, incredibly self-hating and intense. Worthy of DeNiro.
— It was the perfect role for him. He got his start from winning a singing competition and his career took off, but he didn't know how to handle success and got lots of bad publicity from getting drunk and getting into trouble. Things were going downhill. This became the breakthrough film that saved his career. Even today, people still call him Fly on the streets sometimes. *Laughs*.

What about Maggie? Did you see something other directors didn't see in her?
— The way I cast actors and actresses is pure instinct—something in them has to inspire me. For *As Tears Go By*, when I looked at Maggie's face I thought, "This is good chemistry, because she is so different from that gangster world."

Yes, there's something innocent in her face. Was she good from the beginning?
— Yes. Like most new actresses, Maggie wanted to prove herself and worked very hard, but sometimes too hard. I remember at the beginning of the shoot, we were doing a scene of her having lunch with Andy. I kept telling her, "Maggie you have to eat." She said she was. I said, "No, you're *acting eating*." And that made her even more awkward. Those first two days were disastrous. Then one day I asked her, "What would you do if you were in Ngor's situation?" She said this and that. I asked her to show me and I liked what I saw. She has a way with her body. There are two people whose walking I really enjoy. One is Faye Wong. The other is Maggie—"Keep walking," I'd say. The way she walked around and did little things said more than her lines did. From then, I threw away the pages I'd written. I made the lines shorter and customized the role for her. I didn't need her to be someone else. In turn, she became the perfect actor for the role. This was a learning experience for me and it's been useful ever since.

After that, I began to pick up her rhythm, and she began picking up mine. She became more confident. In one scene, she meets Andy on Lantau Island and they spend the night together. First, Andy walks upstairs to his room, out of frame. Maggie is supposed to follow him, but the first time, she just walked right up—*tack, tack, tack*. I said, "Wait. You're not easy. There is tension—do you go up or not? It's hesitation, from your body—you stop there, make up your mind, and *then* walk." She

tried that a few times and it still didn't work, because she didn't know where to stop. I showed her the frame, where to stop, and how that position in the frame mattered. From that day on, she would always look at the frame before shooting and she took off from there.

Let me ask you about Andy Lau. It's more than a quarter century later, and he's still a superstar.
— I like Andy a lot and enjoyed my time working with him. He was the most hardworking actor of his time. He still is. At first he became a very popular actor. Then, he became a very popular singer. And then he started producing films. At the same time, he ran a very successful fan club. He is a true entertainer and is happy to live up to his public image.

Um, I don't know how to put this tactfully. Do you think he can act?
— Yes, but big stars are victims of their success. Back then Andy was already in huge demand. He had five other filmsgoing at the same time. When he came to my set, he'd been shooting maybe 20 hours already. He would take a nap while we set the lights. And he always played basically the same character. He knew exactly which looks would be effective—how to stand, how to smile, how to walk. He knew what people expected, because that's what the audience was paying to see: not the character but Andy Lau.

You had to stop him from doing that.
— Yes.

Was it hard?
— It was very hard for him to shake that off. It's like asking someone who has been smoking for years to quit. Without that cigarette, something is missing and they become insecure. So I would occupy him with other things. In my next film, *Days of Being Wild*, he played a cop. On the first night, when he met Maggie in the film, I gave him an orange. He couldn't be Andy Lau anymore. He was a cop, eating an orange, with juice all over his hands, and caught off guard by this desperate woman. Funny, but warm. Very human and memorable.

Did he like working with you?
— At first, he treated it just like every picture. But later, you realized he was spending more and more time with this film. The other productions started complaining. These were bigger productions, with more established directors. And I was a first time director. The funny thing is, when you look at the films of Andy or Maggie from that same time, you will notice how their look is so close to *As Tears Go By*. That's because we—William and I—asked the cast to let *us* decide on their look in our film first. And all the other films had to follow it. *Laughs.* I was lucky that I started my career with Andy, Maggie, and Jacky. They were being cast as teenage idols, not as actors. So on this first film, our collaboration was very intimate. Andy and I had a great time together as we were both young then. My films, especially

As Tears Go By, set a model for him. You can see Andy doing that character again and again in different films after that. It became his standard role, very successful for him.

Why not work together more?
— We had different rhythms. He was a turbocharged car in the express lane, while I navigated the surface roads. He has made more than a hundred films since then, while I have only done ten. Sometimes I would watch one of his films. I could see traces of the same smile and walk, but now they were much more refined. Maybe we'll work again someday when we cross paths and our paces merge.

In the film, Fly is self-destructive and keeps getting in trouble. I've talked to people who insist that Andy's character, Wah, wouldn't keep bailing him out of trouble.
— Why not?

Because Wah keeps saying, "Stop" and Fly doesn't—even if it will get them killed. He's like the stuntman in the story you told earlier who promises to change then always does the same thing.
— It's absolutely normal to me. They had a childhood together. They were best friends. He's like a brother. Someone you would do whatever it took to help.

But the audience didn't know about their childhood and all that
— But look at *Mean Streets*. Why did Harvey Keitel do all these things for De Niro?

Because he's got a Christ complex.
— That is the Italian side of Scorsese. In this part of the world, especially among the Triads, there is something called brotherhood. Sort of their code of honor. He's like a brother.

Fly is like family.
— Yes, and you look after your family.

This movie—and your directing career—begins with a shot where the left half is of the Hong Kong streets and the other half is their reflection on a bunch of TV monitors showing images of moving clouds. William Chang told me this was a deliberate choice. Why start with that?
— Actually, I didn't plan that shot. It happened purely by chance. You remember, there's a scene when Jacky jumps out and runs into the street, the busiest street in Hong Kong, Mong Kok. It is impossible to get a permit there and impossible to get that many extras. But we had to take a chance to get the shots. So I planned it like robbing a bank. It took two days to set up the cameras. It was a one-off. *Laughs.* I like drama. It makes the whole team very focused, and everybody's so excited. Anyway, everything was set, but we had to wait until the street was busy. And then I discovered that there was this new TV wall—because they wanted to make Hong Kong look like Shinjuku–and what it was showing was clouds. I thought, "That's something that fits this film." Because you need to have something that stands

outside the film's world. It's important to the structure. If you look at my films, most of them will have this element. *In Days of Being Wild*, there's the forest. In *Happy Together*, there's the waterfall. In *In the Mood for Love*, there were the streets. All my films are about relationships, moods, and emotions, which are always changing during the film. But these elements—forest, desert, waterfall—are a constant. I like this juxtaposition between the changing and the unchanging.

While the story seems like a conventional crime movie, I can feel you straining against genre constraints. You're already pushing the style into directions for which you'll become known. Like the way you play with speeds, sometimes making the action scenes blurry. Most gangster movies want us to see all the violence clearly. You don't. Why not?
— After *A Better Tomorrow*, every gangster film was filled with slow-motion. Normally, film is run at 24 frames per second, and for very high speed, it's 100. For someone like John Woo, it's 50. But I wanted to go to the other extreme and do 12, then double-print it. You get a slow motion effect that's different and very strange. During the time of *As Tears Go By*, I'd seen a lot of fights in bars—chaotic, fragmented and you only realize there was a fight after it happened. And I thought, "This is the effect I'm looking for." It's very like manga, very kinetic Things slow down, but because of the blurry image, it doesn't seem real. In a way, it's breathtaking.

William told me, "Kar Wai likes blurry." He said that's why you like shooting rain so much.
— When you work on the streets—which you may not like but you don't have any choice— you have to cover up things. What's the best way to cover up things? You make them blurry or very distorted.

And the effect is quite beautiful.
— Yes. And after *As Tears Go By*, everybody started to use this. It's also something that makes sense in a practical way. You have to remember that, in those days, the film stocks were very slow. If you were shooting at high speed, you needed a lot of light. But shooting at 12 frames, you don't need so much light and it still looks good. It saved a lot of film stock.

Can we talk about the long sequence on Lantau Island where Wah meets up with Maggie's character? You play it like an amazingly elongated music video to "Take My Breath Away." I've heard some critics complain that it doesn't fit the rest of the film.
— I saw the relationship between Andy and Maggie as being like Belmondo and Jean Seberg in *Breathless*. At that time, *Top Gun* was showing, and its love theme, "Take My Breath Away," was everywhere. Patrick thought it was a nice coincidence and suggested the Sandy Lam version as a sort of homage to Godard. You can see other influences from Patrick in the film. Like all the reds and blues. They're his colors. It's his trademark. I developed the story with Patrick and felt that there should be something of him still there.

103

Isn't there some Jarmusch in there, too? I can see it in the plot and even some shots.

— I was very impressed by Jim Jarmusch's *Stranger Than Paradise*. The storytelling is economical. There's no acting, no lines, just moments of a person. And you know that person because of his routine behavior: He does this thing at that time, that thing at this time. He created a gentle melancholy that I thought would work for Andy's character in the first part. The gangsters I knew had their routine: wake at noon, then go to the gym to work out and chit-chat. Their mornings were leftovers, monotonous. Nighttime was the meat of the day, when things would really kick off. That was the main course, more kinetic and dynamic. When night falls, they are in the jungle.

At the risk of turning you into a critic like me, what do you think the movie's about?

— I remember something Fellini once said in an interview: "I don't know what I wanted to say. I don't know now. Maybe once I know, I won't shoot it. Or maybe I don't know so that's why I shot it." In the case of *As Tears Go By*, I never knew what I wanted to explore—I had too much energy and too many ideas. Whenever an idea flashed by, I set off in the direction of the flash, maybe searching for a feeling or an emotion, trying to establish what is real and what is fake. I kept shooting without any idea how the film would end. I wanted to shoot until I dropped — and *that* was satisfying! *Laughs*. Looking back, what stands out is that it was my first film, my first experience. Like a teen who'd never driven on a highway, but was now at the wheel of a Ferrari, overwhelmed by the speed and the energy, dodging cars and switching lanes. And since I work without a script, it was like driving without a map.

The movie was a hit and won all sorts of prizes—all your stars got nominated. Do you like it after all these years?

— Yes. Although at first I thought, "It's not going to work," I soon began thinking, "I was born to do this job." The more I went on, the more I felt sure that I had something and I knew it was going to work. It was just natural to me and I had pleasure doing it. I knew I was going to be damned good. And I knew I was doing something different. After it came out, I didn't worry. It was *proven*. People still say to me, "You should make a film like *As Tears Go By*. It's so commercial, so romantic." They say that to me even today—can you imagine? *Laughs*. I haven't looked at it again over the years, but I've thought of it during some of the most difficult times in my career—the excitement and purity of making that film. For me, it was and is the definition of the innocence of filmmaking. But it's hard to make a film like that again when the innocence is gone and what's left of that excitement is an aftertaste.

And you married Esther right after the film?

— Esther and I had been together more than a decade by then. We actually registered in Hong Kong before shooting and planned to have the wedding in New York when the film was done. She went there first to prepare and the day after the release, we had the wedding and then a party by the water. I had my first film *and* a family. That day, I was the luckiest guy in the world.

Official Selection
Critics Week
Cannes Film Festival
May, 1989

As tears go by

In-Gear Film Production Co. Ltd., Hong Kong

100

109

Days of Being Wild was your first really personal film. Did you think,"I've had success now I can make the kind of movie I actually want to make," or did you think you were making another hit?
— I never considered whether or not it was going to be a hit when I was making it. Nor did I during *As Tears Go By*. I only thought, "If it's good, why would the audience have a problem with it?" Instead, it became the most controversial film of the year and for many years after. That shows you how naive I was.

But it must've felt like you were doing something completely different from everything else being made in Hong Kong at that point.
— That was the idea. I intended it to be different and made it that way. Not just how I told the story, but also the look of the film. I originally wanted to shoot in CinemaScope with sync sound. No one in Hong Kong had done that for almost 30 years, not since the Shaw Brothers productions from the early 50s. But it was too expensive and too complicated to do both. Alan Tang was producing and asked me to choose one or the other. And like the saying goes, it's better to have half a loaf than no loaf at all—so I went with sync-sound. All the actors were totally shocked: "I have to speak my lines and wear a mike *and* we have to clear the set?"

Were they scared?
— No, they felt excited, but at the same time they were under pressure. Back when I was a writer, if a line was not perfect and we wanted to change it later, we'd tell the actors to go, "One-two-three-four-five-six-seven," because we needed to know the line was going to be seven words. Now, the actors actually had to say the line. *Days of Being Wild* was a new chapter for everybody and it created a kind of vibe.

What inspired you to make this movie?
— The '80s started to have a lot of retro. Francis Ford Coppola did *The Outsiders* and *Rumble Fish*. And there was *Back to the Future*. It seemed like the trend to be looking back to the '60s for inspiration. Back to the time of JFK and exploring the moon. People were looking forward to the future back then. But by the end of the '80s, the future was uncertain. We were more concerned about what was happening on earth. So I wanted to make a film about the '60s.

One thing I strongly remember about that period was the 1966 riots. I was only 9 at the time. There were curfews and stoppages in school because of bomb threats. All this changed the course of many lives, but for me it was just an extra holiday. But outside things were changing. There was already a strong feeling of anti-colonialism, and the Cultural Revolution in China was just beginning. This separated the older generation, who saw themselves as transiting through Hong Kong, from the younger generation, who thought of Hong Kong as their home. When we made the movie, it was after the events of June 4th in Tiananmen, when HK wasn't sure what its future would be like after the handover. At first, the story I wanted to make was about the riots—about a policeman and a woman. Then when I started structuring the story, I kept thinking it should be more than that. It shouldn't be just a riot, because a riot is only an incident. It should be about people setting out to find their identities.

Making a period film like this would have been very expensive. So I tried to do it the way Coppola did and split it into two films, back to back. The first would be in 1960, before the riots. The second would be in 1966, right after. Like him, I gathered a dream cast, the most popular teen idols of that time. Then I divided them into two groups of people. One represented the Shanghainese community—Leslie [Cheung], Maggie, and Carina [Lau]. The other group was the local Cantonese—Andy, Tony [Leung Chiu Wai], and Jacky. The story would be about them setting out to find their identities. I was into Latin American literature by then and took inspiration from Gabriel García Márquez's novel *Love in the Time of Cholera*. To me, Leslie's character was like the cholera, the epidemic that changes the course of the two women's lives. The story would be told from their perspectives before and after encountering him. In the first film, one refuses to forget her past. In the second, the other refuses to remember it.

What is it about Latin American novels that you like so much? You often mention Manuel Puig and García Márquez.
— In Chinese literature, it's all about What—what is happening—but there's not much about How. What I learned from Latin American fiction was the way they tell a story. Because How is equally important as What. In fact, somehow, How can

to be a successful gangster in Hong Kong. Everybody knows him. But back then he was just a waiter. As I say, he was very macho and was always late with the rent. Then one time, he said to my mom, "Let's gamble on it." And so they played this dice game, double or nothing. After mom beat him, he never tried it again.

There are lots of memories like that in the movie. When people ask why there's so much green in *Days of Being Wild*, it's because our apartment was green. I remember the light because there were many trees around Knutsford Terrace, even the benches on the streets were green. Everything was green. The color was very popular in those days.

It's a very designed film—the look really stays in your head. The apartments aren't depressing like Wah's place in *As Tears Go By*.
— We were doing the Shanghainese community, not Mong Kok gangsters!

William is also Shanghainese. Did that enter in his production design?
— Yes, of course. The film is very personal to both of us. The story of Rebecca Pang and Leslie—and the way her apartment looks in the film—is based on William's own house. The way he dresses Rebecca is like his mom.

Did your mom dress like that?
— Not all the time. Only when there were guests or on formal occasions.

Did he have more money than you?
— Sure, he came from a much better background.

The Chinese title of the film is The Story of an *Ah Fei*, which was the title that was put on *Rebel without a Cause*. Why did you call it that?
— Because "ah fei" is very specific to the '60s. In *Rebel without a Cause* and *West Side Story*—that's the typical term you used. When you call somebody an *ah fei*, you know you're talking about the '60s and about youth who had a certain Westernized attitude and way of thinking. When I first went back to China in 1974, wearing just ordinary jeans, people looked at me like I was from a different planet. The name gives the impression that this kid is copying the Western style and is not just a kid of the Hong Kong streets.

And Leslie Cheung's character Yuddy is copying the Western style.
— Of course, the way he dresses, the way he looks—the shirts and this hairstyle. *WKW gestures to indicate a slicked back style.* Almost the first thing we see him do is buy a Coca-Cola. With his Pan Am bag. And the way he walks—there's a metal tap on his heels.

Let's talk a bit about Leslie Cheung, who's really terrific in the film as the spoiled heartbreaker who's desperate to find his birth mother. Like your stars in *As Tears Go By*, he seemed to

find a way to *become* What. I wanted to do something like that: a brand-new way of storytelling for Chinese cinema.

So you wanted lots of different points of view.
— Yeah. In *Heartbreak Tango*, Puig tells the stories through different characters' point of view, and it's not in chrono logical order. They may seem random, but they're like pieces of a jigsaw puzzle. Once you put them back together, you'll see the whole picture. By putting different points of view together, you somehow get a sense of fate, of destiny, that there's something beyond the human that you can't control. And *that's life*. That was exactly the point I wanted to make in this film.

If you're telling a story to recapture your youth, why not do the classic thing: Tell a story about a cute, smart little boy growing up in Tsim Sha Tsui and watching stuff go by.
— The characters of Leslie and Maggie and Carina and Tony—all the characters in the film—*are* like people I met when I was very young. In our apartment, we sublet to one guy like Leslie's character, and one of his girlfriends was like Maggie in the film, always sitting outside the apartment, sometimes even until morning. My mom began to worry about her, and the girl would say, "I have to wait for him. I have to wait for him."

And he was as heartless as Leslie's character, right?
— Oh, yes. He was very handsome, very macho, and he grew up

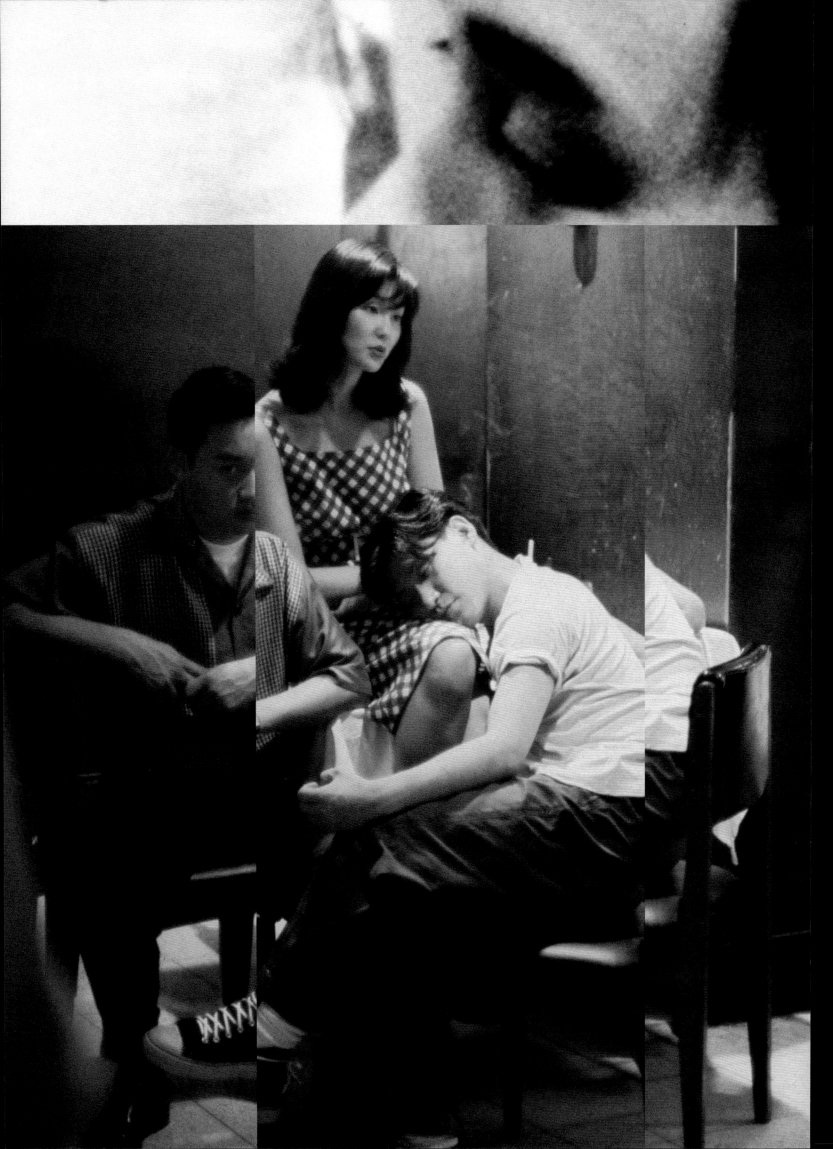

be somebody people didn't take all that seriously as an actor.
— At that time, the focus of Leslie's career was as a pop singer.
He actually went through a very tricky path. When he started,
it was via a singing contest, and people really didn't like him.
They thought he was pretentious and narcissistic. When he had
his first concert, he showed up on the stage with a hat. During
the show, he threw the hat to the audience—and the audience
just threw it back to him! It took him years to get his break
and become a superstar on stage, which led to his success on
screen. After *A Better Tomorrow*, his career as an actor took off.

A week before principal photography, I arranged a full-dress
rehearsal with all the actors and equipment in Queens Café
because I knew doing sync sound would make everyone nervous.
Nobody had done location sound in years, so there was a lot
more build-up just before every shot. When you clapped the
slate in front of the actor's face—it scared them, made them
lose focus. I thought a warm up like this might make them less
tense. But it was quite the opposite. They got more nervous.
Poor Jacky was the first one. He was supposed to talk while
eating this huge steak. He never finished his lines and had to
quit after the 20th take. He was too full to do anything. Leslie
looked calm, but while he was speaking his lines, his hands
were trembling.

Afterwards, I arranged a normal dinner to make everyone
feel better. I took Leslie aside and told him, "To me, you are a
star. A star is different from an actor. A star is, 'I don't care, but
when I'm on set, I need all the attention. I'm the center of the
world.' You didn't give me that, but I know that's what you're
looking for, and that you believe you will get. So from now on,
whenever you're on set, you have to give me that feeling. You
should have the confidence that *you're* the star of the show.'"
And he said, "I get it." And he *did* get it.

How does he compare to Andy?
— Leslie and Andy had never worked together before. By then,
it was like you'd put Tom Cruise and Brad Pitt in the same picture—in their prime. So, they were nice to each other, but you
could sense the tension was there. Both of them did well the
first few weeks, but later on, we could see the differences. First
of all, Leslie only worked on one film at a time. He'd say to Andy,
"You're a very hard-working man. I can only focus on one film,
and I believe that this is the way to have the best performance."
But Andy had to work on five pictures at the time because he
couldn't refuse to do them. So we had more time with Leslie,
and Andy could feel the attention was going to Leslie.

Leslie was better.
— He was more focused, but he had the same problem. He had
a Leslie walk, a Leslie smile, a Leslie turn. I remember the first
day when we shot that opening scene, I started with his walking.
That's how I usually work with actors. And they say, "I spent a
week *walking*! Why?" "Because," I tell them, "you have to find
the right mood and the right rhythm. I have to be convinced that
this is the character's walk. I don't want to see *you* walking. I
want to see *this person* walking."

The film is famous for a production history that was, let's say, troubled.
— I had the idea. I had the structure. And I knew that I would write during the shooting. I was ready to start. As usual, we made our production schedule by breaking up the story into different locations, and put them in order. That way, I could write all the scenes on the set, and William and his team could prepare the next set while we shot in the first one. I didn't expect it would take William so long to build one set. I thought it was going to be fast, but when I started paying attention to how he builds a set, I said, "Shit, we have to forget about our schedule." So I had to reorganize everything.

Was William right? When you look at the film now, the production design conjures up a whole distinct world.
— This film was something very personal to him. He just wanted to make sure every detail was right. I respect that. Even when my actors or actresses complained, "It's crazy to spend eight hours doing the hair," I'd say, "If William needs that time, he needs that time." His issues became my issues, because I knew at the end, it's about the film. It's not about his ego or mine.

Given that you had to improvise so much, I'm curious. Did you know all along that the movie would start with Leslie walking into the snackbar and chat up Maggie's character?
— Yes.

And what about what's maybe the most famous shot in the film, the tracking shot of the jungle in the twilight?
— We shot that almost at the very end when we went to the Philippines. We were on the train because that was the end of the shoot. The film was set to open in Hong Kong in two weeks and Patrick was cutting all the Hong Kong sequences back in Hong Kong. Alan Tang told me, "You have to finish the film no matter what. You have to release part one because it's Christmas, the biggest slot of the year and we have all the cinemas lined up, and all the foreign territories will open simultaneously."

You hadn't even shot the Philippines stuff with two weeks to go?
— No. So Alan went to the Philippines first with the line producer and a bag of cash. And we came a week later. Afterwards, people said, "If you were not part of the Filipino trip, you know nothing about making this film. It was crazy." And it was. There were three units. There was an action unit because Alan said, "You have to have some action. I sold it as an action film. We need something like *As Tears Go By*." So I put in an action sequence. And there was a second unit ready to do one set, and third one to do another set. We would shoot at the train station and on a train because they looked aged and authentic to that period—and most of all, there were no sets to build.

The first night we went to Manila, we were prepping the Chinatown hotel, which was also very aged. I got a call: "You have to come to the train station." I said, "But why?" Because Alan wanted a unit to shoot the sequence there but William was standing in front of the engine, which was about to start moving.

There was a crowd standing around, steam was everywhere, the whistle was blowing, and William just stood there saying, "No, it's not right. We have to repaint it." Alan Tang liked William a lot and didn't know what to do. "Am I going to have to kill him, or what? We have to get it done." All the actors were already there. So I said, "I will figure it out."

I spent one week in Manila with three units shooting 24 hours, nonstop, for seven days. There was a trailer and whenever I was done with one location, they put me in the trailer, and moved on to the next. I would pass out for two hours in my trailer, which was actually a mini-bus, then wake up and start shooting again.

No wonder those Filipino sequences seem so delirious.
— It was surreal. At one point we went to Leslie's mom's place, which is supposed to be a huge mansion, very Spanish. I only saw a photo—it looked spectacular with a huge gate outside. "Okay, good," I said, "that should be fine." I passed out in the trailer and when they finally woke me up, we were there. I looked and the gate was like this—*WKW holds his hands maybe five feet high*. It's a mini-gate! And I said, "Impossible. It's supposed to be a huge mansion." And they said, "We showed you the picture. This is the one you picked." But because there was no background reference in the photo, I couldn't tell: The gate was actually small but in my imagination it was huge. I looked at Chris [Doyle, the director of photography] and said, "How can we make this shit as grand as the picture?" The shot in my head originally would have Leslie standing in front of this huge gate. But once Leslie stood in front of the gate, they were almost the same height! You couldn't show him at the gate—it would look ridiculous. So we shot Leslie far from the gate, did a shot of the mom, and then a shot of Leslie walking away. It was at the point where I had to make decisions very quickly and I did.

From the outside, it's kind of funny. Like the Stonehenge bit in *This Is Spinal Tap*,
— That scene was a nightmare. I chose the location by just a look at a photo, and I chose the mom by a cup of tea. The whole point of this Philippines chapter was for Leslie to find his mom who he believed was a beautiful, aristocratic Filipino lady of Spanish blood. So I had to do the casting for the mom on the first night I arrived in Manila. It was a big thing in those days, a Chinese production in the Philippines. I said, "Give me the best actress, a respectable actress because this mom comes from a very rich family." And so we had casting sessions but I didn't have her lines written yet, so I said, "No lines. Tell them to take off their makeup. No makeup. And give me a teacup with a spoon and a teapot. That's it. Tell them what they have to do is drink a cup of tea in front of me." Because even if I couldn't tell whether they could act or not, by seeing them drinking tea, I could at least know whether they were elegant. That's how I picked the mom! *Laughs.*

This is your first film that touches on the Chinese diaspora. Why the Philippines in this case?
— First of all, Filipino musicians were popular when I was young.

Girls, especially the Suzie Wongs, were crazy about them. They were handsome and very good with women. Second, as I mentioned before, the nightclub where my dad worked was owned by a rich Filipino family, which claimed it had Spanish blood, and they always told amazing stories about their background. And then there was a friend of mine who looked completely Chinese except for some curly hair. He told me that he suspected that he might be a Spaniard by blood, because his great-grandparents once lived in the Philippines and one of them maybe had an affair with a Spaniard! I found his story surreal, and the connection from a Spaniard to a Chinese really got me hooked. It was so Puig! For me, this film isn't really about the Philippines, it's about the Spanish—it was my tribute to all the Latin American writers who had inspired me.

So that's why you chose the Philippines.
— There's like this Filipino part of my childhood and it's connected to the Spanish. It all makes sense to me.

And the great song by Los Indios Tabajaras that plays over the forest shot? The movie would be less magical without it.
— There was a record store in our neighborhood in the early '60s. Back then they played American pop songs and music all day to attract American soldiers and sailors, and "Siempre en mi Corazón" was one of their standard numbers. At the end of the production, Alan asked me to use canned music for the film because there was no time to get a composer and not even any budget left. So what I used was like a soundtrack of the big-band Filipino numbers played by the band at my dad's nightclub. And then Rebecca [Pang] heard that I was looking for this kind of sound. She was a major cabaret singer in the early '60s and recommended Xavier Cugat, the King of Mambo. I loved it. It worked seamlessly with the images, and the film began to dance!

Now, about that amazing shot of the trees.
— We shot it on the last day of the train sequence. It was in the middle of the night and everyone was on the train on the way back to Manila, but I still had one major scene left, Leslie's murder, and there was a helicopter standing by to pick up an aerial shot of the train passing through the jungle during daybreak.

It was a very long night. Leslie was too tired and Andy was trying too hard and became Andy again, as charming as he was in *As Tears Go By*. I had to keep telling him, "You're a cop who's become a sailor." Now, we knew we had about two hours to pass through the jungle and another hour to reach Manila. And we were supposed to stop at a station before the jungle and get a shot of the assassin boarding the train. But at some point, one of the train staff yelled to us, "No more next station!" and the next thing we knew, the train was already in the jungle! The stop before the jungle had been cancelled without any notice! I even used that line in the film.

Everybody was freaking out. I sat down with Chris and we started trimming down the scene—no more assassin boarding. Instead he would walk right in to the compartment and shoot

117

Leslie point blank. "But where the hell did he come from?" I asked. "Who cares!" Chris replied.

The two of us cut the scene to the bones. While the props guys wired the gun and Leslie, I went through the lines again with both of them and explained that we could only afford one take of the master shot because, so they'd better be good. I said, "One hour. We must have this scene. Without it, the film will have no ending." Both actors knew how important this was and they woke up. And because of that, when we shot the scene, Leslie was brilliant, and Andy was the sailor again; he forgot to worry about his best angle, stopped doing *As Tears Go By*, and just used his instinct. We got the shots before the train reached the end of the jungle.

You could see the first daylight just breaking. Everyone was beat. Most of the crew was passed out by then. While the helicopter did the aerial shot, Chris picked up his camera and ran off to shoot the jungle handheld. He shot it at 50 frames per second and kept rolling until the film ran out. I didn't have the chance to look at the rushes until I was back in Hong Kong. I was so moved when I saw it that I totally forgot about the helicopter shot. It was so beautiful and dreamy that it totally captured the essence of the last moment of Leslie's character—the last look a *bird* has at eternity. And that's Chris. Even when everybody is dead, he'll find you something magical you didn't expect.

Just from hearing your pleasure in talking about this mess, it's clear that you enjoy drama. It seems to bring out something in you that you like.

— Somehow it brings out my best. After the train finally stopped at the Manila station, poor Leslie had to rush to the airport covered in blood. He didn't even have time to change or say goodbye. People started packing their equipment, but I still had one more scene before we wrapped: the mom giving away the kid to the nurse. It was a brief scene and I didn't have a plan for it, so I just set it up with a Steadicam set on a 360-degree circular track to cover everything. It was the last shot of the whole production and it worked beautifully.

Afterwards, I sat down with William, who was also very tired. He hadn't slept for five days, and I was 15 kilos lighter. That was the moment we felt like, "We've *done* something." It was amazing. We went back to the hotel and had breakfast together in the room, because by then the tape of Patrick's edit of the film's first 70 minutes had arrived. We looked at it and were so happy. William said, "It's amazing. It's something that we can be proud of."

Cut to two weeks later. You're still putting the film together at the last minute to show at some sort of charity gala. It's supposed to start at eight and you're still working on it that morning. Is it done?

— I was done with the final mix five hours before the premiere. But the lab needed about two hours to turn magnetic tapes into optical tracks and then another two hours to deliver a good copy for the official premiere. When I walked into the premiere,

they told me that only the first hour had arrived. Those days the prints came in reel by reel, each was about ten minutes. So the last 3 reels of the film were either on their way or still in the lab being processed. Alan Tang had to go onstage and tell the audience, "There's still another 20 to 30 minutes on the way, and in case they don't get here in time, we may have to do some singing and dancing." He wanted to warn people. But the film actually arrived on time.

He was your producer, Alan Tang? Had he seen it?
— No.

So who had seen it?
— No one except me and Patrick. William had only seen the first 70-minute version we watched in the Philippines.

So it premieres. You're there. And you like your film.
— I do, but I can sense the reaction.

How soon?
— Very soon. People were in a very good mood when the picture started, especially the first ten minutes, because the film opens with Maggie and Leslie, and they're teasing each other and it's kind of cute. And then later on, you could feel the heat—people began to get restless. *Laughs*. When the lights came on, the whole house was very quiet and you knew it was not in a good way. When I walked out, I ran into Anita Mui, who sang the theme song, which only showed up at the end. All she said about the film was, "My song came very late." And that was it. No one actually spoke to me. They didn't know how to react. I was outside having a cigarette and it was dead quiet. People tried to stay away from me. Finally, John Woo came over and said, "I like it. It's a good film." I think he wanted to show his support.

The next day, the film became a scandal. No phone calls from Alan Tang. I think he was also very shocked. I went to a restaurant with Esther and people around us were talking about the film and how they hated it. We left without finishing our meal.

Days of Being Wild ends with the sequence of Tony's character—who we haven't yet met!—preparing to go out. Are you happy with that? The structure of the movie is almost perfectly balanced without him.

— Because of the contracts with all the distribution territories, Tony had to be in it, even though his character would only do something in part two. Patrick came back with his cut and said, "The only place you can have Tony is at the end because that's where it will make sense. It gives this character the strongest impact and makes people curious about what this man will do in part two"–at that point, we never expected that there wouldn't be a part two. Then he added, "But it's very abrupt." And I said, "Ok. Let's do it." After the film came out, most people said we should take it out because it's too abrupt or because it's too good–they wanted to see more of him and the film just ends. It felt like a metaphor. Life is like that.

Still, watching it even now, that ending feels strange and daring.
— Very daring.

I can only imagine what it was like to see this ending when you already didn't like the film.
— *Laughs.* It really pissed people off. I think the strong reactions when it was released were mainly because of that scene. People felt like, "Are you kidding?"

"You didn't just make this movie. You're messing with us." Especially because it's one of the very best scenes. Did you ever doubt the movie?
— No.

So you always thought it was good.
— Yeah. But I knew it was going to be very, very difficult for me. Most people, even friends said, "It's suicide."

After *As Tears Go By*, you were the most promising director. And now this one?
— But Alan Tang was very elegant about it. He said, "Well, part two has to be very commercial, with more action." He never said anything bad. But I knew part two would never happen.

Had anyone made a film like this in Hong Kong?
— No. No.

So what you did was actually worse than if you'd tried to make *As Tears Go By* 2 and it was just a stinker.
— Uh-huh.

Did other filmmakers support you?
— The critics liked it. Generally speaking the attitude was, "He's very talented, but he's not responsible, he didn't control the budget, and he made the film for himself." In those days, comments like that meant the end of a career.

And yet it didn't end your career.
— No, but I still felt bad for Alan Tang. I knew him and liked him, and I know that it embarrassed him. Later on, the film won so many awards that it seemed like I'd done something honorable. But before that, it was an embarrassment for him. People were saying, "You were silly to support a director like that. You're the biggest sucker in town." I realized that if I wanted to take a risk, I should take the risk on my own account. And realistically, nobody else was going to give me any freedom going forward.
　I met with Alan and said, "I know you want me to make films like *As Tears Go By*."
　And he said, "Yes, because it's good for you. It's proven, it works, it's what the market wants. Why not take this path?"
　And I said, "I cannot go back. It's gone."

123

HONG KONG
NOCTURNE

After *Days of Being Wild*, you took a great leap forward and started your own company.

— I did it out of necessity, not choice. It wasn't what I wanted. But I had to have my own company because it was the only way I could make another film after *Days of Being Wild*—no producer would give me a chance. Of course, I didn't have any money or any experience running a film company, so I needed a partner.

Now, I started at In-Gear around the same time Jeff Lau did. He came from a different background—he'd been a producer who ran a film company. I showed him how to develop a story and he showed me how to sell it. Jeff always said, cinema has two sides, industry and art, and one cannot be without the other. After *Days of Being Wild*, he told me, "The only way you can go ahead is to set up a company. I will be your silent partner. Because you have credit with actors." So together we set up Jet Tone Films in 1991. From that day on, I became a "filmmaker," as opposed to merely a director. This meant I would have to deal with both sides of cinema.

Why, exactly, did you call the company Jet Tone?

— Our first office was in Kowloon City, which was close to the old Kai Tak Airport. Jets flew over our building for hours every day. From our windows we could clearly see the wheels of the planes—that's how close we were to the jet tone.

Was it hard starting off on your own?

— Hong Kong was in its Golden Age of independent filmmaking by then. The studio system had collapsed. Independent producers could easily raise money by pre-selling pictures to the South East Asian market and to overseas Chinatown. All one needed was a genre and a list of attached actors. At the time, Tsui Hark's *Swordsman II* was a huge hit in those markets and set the trend. It made Brigitte Lin the hottest star in Asia after Chow Yun-Fat. Martial arts were now in and gangsters were out. So, Jeff and I decided to make a martial arts film as our first production and we set our eyes on Louis Cha's novel, *The Eagle Shooting Heroes* [published in English as *Condor Heroes*]. Even today, it's one of the most popular martial arts epics, like a Chinese language *The Lord of the Rings*. Cha's novel has many characters. Among them are four legendary swordsmen, coming from North, West, East, and South. After we got the rights, we managed to secure a stellar cast of eight of the hottest stars of the time and we announced the film.

Given your reputation, how did you get them?

— The first person was Leslie. He had been worrying about my career and once in a while would ask, "What are you going to do next, Kar Wai?" When I approached him with the project, I said, "I'm going to be setting up a company and I want you to be in this film." He'd already announced that he was going to retire, but he said, "Okay, I'll do it." The next was Brigitte Lin, who was very close to William [Chang]. I offered her a schizophrenic character who was a princess in exile and would turn into a deadly swordsman when

enraged. It was a challenging role and she accepted. Soon, Tony [Leung Chiu Wai], Maggie [Cheung], and Jacky [Cheung] joined the film and it was like a reunion of *Days of Being Wild*.

So you started to make *Ashes of Time*, but for all sorts of reasons we can talk about later, it wasn't ready for a long time. It didn't come out until after you'd done two other movies.

— Yes, *Chungking Express* and *Fallen Angels*.

I want to skip ahead to them. Let me begin by saying that *Chungking Express* is one of my favorite films ever. But every time I say this, you seem slightly unhappy about it.

— No, I'm not. Why do you think that?

I just get that feeling—maybe because you made it quickly.

— Well, I don't have that feeling. Normally when people tell me which films they like, it says more about them than the films. *Laughs.*

Spoken like a true director! So why did you make it?

— It's like what Chris Doyle says: What came before creates what comes after. I had been working on *Ashes of Time*, but it was a complicated shoot. After 24 months in China, we finally finished filming by the end of 1993. The company was financially in trouble and Jeff had left to take on his other projects. To keep our heads above water, we decided to start another production before the release of *Ashes of Time*, which was scheduled to go to Venice in September. So we started *Chungking Express* in May 1994, while Patrick was still cutting *Ashes of Time*.

And what was the idea?

— Instead of an epic, the idea was to do a collection of short stories that I'd developed over the years. I called it "the days and nights of Hong Kong." The day would be in Central, on Hong Kong Island, which is where Chris used to live. It was the new Soho of Hong Kong, with fancy bars and that long escalator passing between the buildings. Night would be in Tsim Sha Tsui, Kowloon, where I grew up. That story would happen in Chungking Mansions, with gangsters.

For the first story, we started with Brigitte Lin playing a retired actress, à la *Sunset Boulevard*, because she was getting married and it was going to be her last film. So we imagined her going out at night and playing different roles. One night, it's *A Streetcar Named Desire*. The next night will be *Gloria*. We started with her in her apartment. And when we started shooting that first night, I looked at the set and watched the props man place her glass on the table like this—*WKW sets a cup down and arranges it with extreme care*—I knew we'd be in trouble if we shot the film in this spirit. It would be another *Ashes of Time*. We simply couldn't afford it. So I said, "Forget about this place." Chris was setting all his fancy lights and I said, "Forget about dollies and lighting—let's go out on the streets." And so we shot this scene with Brigitte putting on the blonde wig on Nathan Road, and the film took off.

What's great is that the whole film feels like it was made in that spirit.
— I told Chris and William, "Don't repeat *Ashes of Time*. We need to make this film like a student film. We can't have lots of camera moves and complicated lighting."

The voice-overs for the movie are very clever and memorable. You must've had some of them before you started.
— No, I wrote the voiceovers for both *Ashes of Time* and *Chungking Express* around the same time because we were doing post-production on one while we shot the other. I would get up at 8am and sit down at this quiet deli in the basement of the Holiday Inn right by Chungking Mansions. Jacky [Pang, then a production supervisor], would come around 3pm to pick up the scene for that night to prep and then I'd start writing Ouyang Feng's [Leslie Cheung's character in *Ashes Of Time*] voiceovers until 7pm, then walk to the set.

Esther was pregnant at that time, but I only saw her briefly each day because I was so tied up with the two films. One day, I noticed she was speaking to herself in the mirror. I asked her why. She said she had no one to talk to except herself. It broke my heart. That was the most powerful scene of loneliness I had ever seen. Most of the time voiceovers are used for narrative purposes. But for *Chungking Express*, they're about loneliness. All the characters are basically lonely people, but being alone doesn't necessarily mean they are sad. Haruki Murakami was very popular in Hong Kong then, and because Kaneshiro Takeshi is half Japanese, I thought it would be funny to have his voiceovers written in Murakami style.

A lot of the movie's charm depends on the buoyancy of its actors. Kaneshiro is an amazingly light spirit.
— *Chungking Express* was also about contemporary Hong Kong, so I decided to look for new faces to play the roles opposite Brigitte and Tony. The first one was Faye Wong.

I'd met Faye when we were doing *Days of Being Wild* and she had come to the auditions under her real name. She was supposed to be Maggie's sister in Part 2, but Part 2 never happened. So she went off to study in England. Later on, she came back and became a very popular singer. She had something in her that just attracted a lot of attention. After the film, she became a phenomenon. She came from Beijing and it was obvious she wasn't a local girl. So she was something new—very modern.

I also looked for a young actor to play the role of the young cop who had to follow Brigitte. One day I had a meeting with Jacky at a coffee shop and a young man sitting a few tables away caught my eye. I asked her who he was and she said, "He's a new actor from Taiwan called Takeshi." I said, "Well, I like this guy." We called his manager and made a deal soon after. People then started warning me, "Do you know his reputation?" because he'd just been in a film with Maggie and Michelle Yeoh. "They call him The Wooden Man." Why? Because he was stiff—he couldn't act. But he had the look that I was looking for. So I said, "Let me try." On his first scene, I didn't give him any lines because he spoke only Mandarin, and we shot the film in

Cantonese. It would be hard for him to memorize all the lines. He was supposed to wait outside Brigitte's apartment and keep her under surveillance. I said, "Just linger outside. You are bored because you have nothing to do. Take a Coca Cola can and you can do what you want. And once in a while look up." He started playing soccer with this can like a kid and it was funny. His timing was very good. From that day on, I changed all his lines into Mandarin and in most of his scenes he was speaking to himself. He was liberated. The way I saw Takeshi is that he's not a man, he's a kid. That's the direction I chose, and it became a breakthrough film for him.

There's almost no actor who could pull off the scenes he does in *Fallen Angels*.
Massaging the pig? *Laughs*.
— Yes, massaging the pig. He's really funny doing all those crazy things. And like Maggie, there's an innocence to his face. It makes the scenes with his father very touching.

Takeshi has very good sense of humor and is good at making fun of himself, which is a great quality for a comedy actor. I still remember all these nights when I was working on the final mix of the film, he just stayed there in the studio, lying on the floor, looking at the stuff. Like a kid. There's a purity in this man. He is the male version of Faye Wong. Both soon became the hottest stars with young audiences. The fact that neither were locally born actors brought freshness to their performances. They were like fresh air.

He's also good at the kind of business you have in these movies. I like that great bit with Tony throwing away the letter with the ticket, it getting rained on, and then him drying it on the convenience store food-heating rack.
— I was very lucky—and it's very rare—to have the perfect cast for *Chungking Express*. At first, I thought, "I have Brigitte, I have Tony—he'll be able to do everything. I'm safe." Tony can do almost anything you want him to, but Faye was an unknown and so was Takeshi. And Brigitte, after *Swordsman II*, every shot she did was—*WKW leaps up and imitates her swordsman pose*. Turning her into a believable person was a challenge. I remember the first two nights she played Blanche DuBois. She was so serious that you didn't feel the humor in it. The scene wasn't about actually doing *Streetcar Named Desire*. It was about this retired actress pretending she was Vivien Leigh. But for Brigitte, she played it so straight, it was, "This is my moment."

That's interesting, because once she gets going in the movie, she's funny bossing all those Indian extras.
— Brigitte is very Method. She needed reasons. She would ask, "Why do I suddenly become a smuggler?" And I said, "No, you're a retired actress, and this is one of your fantasies. That's why." Otherwise there would be endless questions about her motivations. Then she said, "Do I have to do something to make people know it's a fantasy?" And I said, "No, you have to do it as serious as possible." But one thing about Brigitte, she was her generation's biggest movie star. Truly. We shot the whole film

135

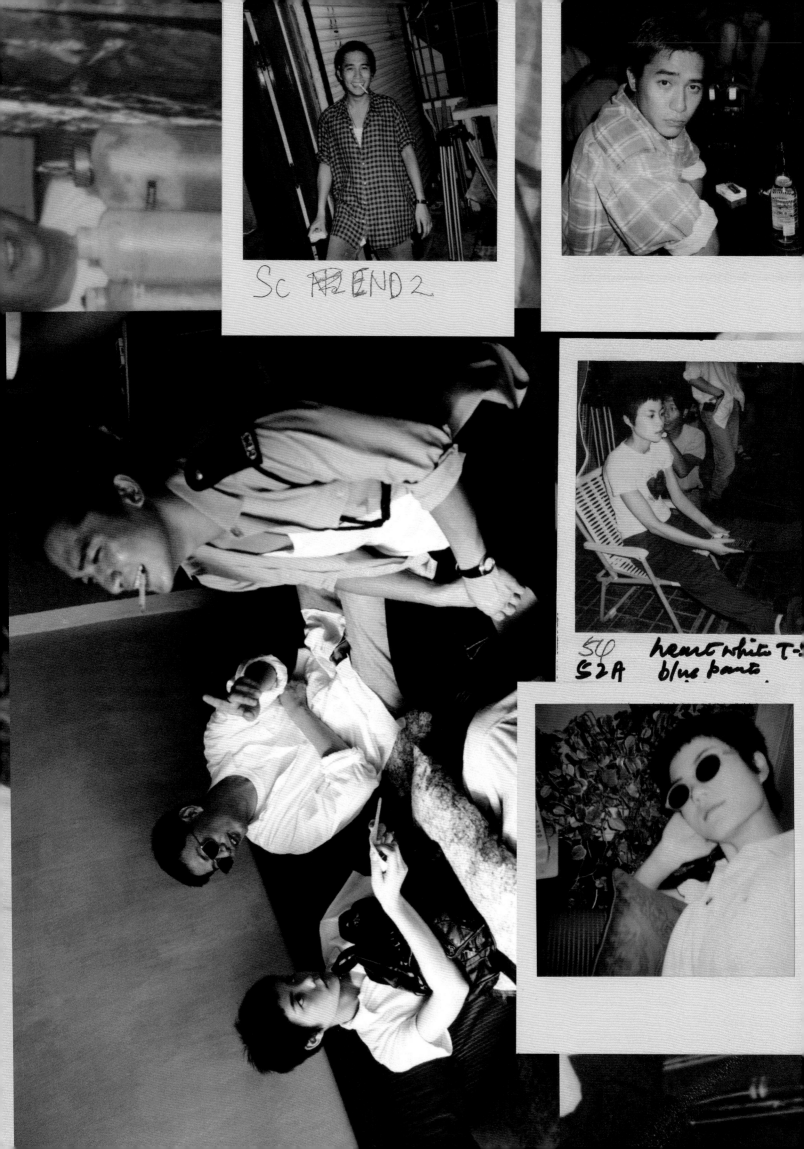

SC 阳 END 2

5Q
S2A   heart white T-
       blue pants.

139

But if you really wanted to do something new, why do something you dropped from *Chungking Express*? Given the way you work, that third story would've been little more than a piece of paper.
— No. The challenge was not about the story, which was actually very precise, but about how to shoot it. Given that the story was originally intended for *Chungking Express*, could we find a different way to shoot it? A director's job is to provide the best solution to shoot a film against time and money. And what would be the best solution for *Fallen Angels*?

On our first night, we shot the scene of Takeshi getting beaten up in the tea-house. We opened with a close-up on Michelle Reis who was a former Miss Hong Kong. At that point, she was considered the best looking woman in this town, but she had little experience acting. She was doing okay during rehearsal, but once we set up the camera in front of her, she lost her magic. She was very nervous and her hands were trembling. I said to myself, "Oh no, this is going to be a nightmare." We did more takes and more takes. Michelle kept eating noodles, and you have to imagine Takeshi getting beaten up in the background again and again and again! Michelle was getting so nervous that even the muscles in her face were trembling! Finally, I said, "Chris, let's try different lenses." Eventually we brought out the 9.7 millimeter, the extreme wide-angle. Now, in the business, there's an inside joke: If you hate an actor, use the 9.7 millimeter to shoot his close-up. *Laughs.* It's very distort-ing. So I said, "Let's try this." Not that I hated Michelle, but I needed to do something to make her look different or at least special. I wanted to make use of her nervousness. So I shot with 12 frames-per-second and said, "Michelle, do everything I told you to do, only two times slower." To act slowly brought a different layer to her performance. Instead of looking nervous, she looked 100% stoned which was perfect for a woman who handles hitmen for a living. It was a very powerful shot!

So I said to Chris, "Can we use this lens as the standard lens of the film?" He said, "Yeah, but why?" I said, "Maybe the film is about distance. They're so close to each other but they seem so far away. Does that work with the film?" *Laughs.*

It does.
— Yes, it does. In my experience, a film works best when its theme goes hand in hand with its form like ham and eggs. Thanks to Michelle we found both on our first day of shooting, which is rare. And the 9.7 millimeter lens became our standard. In *Chungking Express*, we opened the film with Takeshi walking by Brigitte and he says, "We were that close, and many hours later I fell in love with that person."

The characters in *Chungking Express* are strangers, but some-how, they finally connect. In *Fallen Angels*, it's the opposite. With the 9.7 millimeter lens, the characters are always far away from each other even though physically they're very close. They never connect. Even Takeshi and his father, they only connect through the video screen. In fact, *Chungking Express* and *Fallen Angels* are like two sides of a coin. Both address human distance, but in a very different way.

You told me once that, if you could change anything, you would have less good-looking people as the Killer and Agent.
— Yes. Michelle did great in the film but when I look at the film today, I wish I had cast someone who wouldn't draw your atten-tion. A striking beauty like Michelle defeated that purpose.

You ask yourself why she's a hitman's agent when she could be the most famous model in Hong Kong.
— The Agent should have been less attractive, someone who can't easily find a guy, maybe three times bigger than Michelle. And the character of Leon Lai shouldn't be that good-look-ing, either. He should be a rough guy, much grittier and more believable and moving. Just imagine if they're people treated as shit who earn their living in a very hard way. That could be very moving.

Leon Lai's not exactly an expressive actor.
    Leon Lai was very popular then as a singer and a handsome man, so he was always concerned about his look. And some-times, his biggest argument was with William. At one point, William told him, "In this scene you should take off your shoes and socks." Leon Lai said, "Why?" And William said, "Because you're a *person*." *Laughs.* They drove each other crazy.

In talking to William about this, he said that when he edited the film, he told you that it was too cold and inhuman. That's why you shot the stuff with Takeshi and his father, right?
— Yeah. By now, we were welcome in Chungking Mansions. We used one of the guest houses there to set up our base camp, and dressed up one of its rooms as the hideout for the Agent. The actor who played Takeshi's father was actually the night manager there. He had an interesting face and was always helpful. Because he spoke many dialects, he spoke Taiwanese with Takeshi all the time. The two of them got along well. So I thought it would be interesting to have him playing Takeshi's father. After the film's release, he became very popular; fans even checked into his guest house just to know him. He was nominated for the Best Supporting Actor that year in Hong Kong.

It's probably the most touching thing you've done. In fact, the stuff with the father is the only time I ever thought you'd done something to make people cry. You hold the final video image of the father so long, you clearly want people to feel it.
— The fact is, in *Chungking Express*, all the characters except Brigitte are people you can easily find in your daily life; they are the "commoners". Whereas in *Fallen Angels*, most of the characters are exceptional. You seldom find a hitman or a crazy kid like Takeshi around you every day; they were like "fallen angels" who wander around the city like ghosts. And the father is a "commoner." That's what makes this character so lovable. And once the audience falls in love with a character, it breaks their heart when they lose him. On *Fallen Angels*, we shot the second to last scene on the first night. We

shot the last scene with Michelle and Takeshi on the motorbike the night after. So basically, the sweetest scenes for me happened in the first two days. *Laughs*. It wasn't very nice.

Your movies glamorize Hong Kong, and shooting at night, the city becomes more glamorous.
— It does, at the same time it is easier. First of all, it's less crowded, with less noise. It's less hot —

And you have time to write during the day.
— And I have time to write during the day.

Can I ask you about Michelle's masturbation scene. Why is it so long? Watching it again recently, I was thinking, "Jeez."
— I played music on the set while we were shooting that scene. I had this Laurie Anderson music, and I thought it'd work perfectly. I remembered Hitchcock said that film is either about surprise or about suspense; and this scene had both. The audience was surprised when they saw the Agent was lying on the hitman's bed, and once they realized what she was doing, they were shocked. Then they were dying to see *how*? There are the feet and there's a clock at the end, almost like sunset. So for me, I saw the body of Michelle as a landscape. Chris at that point had many offers to do commercials and wanted to sneak out to earn some quick money. So I had to work with another D.P. Mark Lee Ping Bin. This was the first time I worked with Mark. So I shot with him and instantly could tell the difference. It's a very tricky shot. It's hand-held, and the night was very hot, and he had to start off very low and hold the shot a long time and go down again. We tried many takes, and he never got what we needed. I said to Mark, "What are you doing? She's masturbating. Where the hell are her fingers? I only give you a few seconds to get a glimpse of it and you have to get it." Later on we shot it again with Chris, and he got the point—he knew exactly where to look.

I don't doubt that for a second.
— The difference between Chris and Mark is like that between a sailor and a soldier. Chris is a sailor—that's who he is. Mark is a great cinematographer, very disciplined, very hardworking, he knows exactly how to do all the things you want him to do. But he's so decent he didn't want to look at where her fingers went. It's against his nature.

Speaking of Chris, he did a brilliant job on *Days of Being Wild*, but it was *Chunking Express* that really made him, and *Fallen Angels* only added to his reputation. What did he bring to your movies at this point?
— Any capable cinematographer can normally deliver what you want. Chris can surprise you. He has the best qualities of a great cinematographer: the eyes, the rhythm, and most of all, the heart. He is the Charles Bukowski of cinematography.

He's a different kind of cat than you or William. What is his presence like on the set?
— Chris went through a few stages during our collaboration. When he first started on *Days of Being Wild*, that was his second or third film shot in Hong Kong. He didn't speak the language, didn't have a team, and was shy. He took a lot of notes, writing, writing, writing, and analyzing the film and doing tests with different film stocks. He knew he was good but he didn't know *how* good he was. *Days of Being Wild* made him confident. In an interview about it, he said, "After this film, I know what I can do." Later when we shot *Chungking Express*, he thought I was joking when I told him to forget about the dolly because the camera had to be on his shoulders. There was only one hand-held shot in *Days of Being Wild*, and he was very clumsy then. But Chris picks up things very easily. He picks up languages very quickly. He speaks Mandarin better than I do. He speaks Cantonese. When we shot in Argentina, he picked up Spanish. And very quickly, hand-held became his trademark.

He soon became the most sought-after cinematographer and offers kept coming in, as well as girlfriends. *Laughs*. He's a loyal person and he had been a great help in many ways— translating our subtitles and synopsis when he felt they were badly translated, charming the owner of the locations whenever it's needed. He could be fast and was very inspiring on set. But Chris is Chris—his patience is very short. He can't handle spending three weeks waiting. "Kar Wai," he'd say, "there's a commercial" or "Kar Wai, they want me to do a film," or "I want to go to this film festival." He has so much energy that he just has to be going non-stop. So in *Fallen Angels* we started using second units because sometimes he had to go away. The same with *In the Mood for Love*. Because he had so many offers and preferred to keep himself busy, he couldn't be a regular anymore.

But you would still use him?
— Yes, of course.

And you're personally close.
— Yes. But we don't hang out because I don't like parties. We only hang out when we're shooting a film. His life is very different from mine. But we are family and he's always a member of the family. As I said before, Chris is a sailor by nature and you have to accept that sometimes he has to move on.

He seems to fit into your traveling circus.
— Yes, he did. In fact, he's the one who's closest to the actors and actresses. He is a charmer and he can be funny. He makes things smoother. People feel relaxed with Chris because they'll be laughing and saying, "Stop doing these silly things. Chris, stop taking off your pants." *Laughs*.

I remember at the *Temptress Moon* luncheon at Cannes, Gong Li adored him. He really made her laugh, and she knew he'd made her look beautiful.
— That's why I always say that D.P.s get the best girls. *Laughs*. His girlfriends all seem the same. They admire him, and at

the same time, they take care of him and they worry about him. But as a cinematographer, Chris is someone who can *surprise* you.

Like what?
— All the shots above the desert in *Ashes of Time* were done by Chris. In *Chungking Express*, where there were shots of steam or moving clouds above the buildings—that's Chris. All the cutaways in Buenos Aires, too. They were his poetry.

One thing I like about *Fallen Angels* and *Chungking Express* is that they show you a lot of Hong Kong. People are constantly moving around.
— Since *Days of Being Wild*, we wanted to capture Hong Kong at that moment as much as possible. Especially places we imagined would be gone soon after '97. Like the Goldfinch Restaurant in *In the Mood for Love*. And it's natural to have people moving around when you are shooting on the streets of Hong Kong. *Laughs.*

But *In the Mood for Love* is a very art-directed movie—William even changed the restaurant. In these movies, it feels like the art direction showed what was here. You came in and just grabbed it.
— That's the magic of William: He knows how to steal the shot.

William often makes every corner of every place interesting, but in these movies people are leaving their crummy apartments and taking us onto the streets.
— That's the way it is in Hong Kong. Everybody always goes out. Everything is in walking distance. It's 24-7. It's almost like your living room is outside your apartment. What's the point of staying in your crummy rooms if the streets outside are so full of life?

If you tried to find the glamorous Hong Kong of your films, it would be hard to find because you've made it that way. Like those trains racing by in *Fallen Angels*. If you lived there, they would be loud and annoying, but watching them is magical.
— Right. It's just in the way we shot it.

You said you wanted *Fallen Angels* to be different and you really succeeded. Even though there are lots of deliberate echoes, *Chungking Express* makes Hong Kong seem like a place you'd want to be. Fallen Angels makes it seem like a place you don't want to be. It's beautiful, but it's cold.
— The film is much more challenging than *Chungking Express*, and it is much darker. *Chungking Express* is sunny even at night, but in *Fallen Angels* there's no day. The whole film happens at night. That's what I felt about Hong Kong at that point. I put Shirley Kwan's song, "Forget Him" in the film. It seemed like it was time for us to move on and do something else.

Chungking Express and *Fallen Angels* made you The Cool Guy in international cinema. For years after—even though you didn't

make a movie like this again until *My Blueberry Nights*—you had the image of this guy who makes hyperkinetic romantic movies in love with youth.
— But that period was over because I was beyond that stage. I was a guy who had a wife and a kid who was learning to walk.

Before long, you began making movies about middle-aged people.
— Yes, I think the films age at the same speed I do!

Anyway, we both know that back in the '90s you began to be thought of as a hip director. The sunglasses became part of it—your trademark. Did you ever think about your persona as present in your films?
— I didn't set out to create a kind of image of myself, but especially after *Days of Being Wild*, I basically became someone people would talk about. We seemed to be doing the most exciting projects, so people wanted to know what we were doing—like when we shot with sync sound. They began saying, "He doesn't have to look at the monitor because he wears sunglasses all the time. He can tell whether the actress is good enough by hearing them speak the lines." Or they'd say, "He doesn't look at the monitor, he just feels it." There were so many stories about this Wong Kar Wai. And because I don't work with a script, that was something else to talk about. With our way of making films, there is always something that people can talk about. It's hard to shake off the myths that have somehow accumulated over the years. Sometimes, they are completely off the wall, but they have been told so often that everyone believes they are true.

And then there are the sunglasses. When people learn I know you, they always ask about the sunglasses. Always. Was Chris right when he said that you wore them to separate subjectivity and objectivity?
— He phrased it beautifully and he believes it. But for me, the sunglasses give me the time that I need to react. Whenever I was shooting, there were too many things to deal with that I needed the time so that I have a second, or two seconds, to respond, and the dark glasses actually helped. It eventually became a habit and a way to have my privacy. It's like the difference between Chris Doyle and Du Ke Feng.

An imaginary alter-ego, yes?
— This is WKW [*he mimes putting on sunglasses*] and now this [*he mimes taking them off*] is Wong Kar Wai. I don't understand why people are so curious about my sunglasses? Godard wears sunglasses. Kiarostami wears sunglasses. Kurosawa wore sunglasses. But nobody ever says, "Kiarostami wears sunglasses." I don't understand why.

Well, they don't always do it. Anyway, Kiarostami doesn't seem like a hipster or a young person's director. You have the reputation. Which may have been good for business, actually.
— It was, but not always. Being young or hip doesn't matter. In fact, all my films are related to the way I feel about this city,

whether subconsciously or not. When we did *Chungking Express* and *Fallen Angels*, I had this new company. We had to work fast and were young. As far as I know, these movies captured the essence of Hong Kong at that time. People were really aware of '97. You felt like there was a deadline—you had to rush. Foreign journalists began coming in when we were shooting *Chungking Express* and *Fallen Angels*, asking, "What do you think about '97?" I wasn't making my films to address that, but somehow it went into them. Nobody knew what was going to happen, but I wanted to capture on film the Hong Kong I knew the way it was—I knew every street, every neighborhood— in case everything changed.

And you haven't made another movie about contemporary Hong Kong since. Does that mean something?
— I don't know. What do *you* think? I think my movies are still about Hong Kong.

147

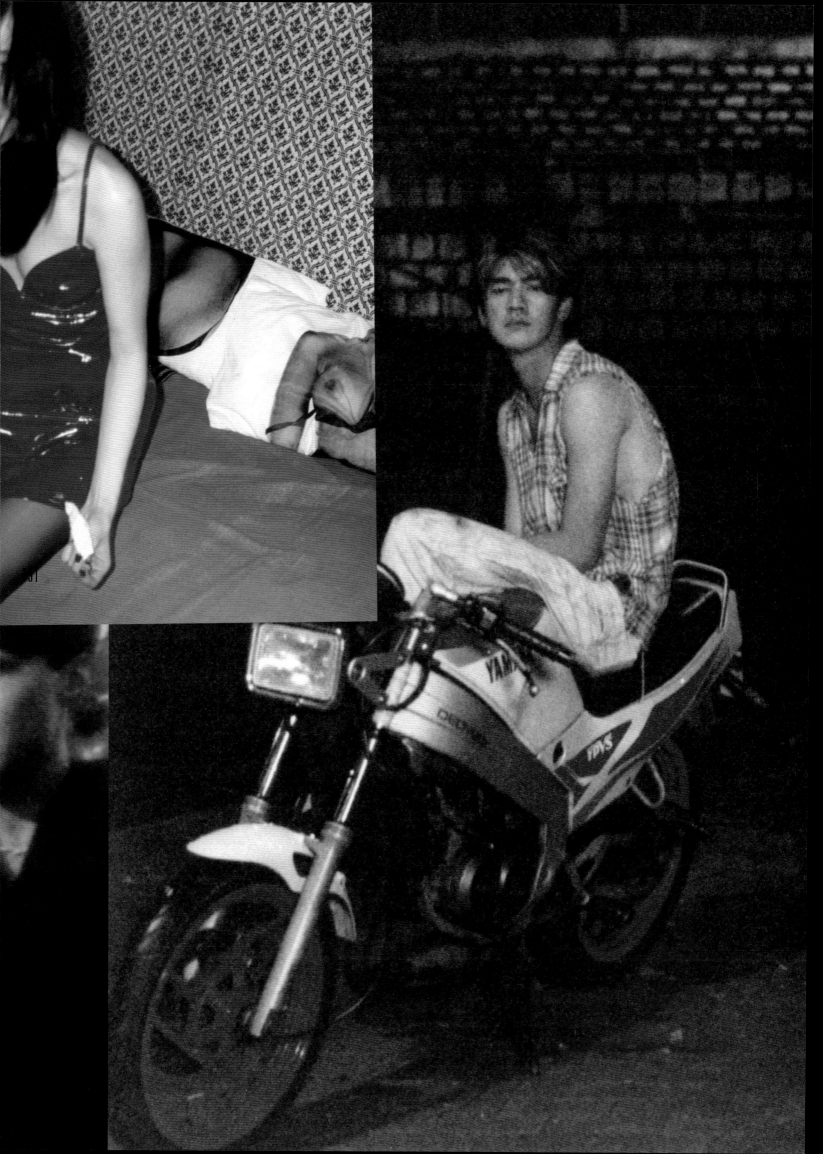

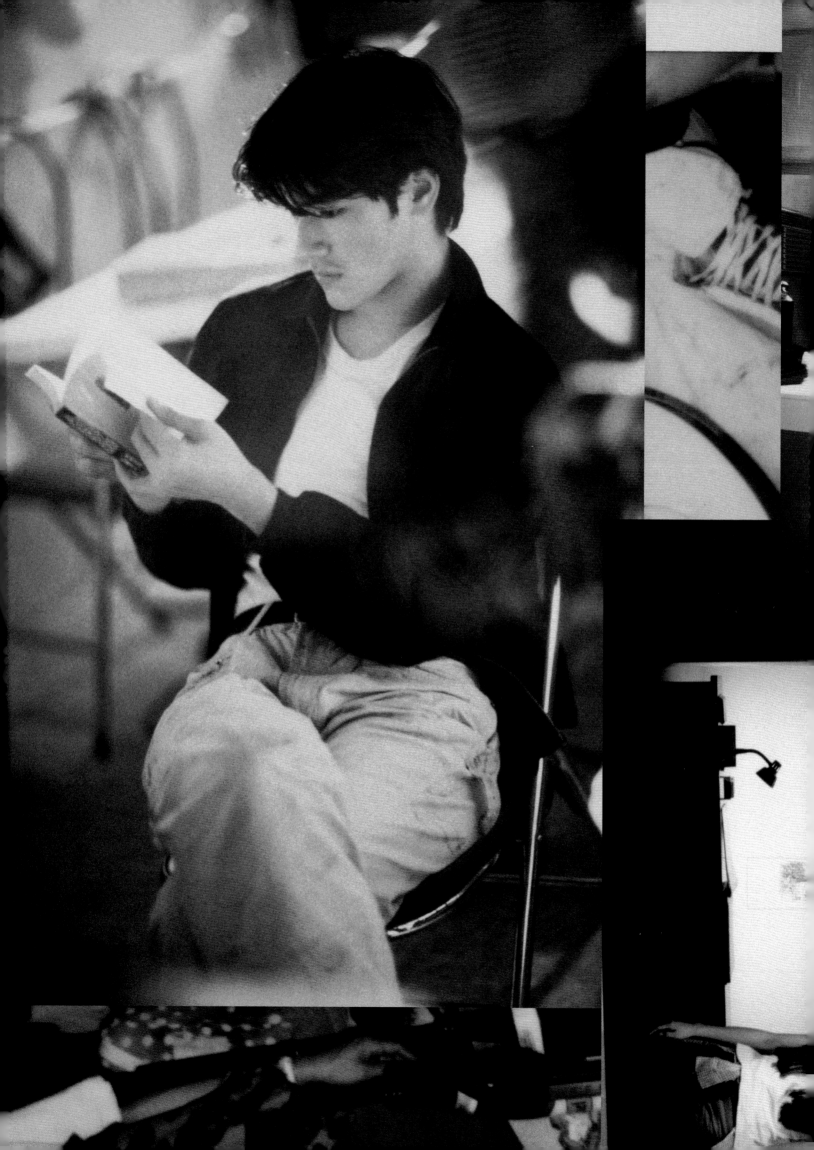

PERFIDIA

In the Mood for Love is probably the film of yours that international viewers know and love best. Critics, too. In the last big *Sight & Sound* poll, in 2012, they voted it one of the 25 greatest films of all time. Like most of your films, it wasn't really planned out in advance.

— I was in Paris doing promotion for *Happy Together* and had dinner with Maggie [Cheung]. She had finished *Irma Vep* and was living with Olivier [Assayas]. We hadn't worked together since *Ashes of Time* and she hadn't worked in Hong Kong in a while. Over dinner, she said, "We should do a film together." She wanted to work with Tony [Leung], who was her first partner from her TV debut.

I said, "Why don't we do a collection of stories, and both of you will play all the characters." "And what would be the topic?" she asked. "How about food?" I was reading a book *The Physiology of Taste* by the French gastronome, Jean Anthelme Brillat-Savarin, whose famous quote was, "Tell me what you eat and I will tell you who you are." There was also a quote that said, "The pleasure of the table belongs to all ages, to all conditions, to all countries, and to all areas: it mingles with all other pleasures and remains at last to console us for their departures." It was a perfect theme for our project, which had the working title *Three Stories About Food*.

We shot the first story in an all-night convenience store in Central. Late at night, it was a natural stopping place for broken hearts and lost souls. The place reminded me of Edward Hopper's painting, "Nighthawks." Tony played the owner who had a hobby, which was collecting the keys customers would leave behind, the remnants of broken promises. Maggie played a woman who'd left her key before, but then comes back, very upset. She gets drunk and wants to eat whatever food he has. He's only got cakes left and she eats them, one after the other. After the last piece, she passes out with a bit of frosting on her lip. This bothers the owner, who is very tidy and keeps an immaculate restaurant. He wants to clean it off of her, but instead of a napkin, he uses a personal touch. We shot the whole story in 10 days and started prepping the next one.

The second story was about a man and a woman, neighbors, whose spouses were having an affair. They were devastated when they found they had both been betrayed. They wanted to know how it happened and why. So they each played the other's spouse and re-enacted the affair as they imagined it, until the point where they confused the line between "acting" and reality.

The idea was inspired by a short story written by the Japanese novelist Sakyo Komatsu and by the works of Liu Yichang, a very influential writer in Hong Kong. Liu, like most of the writers in Hong Kong of that period, made a living by writing daily columns for newspapers. I took him as the model for the betrayed husband. One of Liu's novels has the title *Duidao,* which means *tête-bêche* in French, or head-to-tail. I took that as an inspiration for the structure of the film: to have the story center around the intersection of two parallel affairs. Both actors play the victims and also "act" as each others' spouses. What intrigued me most about the story was not the affair itself but *how* it happens. I wanted to tell the story with a Hitchcock twist,

155

like *Rear Window*—neighbors playing a significant role because the two characters were always under the surveillance of the neighbors. They were actually the catalyst: Because of them, the victims share a secret.

And why the '60s again?
— I decided to set the story in the '60s because it was a time in Hong Kong when most of the people were still very conservative and adultery was not as "accepted" as today. It was a pretty big deal. And the idea of neighbors then was very different than today. They were not the people who were living next door, but the people who shared your toilet! They were the last ones that you wanted to know about your affair. In our original plan, the affairs would unfold over the course of 10 meals. It was a challenging shoot. The story was so rich that it became a drug we couldn't quit. The film got longer and longer and eventually we decided to forget about the idea of having three stories and just focused on the one. We borrowed the title of a Langford song and called it *In the Mood for Love*. The first story that we shot eventually was shown as a short film at my master class in Cannes 2003 under the title "In the Mood for Love 2001", which a few years later was developed and became *My Blueberry Nights*.

It also let you go back to a time and place you like—Hong Kong '62 or '63.
— It was a way to revisit the 60s. At the bottom of my heart, I saw the film spiritually as part two of *Days of Being Wild*. It was impossible to make an actual sequel, but it does have Tony and Maggie, and I even call her the same name from *Days of Being Wild*. Bringing them back together was kind of fun.

And like a rhyme. You like self-referential things.
— Yes. William and I had a great time while we were shooting. Sometimes, he would put Maggie in a certain dress and then give me a look. I'd go, "I know. This is from *Days of Being Wild*." Of course, this was a very different film and our approach was different. With *Days of Being Wild*, I had a specific date and year; with this film, we revisited the period in a more impressionistic way.

In the first one, we learn the exact month, day, hour and even minute.
— *In the Mood for Love* is less precise. We were looking for a flavor. The film is actually about the *mood* of the '60s.

Did the story interest you? Was it an exciting film to make?
— The story wasn't that complicated. Most of my energy was focused on creating the mood. I even went so far that I actually designed a menu of what Shanghainese people like Rebecca Pan's character would be eating, because they were very specific about food—some dishes only belonged to a certain season. I set the menu based on my memory of what my mom made. Then I had to find a Shanghainese lady to cook them because it had to be very accurate. I also designed the soundtrack of the film—not only the music, but the whole ambience. In a neighborhood like this, you would hear Beijing opera, Shanghainese opera. I actually re-created the soundtrack of my childhood, hiring retired radio broadcasters to re-record radio programs and weather reports like the way they used to do. I conducted the soundtrack of the film like I was a radio DJ in the 60s! *Laughs*. Personally, *Days of Being Wild* was less intimate to me because I didn't come from a background like Leslie and his mother. But with *In the Mood for Love*, it was very personal. The character

Maggie 一人食譜.

早餐. 泡飯
苦瓜
咸菜毛豆百頁 加紅椒絲
皮蛋 (或咸蛋)

晚餐. 咸菜毛豆百頁 加紅椒絲
陽春麵

Maggie 羹 (苦瓜)

① 金針雲耳元蹄湯:
瓜肉百頁.
蝦子海蚕
清炒黃芽白肉絲年糕

Maggie 羹 點心 (夏季)

① 桃圓湯.
② 酒釀圓子.
③ 百合紅棗湯.
④ 生煎饅頭.

Maggie 羹 水果 (夏季).

① 苦瓜
② 桃
③ 梨.
④ 楊梅.

Maggie 羹 點心 (苦季)

① 西八民飯.

CONVERSATION FOUR PERFIDIA

Rebecca Pan played reminded me of my mother—all those mahjong scenes, all those dinner scenes. It's my childhood.

It's interesting that you were so obsessive about the precise details of the food. Because it doesn't really figure very much in the film.
— The food wasn't for the audience to see. Usually, the actors aren't supposed to eat it, but this time it helped them create the mood. For instance, with the wonton noodles, what matters is it's an excuse. Maggie walks out every night with this [*WKW holds up an imaginary container*] which was very typical in those days. It was an escape. It was my escape as a child, going out to bring snacks for my mom's mahjong group.

Well, it's a very claustrophobic world that Tony and Maggie's characters inhabit. Even if everybody doesn't know what they're up to, the world is always very snug around them.
— Neighbors were close by. And they had rumors. Rebecca's character here is typical Shanghainese. They know everything and would never tell, but they will "pinch" you at certain points to make sure you know that they know. That's what Maggie deals with. On Tony's side, the landlord is Cantonese and much more explicit. If you look at the apartments, it's two cultures—the Shanghainese and the Cantonese. On one side, everybody's well-dressed. Even if they're playing mahjong, they have suits and ties and cheongsams. On the other side, the landlord is basically wearing his pajamas.

Imagine living in a neighborhood like this. You would need a private place to talk about your secrets. Originally, I wanted Queen's Cafe, but that was gone. So I found a similar place, The Goldfinch. Those places weren't real western restaurants. They just served western food with Chinese ingredients and catered mainly to Chinese. They were popular at the time for not being expensive and seemed to have something special to offer. It was a place you could bring a date.

Both affairs actually start from the rice cooker, which was a new invention from Japan. Maggie's husband bought her one. Tony then asked the husband to get one for his wife, because she was tired of being a housewife—she wanted to work, and the rice cooker would release her from the kitchen. When he buys her the rice cooker, that's the beginning of their affair, which eventually kicks off the affair between Tony and Maggie. To me, the rice cooker was the most important invention in Asia to help liberate women, because they no longer had to tend so much to the cooking. That and instant noodles completely changed the lifestyle of Asian people.

157

You've never made a movie before or since where the clothes matter so much. Every time you see Maggie, she's wearing a different outfit. I asked William how many outfits she had and he said he wasn't sure—maybe 30. For a 90 minute film!
— First of all, realistically, this was normal. In those days, Shanghainese ladies did not wear pajamas at home or in front of people. They were always well-dressed. Maybe they didn't have as many Maggie's character, but every day they dressed their best. The second thing is that, in this film, the dress is not just a dress. It's Maggie's character's mood. It's as if she's wearing this mood that day.

William also told me that because Maggie's not rich, he thought it would be good to give her some fabrics that weren't beautiful. But even with clothes he thought ugly, Maggie always looked terrific—she made plain fabrics look gorgeous.
— She did. And it's her iconic role, although she kind of doesn't like that.

Why not?
— She and the dress had chemistry. They brought out a kind of elegance in each other. In a way, the dress captured a part of her essence and so she will always be associated with it, but nobody likes to be thought of as one thing.

This seems like a good place to talk about her. You were the first person to reveal her as a serious actress, and this was her last big role for you. It's so iconic that Cannes used her image from this film for its poster.
— Maggie started differently from the other actresses of her generation. But she was a natural and brought together two things. Her British childhood lent her a carefree spirit, so she was very modern. Everybody thought, "Maggie's the hippest girl". Yet her features were very classic. She is like the *qingyi* in Peking Opera terms, the virtuous and elite one. But nobody considered her classic until *In the Mood for Love*.

So you carried her from hip through classic.
— I had to bring it out of her. I showed her how to sit, how to eat—how to behave. She went through what Audrey Hepburn did in *My Fair Lady*, she had to be a real life Eliza Doolittle and it wasn't something she got used to because she prefers something more carefree.

I can understand. In *In the Mood for Love* she had to spend hours getting dressed and having her hair done.
— That's true, and it was hard for her. We shot long hours in Bangkok, mostly at night and wrapped around daybreak, when everybody would go back to the hotel and take a rest while I wrote my script. But not her. One day when I went down to the dressing room, I noticed Maggie was there, sitting like this [*WKW leans his head forward propping it on an imaginary dressing table*]. You see, it took hours to do her hair, and William was very exact. He had to make sure she had this particular kind of Monica Vitti curl to her hair. In Hong Kong, the old barbershops could do it,

but we couldn't take those hairdressers with us. So in Bangkok, we ended up having to rework it. Over and over. It was ironed and blow-dried a certain way, which took hours. And if he didn't like it he'd say, "Do it again." That meant another two hours. And then an hour on her eyebrows to make sure they were right. If they weren't, it was, "Clean it and do it again."

Did she want to kill him?
— Everyone respects William, but you knew she was pissed. Very pissed.

Was she easy to direct?
— Yes. I've worked with Maggie since my first film, so I know her very well. So well that she is someone whose take I *could* tell was good just by listening to her delivery.

Do you think she's a good actress?
— There are many good actresses out there, but she is more than that. To me, she is the face of Hong Kong cinema in the '90s. Girls looked up to her. She is both east and west, modern and independent. Urban with an Asian elegance. She is the embodiment of the culture from that time.

What's her special gift?
— Actors communicate with their lines, but what is magical with her is what she says in between. The way she says it with her movements.

She and Tony are so good together in this movie. But from meeting them, I have a sense he likes acting more.
— Tony is a born actor. The only thing he really cares about is acting. He is able to present himself to a director as a clean canvas. Odorless and tasteless in his own way. He doesn't force anything on the character. For the last 20 years, it's been film after film. He needs time to get into character and then needs time to get away from that character. So in a way he's always in-between roles. Maggie, I'm not sure that she really enjoys being an actress. Acting was one phase for her and after a point, I think she had a bigger picture of her life and wanted to have more control over it.

Well, you're a film director so you must like control, too.
— Film production sometimes is like a runaway train, and someone has to take the controls. The job of a director is to make decisions; he has to be both an angel and a devil.

I'm curious about your musical approach in *In the Mood for Love*. It's all about movements and glances and that haunting theme by Shigeru Umebayashi—a few notes conjure up a whole feeling. Have you ever thought of doing a musical?
— Most of my films are already musicals, in a way. Just that the actors don't sing.

Even then you might not like having to plan all the shots.
— I'm too impatient. I don't have the patience for rehearsals.

159

Some directors enjoy that, but not me. I believe in surprises when you're making a film. I guess I have a pretty good sense of rhythm. In the final shot of *Days of Being Wild*, where Tony gets ready to go out gambling, I didn't time his movement with music—I didn't even know we were going to use Xavier Cugat's piece for this scene. But when we put his music over the shot, it synced perfectly. The music ended when he walked out, and we could fade out. Amazing. I've had many more experiences like this.

Well, you care a lot about the actors' physical rhythms.
— Later on, I began to have a habit of playing music while shooting because it sets a rhythm and a mood. The rhythm creates the dance between camera and cast. *In the Mood for Love* is, as you say, almost like a musical. So the choreography of the actors had to be in sync with the camera movement. We shot most of the scenes in tiny rooms, so the set up was very, very tricky, sometimes—almost like doing *Swan Lake* inside a 10' by 10' room.

You use music in nearly all your films and in a strikingly overt way. It's rarely background. In *Chungking Express*, you keep playing "California Dreamin'" and that reggae song my wife hates, "Things in Life." Over and over.
— I like that song, though I've forgotten where I got it. It set the tone for Brigitte's character.

It reminds me a bit of the way Altman used the theme to *The Long Goodbye*.
— Repeating it is a way of making it register. If you play the same music again and again— and a long chunk of it—it becomes a signature, not background music. But the character changes, even though the music does not. Fellini once said, "Show the changes through the unchanged." A song is something more than just the music. In *Chungking Express*, it started out as a coincidence. We were shooting in Lan Kwai Fong at the Midnight Express snackbar. The other side had a restaurant called California because it had Californian cuisine. And I thought, "Yes, California Dreamin'." Later, I realized the song was more than random because it provides an undertone to Faye's character. In those days, Hong Kong people talked a lot about immigration, but for Faye's character, California doesn't mean a passport or moving away. For her, it's something bigger than that—an experience or a possibility. But I knew at the end she'd come back to Hong Kong.

In the Mood for Love is shot very differently from your earlier work. In fact, you shift your style, at least a bit, in every single film. Maybe that's one reason why people think you only care about style.
— People usually mix up style with *form*. Every movie has to have a form. It's about the best way to tell a story visually. When we shot the first story in Central, we did it the same way we did in *Chungking Express*. For the second story, I intended to do it differently. I told Chris, "No more hand-held for this chapter—put

it on a tripod or a dolly." He thought I was joking. But once we started, the contrast with what we'd been doing was so strong that it felt like a new beginning, even though we were going the most traditional way.

It's a lot more stylized than a traditional film.
— It's formal.

It feels like the most disciplined film you ever made.
— Most of the characters in the film are very formal people. So the film has to be formal. Everything is formal and rigid. The settings were constants, but the characters changed. And what's underneath in the darkness is very interesting.

Did you always know how the story would turn out—with them apart and Tony in Cambodia?
— No. About halfway through, I realized it was not going to be a short film, it would be a full length feature. And for that, we would need four acts. Act One introduces these two people. Act Two, they find out about the affair. The third act is about the revenge. But what would be the final act? I only knew one thing: We couldn't end the film saying these two people lived happily ever after. It couldn't work that way. Their relationship would always be under the shadow of their spouses. I expected it to end like The *Umbrellas of Cherbourg*—there's always a regret.
   One day, Tony asked me a big question: "Why am I spending all this time with this woman? Am I falling in love with her? Do I want to get laid, or what?" I told him to think of it as revenge. This woman, Maggie, has always said, "I'm different. I'm not like your wife. I won't have an affair." So your character should be thinking, "What makes her think she's better than my wife? Why is she so sure?" So in a way he's plotting—he wants to get revenge. Not on her husband or his wife, but on Maggie for thinking she's superior to his wife. So I gave him a dark side, and I had an idea for the final act.

But we like the nice, soulful Tony.
— In my original plan, Tony bids farewell to Maggie, filling her with a sense of loss when he goes to Singapore. She finally goes there to find him, and they spend the night together. Then he tells her, "I did this for revenge. I just wanted to prove you're no different from my wife. You're also a slut." This breaks her heart. Then the end of the story happens a few years later, in the 70s. He comes back to Hong Kong for Ping's wedding, and at the wedding party, comes across Maggie again. She has a kid, but never mentions that it's his. At the end of the film, you sense his regret. He realizes he still loves Maggie after all these years, but can never be with her again.

I think the audience would've liked that film a lot less.
— It's hard to tell. Just imagine the ending of *La Strada*, when Anthony Quinn goes back to the place where he left Giulietta Masina. His sense of loss is heartbreaking. Of course, it's satisfying to have a film embraced by the audience. That doesn't mean it's necessarily a better film.

I think that what audiences love is that Tony and Maggie are likable people caught in a tough situation. It gives their romance a muted sadness. Anyway, the revenge version isn't how you ended the actual movie. Why not?
— The film was a year behind schedule and way over budget. We'd shown 60 minutes to Cannes and they'd accepted it for competition, so we had to get it done. And *2046* was already going into pre-production while we were shooting this one. Working on two films back to back was suicide. Most of my days were about the number of bills we had to settle and the hours of sleep that I managed to get. Some people say that filmmaking is like bullfighting. Here I was, like a matador facing his bull, I had to finish the film before it finished me. So we had to stop. We wrapped without being able to complete the final act, cut the film in a month, and sent it to competition with only mono sound. The film was a success and it saved our company.

I find it slightly unnerving that our whole idea of *In the Mood for Love*—especially Tony's character—is radically changed because you were running late for Cannes.
— But that happens all the time. When you make films the way I do, you realize that a story doesn't go just one way. All along, you keep having choices–does this character do this or that? And each of those choices leads to more choices later on. The possibilities seem endless. And you try some of them. But each possibility carries a price tag and "let's try" are the most expensive words in the business. In the end, you wind up with one film, the only one you could have, yet somehow it didn't *have* to be that film. To an extent, making a film is like offering the audience a deep drag off your cigarette. The drag is what's left on-screen. The rest is just ashes.

In the finished *In the Mood for Love*, Tony winds up whispering into a hole in Angkor Wat. Why?
— I knew the film would end with a secret, but where? One day, I woke up and asked Jacky [Pang, now his producer], "Have you heard of Angkor Wat?" She said, "What's that?" "It's in Cambodia," I said, "and nobody has ever shot a film there. I want to end the film in Angkor Wat." You see, I remembered the scene when Tony was speaking with Ping and they talked about the guy who, when he had secrets, speaks into a hole. I could imagine Tony speaking his secret in Angkor Wat.

And why Angkor Wat?
— Because it was almost impossible.

Surely there has to be more meaning to it than just that.
— Because it has a sense of history. The place is a mystery. It has been forgotten for years. And when you look at all the reliefs on the buildings, they tell stories like this one, stories about human beings over centuries and centuries. Tony and Maggie's story would be only *one* of those reliefs, one of those stones. The film is chamber music and I wanted a coda that was from a different level. *In The Mood For Love* represents how I felt about post-colonial Hong Kong. Ending the film in

Cambodia, which used to be a French colony, was my farewell to our colonial days.

Yes, it lets you shift the perspective.
— Exactly. I learned it from Antonioni. He ended *Eclipse* with a long montage without the characters, only the empty piazza where the main characters used to visit. He later explained in one of his interviews that for him, this place served as a witness. So instead of ending on a single couple and a single relationship, which most of the film has been about, he switched to the angle of the witness. That was really inspiring.

And you always like something outside of normal time—like the TV monitors at the beginning of *As Tears Go By* or the forest in *Days of Being Wild*. Angkor Wat feels magical and special.
— There is a sutra which goes, "Mount Sumeru hides mustard seed; mustard seed contains Mount Sumeru." To me, those images were my "piazzas."

What did Tony think of the ending?
— He said, "What happened to my story—to my revenge?" I said it became his secret. *Laughs.*

But Tony gets his revenge in *2046*, where that sweet-faced cuckold from *In the Mood for Love* turns into a heartless ladykiller.
— He was not heartless. He just lives in his past. The room 2046 is like the hole in Angkor Wat, where he buried his past with Maggie. It's a wound that never healed.

163

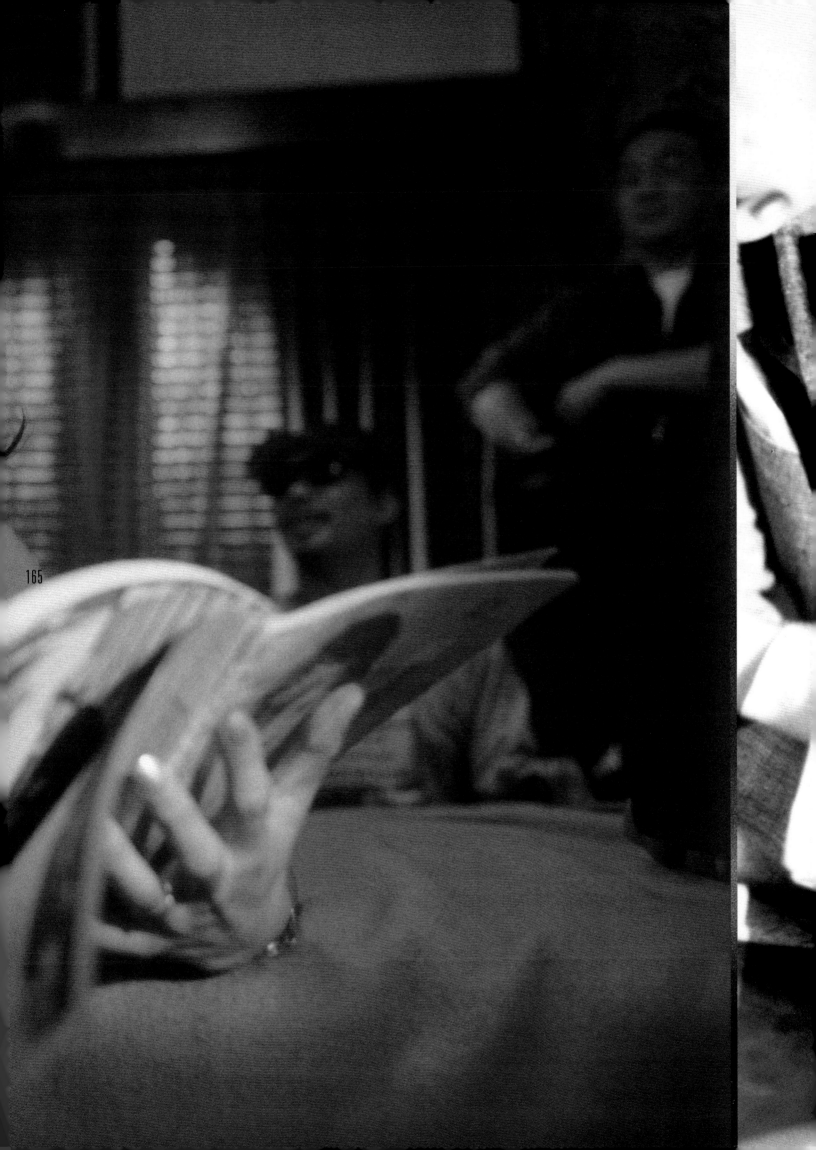

179

But he's also cruel to women.

— He never treated them badly in *2046*. He was just cynical. He treated each woman like the Cole Porter lyric from *Kiss Me Kate*, "I'm always true to you, darlin', in my fashion; Yes, I'm always true to you, darlin', in my way."

What about that scene where he sleeps with Zhang Ziyi's character and makes her cry by giving her money—turning it into a transaction.

— He was just being honest. A woman like Ziyi's character would only refuse a guy's money for two reasons. She could treat him as a sucker and the guy would feel flattered, eventually costing him much more because he thought the relationship was personal; or she could treat him as a lover. Tony wanted to be neither. By giving her money, he's saying, "If you think I'm going to be a sucker, you are making a mistake. But if you really think we are going to fall in love, that's not going to happen. It's business, and I don't want to waste your time." He's Dean Martin singing "Sway," because they shared this dance together, but at the end, it's just a dance.

But she doesn't feel that way.

— Either way, she feels hurt.

But because he's a beloved star like Tony Leung, the audience will also think he's the special one and that even a prostitute like Ziyi will naturally fall in love with him.

— Ziyi's character is not a prostitute. She worked in the bar as what was called a dancing girl. To dance with them, you had to buy them a drink and they got a cut of that drink. That's all the arrangement was. But a man wants more. And even though writers like Tony were very popular with ladies, they still had to invest time and effort in these women who had their own power and weren't easy to get.

In the original conception, *2046* would have to have been a very long movie. It's got the story in the '60s, with Tony's character going through all those women, and the futuristic train to and from *2046*, and then the city itself filled with all these women in crazy costumes—that part didn't really make it into the film.

— *One Hundred Years of Solitude* opens with one sentence about an imagined future from a man in the past, but it applies to the present. I wondered if that could be done on film. I started with the famous promise that, after the handover, Hong Kong wouldn't be changed for 50 years. I thought it would be interesting to make a film about this promise. It's a kind of metaphor. I tried to imagine what happens to a city if it has to remain unchanged for 50 years. That's the origin of the film. When we shot *In the Mood for Love*, they asked me to choose a number for the hotel room, and I said 2046.

When you said 2046, you were thinking of the fiftieth year after the '97 handover.

— The number just came out from my mouth. Since we had already planned *2046* as my next film, I thought why not?

But you also have him writing about the future—the trains and women in weird costumes.

— This made sense for a writer in the 1960s. I remember the science fiction I read as a kid. It was, "By the year 2000 people don't have to walk, they can fly!" *Laughs.* So I thought why not create a low-tech futuristic city imagined by a writer in the '60s. It was even harder for William. First, he wasn't interested in low-tech sci-fi. Second, he hates CGI because it's beyond his control. I said, "Why don't you just do a drawing of the city, and I'll have other people do the CGI—that way you can keep the art direction." And he said, "Let's do the '60s first." *Laughs.*

To be honest, most people don't like the science fiction part very much. A friend of mine watched it, then called me: Do I really have to care about all that futuristic crap?

— Compared to most of the big Hollywood sci-fi pictures, your friend's disappointment is understandable. In fact, it would have been much easier for any decent CG company to create a standard hi-tech city than the other way around. To create an interesting lo-tech futuristic look would require taste; and taste is subjective. Finally, we contacted a French company, BUF, which was responsible for some of the work in *The Matrix* and *The Fifth Element*. They took pictures of Hong Kong from different periods to create the look of 2046, but they had difficulty reading Chinese, and most of the time the signs in the composites were reversed, so we had to redo them over and over. It was painful. Eventually we ended up with a few shots of the city and an express train on the way to 2046 that never arrives.

Also the stuff happening in the '60s with Tony and the women—Ziyi, Gong Li, and Faye Wong—is so much better. And sexier. Usually your movies are extremely chaste. But the bed scene with Ziyi and Tony is racier than almost anything you've done.

— It was actually very mild. In fact, it should have been much more straightforward.

There's that Orson Welles remark where he says that there are two things he never believes when sees them on screen—people praying and people making love. And I thought you might feel the same way.

— What's really stimulating and sexual is in the mind. Normally, a love scene doesn't give you more information about who the characters are. So there's nothing more to know except their body. Of course, if you said, "I want to see this movie so I can look at the body of Nicole Kidman," then that's maybe the main point.

How old-fashioned of you. These days, most people like things explicit.

— When I look at *Lust, Caution* I know that. But I've known Tony [Leung] for so long, I don't want to see his ass! *Laughs.*

When I saw *Eyes Wide Shut*, I'd already spent time with Nicole Kidman, and I certainly didn't feel that way.

— I'm not surprised.

People often say that *2046* is about memory or nostalgia. Do you agree?
— It's about letting go. In a way, memory is a curse to Hong Kong. After '97, people got afraid of change; instead of looking forward, they preferred to stay in the past. It is very unsettling.

So *2046* is about the fear of change?
— Once you say you want things to stay the same forever, that means you don't believe that things could be better. It's lack of confidence. It's fear of losing. That's the complex. In *2046*, I'm not using the love story to be a metaphor for the future of the city, but the other way around. I'm using this political metaphor to tell a love story. In relationships, people always say, "We can't change. We have to be like this forever."

Was Tony afraid to lose?
— He was afraid to let go of his past with Maggie. His heart stayed in 2046. So he refused Zhang Ziyi, he refused Gong Li, he refused Faye Wong. That's why, at the end of the film, Faye told him, "Maybe you should start writing a novel called '2047'."

And move on.
— Yes.

I would find it hard to resist Zhang Ziyi in that film. She's really good. How was she to work with?
— At first, she was very suspicious. It was her first Hong Kong production and she didn't understand the language. She felt like a foreigner and was always on her own—very alert. But that was good for her because it kept her on eggshells. I told her later, during *The Grandmaster*, "There are two kinds of actors. Some need to be encouraged and others work better under pressure. You work better under pressure."

   When I cast Ziyi, a lot of my people were saying, "What do you like about her?" I said, "You'll see." Remember the scene at the restaurant where she's about to say goodbye to Tony? I said, "Ziyi, you are very vulnerable and alone on Christmas night and you don't know about your future and you're pretty drunk. I want to see tears in your eyes." And she said, "Okay"—and she delivered. So I said, "Very good, but I think this shot will

not end here. You will seem too weak. But you have strength and spirit, so after the tears you will smile, like you're saying, 'I will move on.' Can you do that?" She said, "Let me try." And she delivered. The people around me were going, "Hmm. Not bad." And I said, "Ziyi, the shot will not end here. After the smile, you are questioning yourself. You're wondering am I really that strong? So you feel puzzled. Can you do that in one shot—tears, then smile, and then puzzled." "Let me try." And she delivered—perfectly. And my team was going, "Fuck it, she's really, really good." *Laughs.*

Give her a good role and she can be a great actress.
— She likes to be challenged. She is a very powerful actress.

Gong Li was also in *2046*. It was the first time she and Ziyi had been in a film together.
— Yes, but before that, Gong Li and I did *Eros*.

I'm curious about that project. Although it doesn't seem really new, "The Hand" is one of your most perfect films.
— *Eros* was commissioned. Antonioni wanted to make this film, and he wanted two partners [Steven Soderbergh was the other]. I'd only met him briefly before at Cannes. For me, it was an honor. I thought it would be challenging, as I was shooting *2046* at the time, but how could I say no to Antonioni?

Did ordinary women wear cheongsams like the women in these films?
— Yes, but only for formal occasions, parties. You have to understand that cheongsams are not very comfortable.

   I'd seen the women around our neighborhood get their fittings. In those days, a good tailor was very popular. He could enhance your figure and cover up things. But they didn't work by themselves. They had workshops. And there was an apprentice who had to do everything, and he would have extra help. When you watch *Eros*, you can feel that. It's long hours, with a radio on the side and a lot of cigarettes, and they worked mostly at night. If a woman had a favorite tailor, like Gong Li in *Eros*, it would be a friendship that lasted for years. She'd always go back to the same tailor because the tailor knew her body so well.

In this movie, he's Chang Chen. When he first meets Gong Li, they have an erotic encounter–which is partly why it's called "The Hand." It sounds rather simple.
— But there was more going on with *Eros*. Our second night was the night that Leslie [Cheung] committed suicide. We were about to leave the office. Gong Li was doing her makeup and we got the call. I'll never forget it. It was the first of April, 2003. We were shooting in Admiralty and he jumped at the Mandarin Hotel, only five minutes away. So close. Most of our crew knew him and liked him. That was a terrible night.

Did that change the film?
— We had to stop the production soon after because the city was hit by SARS. I've never seen a time like that before. The whole city was dead. Every night you'd go to Nathan Road and the street was empty. There would be a line of taxis with their lights on, available. You walked into the busiest restaurants and they were empty. It was very scary. And the thing that people always reminded each other was, "Don't touch any-thing." You had to wash your hands all the time. It was always about touching. Even touching could be contagious. I thought, "Maybe it's time to make a film about touching—about how that can be contagious." So that was the idea. We'd already started shooting the film, set in contemporary Hong Kong, but I liked the idea about touching. It wasn't about SARS; it was about EROS. I rewrote the script and set the story in the '60s.

The story seems better in the past.
— It also made more sense to shoot the film at the same time as *2046*. We only had a few days to work with Gong Li after SARS was over and I soon realized that she didn't understand her character. Having grown up in China, Gong Li had no idea what a woman in '60s Hong Kong was like. So she played the role like a classic 1930s Shanghainese courtesan, a role she learnt from plays she studied at the Beijing Performing Academy. But performing for film is very different from doing a play. So I tried different approaches. In the end, we had only three days before she had to go to Italy. I told her, "We have to finish this. We have only 72 hours, and we'll make full use of them." And she said, "Yes, but you'll need to give me a short

break for two or three hours to rest. I can do it." So we shot non-stop for 72 hours with only a couple of hours off for hair and wardrobe changes. We shot in chronological order, and as she got more and more tired, her performance got deeper and more vulnerable. She was no longer a 1930s Shanghainese courtesan.

And then *2046*.
— Our experience on *Eros* was very brief but very satisfying. By the time we finished the last scene of the film, we both felt we should work together again soon. So in *2046*, she became The Gambler. In this film, I intentionally made reference to our first collaboration. Because *Eros* is about her hand, in this film she's always wearing a glove. We shot all her scenes on our last week in Bangkok and Gong Li kept asking, "How long do you think my chapter will be?" "I don't know. 10, maybe 15 minutes." On the last day of shooting, we did the scene of her doing the goodbye kiss with Tony. And that really showed me how great an actress she is.

So it's a kiss. That's normally one minute, two minutes. Chris would load the camera with a four minute reel. I'd normally sit in front of the monitor and say "Cut" when I feel the emotion is there and it's okay to stop. But no matter how I looked I couldn't find a way to cut, because she's so skillful. The camera can't stop looking at her because she has so much emotional variation in this kiss. So the kiss lasts *exactly* four minutes. Just before the camera rolls out, Gong Li walks out of the frame and the camera goes *click!* I tried three times to make sure, trying to figure out how she could do it.

It's not four whole minutes in the film, is it?
— Four minutes, four minutes, *four minutes*! She's not doing exactly the same thing each time, so you just can't cut it. That's incredibly skillful. Afterwards Tony said, "She's the best kisser I ever had." *Laughs.*

Well she's one of the world's great screen actresses.
— The truth is, really great actors are so good that they only have to give very little and people already say, "That's amazing." It's hard to motivate them for more. Sometimes, you might have

to put them under some kind of pressure, like with a time limit in the case of *Eros* and *2046*. Then you might get something exceptional.

I want to end by talking about something more abstract. *In the Mood for Love*, *2046*, and *Eros* are consciously beautiful movies with a glamour I associate with old Hollywood. Even when you shoot in shabby places, they seem somehow romantic.
— I'm very old-fashioned in that sense, I enjoy watching stars. I remember during *Days of Being Wild*, Andy Lau said to me, "If you don't want acting, why don't you find a non-actor?" I said, "It's different. To look at a film with a non-actor and a film with a star who's not 'acting' are two very different experiences." I feel that a movie should be something larger than life.

But even when you're shooting ordinary people, like Ping in these movies, you light them so they'll look great.
— I like my characters and when you like your characters, the way you see them will be kinder. When I look at a film, I can easily tell whether the director likes the actor or not. It's very obvious. It's not that they have double chins or bad lighting. It's something larger than that. The tenderness isn't there. I like to be *with* the characters, not superior to them. One of my problems with *Fallen Angels* was that I didn't know how to be with Leon Lai and Michelle Reis.

So your love of beauty is born of affection?
— The beauty in a film is more than how it looks visually. A good film should have an *aftertaste*; maybe a shot, or a line, or even a moment. Something that stays with the audience for a very long time.

199

203

205

PAN-AMERICAN HIGHWAY

You've made two films that are geographical outliers—set in the Americas, not Asia. The first was *Happy Together*, which you made in Argentina and premiered at Cannes in '97. I was at that first screening and remember people thinking it slightly daring because it was a gay love story with two huge Hong Kong stars. Is that the best way to see it?

— With *Happy Together*, you have to go back to the time before '97. In those days, people were really worried about life after the handover. There were people trying to get green cards to Canada, the United States, or Australia. There were lots of tragedies and broken marriages. One of the biggest disappointments for the people of Hong Kong came when they received their UK passports that bore the letters BNO—"British National (Overseas)"—which meant they were British subjects with a British passport, but with no right to stay in Britain after the handover. It meant that you were an illegitimate son.

I felt we should make a film about this, a story about being rejected when you expected acceptance. A film about a "non-accepted" relationship, perhaps a gay one—especially because I wasn't sure that, after '97, you'd even be able to make a gay film in Hong Kong. So I went to Leslie and said, "Let's make a gay film." And he said, "Why not?" I said, "Are you sure?" He said, "Yes, with you I am sure. And who will be my partner?" I said, "Tony" and he said, "Good."

Leslie obviously trusted you.

— Yes, of course. It was something he wanted to do for a long time, but never found the right opportunity. He also felt the same urgency as we did. This seemed like the right time. He trusted our team and believed that we wouldn't do anything exploitative.

I'm told that you have long been known for being what people call "gay-friendly."

— I have many gay friends and a lot of the people I work with are gay. It's never seemed like a big deal to me. And really it wasn't a big deal in Hong Kong or the film business back then.

Anyway, Leslie was gay so you knew he wouldn't feel uncomfortable playing a gay character. I wouldn't have been so sure about Tony.

— I talked to him in his apartment. He said, "My character's gay?" And I said, "Yes." And then he said he would do it. I asked if he was sure and he said, "You're not asking me to do a love scene, are you?" I told him the film didn't have to have a love scene. It's about two guys leaving Hong Kong and we'd be shooting everything in Argentina. He was intrigued by that and said, "Well that's interesting . . . Are you *sure* there will be nothing explicit?" I told him there would be dancing because Argentina is known for tango and when we announced the film, we'd say that he and Leslie would dance the tango. And he said, "OK." So we did the press conference, the press took pictures, and it was big news: Tony and Leslie in a gay film! And so we moved on.

But when you watch *Happy Together*, the first thing that you see is the passport with the BNO on it. It starts where *I* started.

So why Argentina, of all places. Is that because you'd liked the novels of Manuel Puig? You said he influenced the way you tell your stories. And he himself was gay.

— That's right. Among all his novels, *Heartbreak Tango* is my favorite. I think it is a great title. We even used it as the working title of the film. But when we applied for the permit to shoot in Argentina under that title, people asked, "Do you have the rights?" and we said, "We're working on it." At the end, of course, the answer was no.

To shoot a film about tango, where else could you go except Argentina? Besides, I was fed up with the question that every journalist kept asking about whether my next film was going to be about the '97 handover. I thought, "I want to get as far away as possible from Hong Kong. I want to go to the other side of the world and tell a story of these two men." I then realized Argentina is actually the furthest place from Hong Kong on earth. *Laughs.*

By now, I think I'm safe in assuming that you didn't have a script. Did you have a story?

— I had only an idea. I told everyone, "We are going to shoot a road movie in Argentina, like a traveling circus, but exactly from where to where, I don't know yet. We're going to spend three months there and that's it. Now, let's go!"

That sounds so glamorous and fun. But this is a Wong Kar Wai film, so I suspect that things spun out of control.

— Naturally. The first production house that we hired was crooked, so we had to find another one. Then the first one began to cause trouble—they called Immigration and made a fuss about our permits and working visas. Meanwhile, I had a kind of mini-stroke. Half of my face wouldn't move. I had to put tape over one eye when I slept—*WKW mimes taping his eye shut.* When I ate, food dropped out of my mouth. It was terrible. And Esther had just joined me with my son, Qing, who was only 18 months old. Anyway, I went to the doctor, who did all these X-rays, and told me that I had to stop working for a month. That just wasn't possible. But I was very lucky. Jacky [Pang] found an acupuncturist—from some local Chinese restaurant. So I had this Chinese doctor and somehow the treatment worked. Soon I recovered.

You've made so many films about the diaspora—your Chinese characters are always moving around—that it seems inevitable you'd go to Buenos Aires and wind up in a Chinese restaurant.

— In every city I visit, I always find a Chinese restaurant. That's where I find out the most about a city.

In New York, you took me to Joe's Shanghai on West 56th. What do you know about New York from that?

— You'd learn even more from going to Chinatown than staying in a midtown restaurant. When I first went to New York's Chinatown, most of the people were from Hong Kong. They spoke Cantonese, but it was very old-fashioned Cantonese. Now it's mainly Mandarin, so you can see the changes.

Anyway, I got along with the restaurant's owner. He had a long story. I said, "Why did you have to come all the way to Argentina to open a Chinese restaurant? Do you have relatives here?" He said no. He'd come to Buenos Aires in the '70s. He'd been a cop, but because of the ICAC [Independent Commission Against Corruption that cracked down on police] he had to flee. Police corruption was common in Hong Kong then; taking bribes was like accepting a cup of free coffee today. He was very helpful and we got along well. He said, "You can shoot here. And I have some Chinese friends who speak Spanish and they'll find you a production manager." So that's how we made the film, with the restaurant doing the catering. By then, we had already been sitting in Buenos Aires for two months without a production house and a permit, and we'd be either arrested or deported if we shot anything without them. We missed Hong Kong! *Laughs.*

By then, did you have your story?
— To make a road movie the first thing you need is a map. You have to find the route and figure out the places, cities, and landscapes along the way. Because we knew most part of the film would take place in Buenos Aires, I spent most of my days touring the city. Meanwhile, Tony and Leslie were taking tango lessons. At the same time, Tony was doing all this training because I'd told him, "You're going to take off your clothes, so your body has to look nice." He worked very hard. And then Leslie got this amoeba thing and became very sick. Tony was the guy who fed him every day. But you could feel that there's a tension in Tony's mind: "What am I going to do?" He didn't know how to act like he was part of a gay couple. He was restless all the time. And I could see it.

Then I found this picture by Nan Goldin. She does lots of photos of unhappy relationships and I think they're very well done. So I went to William and said, "I want to start the film like this." I handed him a photo. "Let's open the picture with a love scene. This is the room that I want when they're making love to each other. There will be two beds. And the light will be minimal." William said, "You'll have to give me details," and I said, "There are no details. But we have to do this now because I need to know whether Tony will be able to do it or he will quit the film." I wanted to open the film at the moment when the characters were closest to each other and from there they would go further and further apart. I had to be sure that Tony would be able to do it. It was the make or break point of the film.

And Tony had no idea.
— I set up the scene—*WKW giggles*—and Tony is pale. He didn't expect the first day to be the love scene. Now, normally with all my films, I demonstrate what I want. For Tony's love scene with Ziyi in *2046*, I acted it out with my assistant, Johnnie [Kong] to show how far it would go. But this time I said, "I leave it to William and Leslie." Nobody really knew how to start. So I set up the camera, Chris put on the lights, and Tony sat there in his towel, just looking at Leslie. There was no one on the set except for me, William, Jacky, the camera assistant, and Chris.

Leslie took off his towel and said, "C'mon." This was the moment and it was really about who's on top. Because I never said who was on top. Then Leslie just goes and lies down on the bed—so it's very obvious. Tony said, "Okay, let's go," and it got very quiet. Tony took off his towel, but he still had boxers on and I thought he should take them off, but he said, "No! I won't do that. That's my bottom line." So I said, "Okay, let's go." And Leslie led him. We did a couple of takes and then I said, "It's done."

After that scene, Tony just sat there, totally shocked. Leslie told him, "Now you know how I felt all those years playing guys who are with women and having to pretend I enjoyed it." It was a big moment for Tony. A few years later he told me, "The biggest regret I have is that I didn't have the courage to take off my boxers that day." I think this is one of the reasons he did *Lust, Caution*.

So your tip to young filmmakers is to get the sex stuff done early.
— It works better that way. On the first day of *Eros*, I did the scene with Gong Li touching Chang Chen. It was the first time they'd ever acted together and it really helped them to know each other. It's always good to start with a kiss or something intimate because everything afterward seems much easier.

So now you've got an opening scene, but what about the rest of the movie?
— First, we planned to do it on the Pan-American Highway from the U.S. border to the furthest point in south Argentina. I began to check all sorts of places. I went to northern spots like Jujuy and then to Mendoza. Finally I found Ushuaia, which is very nice—it's the end of the world. I felt that we should end the film there because I liked the idea of ending the film at the End of the World. Ushuaia was then and still is a tourist town where you can find places like: The Last Coffee Shop at the End of the World, or The Last Hotel at the End of the World, etc. I remember that on the main street there was a phone booth, where you could call your friends from the end of the world. I found it really romantic. Besides all these, there's one casino catering mainly to the Japanese tourists on their way to Antarctica. But it wasn't like the ones in Macao. It was much smaller, with ten dollar bets. At night, that casino became strange, deserted like a ghost town.

You were basically trying to improvise another film. Does that get easier over the years? Were you ever terrified that you'd wind up with nothing, or had you been through this process so many times that you were used to it?
— With a team like this, I never worried about whether we were going to finish the film or not. My only concern was how good we could make it. In a way, most of my previous films were sort of road movies, but on a much smaller scale: We were just jumping from one street to another within Hong Kong. I didn't feel any pressure. But when you had almost 50 people from Hong Kong stuck with you in a totally foreign country, and they couldn't do anything except to wait for you—well, that's

something new. I felt responsible. For the first few days, everyone was happy because the wine was so cheap and the steak was so nice—there were parties every night in their rooms, and wine bottles were everywhere the next morning. But after two months, everybody started wondering, "What are we doing *here*? Are we going to shoot tomorrow?" Leslie had a concert he needed to go back for, and William would say, "There are two films waiting for me." It was like a boiling hotpot. And my kid was over there and I couldn't spend time with him; even on my son's second birthday, after the birthday cake, I had to go. I could only go out every day to a nearby coffee shop and write.

You were shooting some scenes with Tony and Leslie, though, right?
— Yes, and Chris had been shooting cutaway shots on the 9 de Julio Avenue [the main street of Buenos Aires] for weeks!

What was the first moment you felt you had something?
— When Leslie said, "I cannot stay any longer," somehow it narrowed down the possibilities. I knew the film would be more from Tony's perspective. There were times when Leslie talked about how he could come back, but after a certain point he said, "I can't come back. It's a world tour." That meant for sure that we had to shorten his part. In Hong Kong productions, this happens all the time. You only have a week with an actor, so you shoot all the scenes with him and let him go. But that can only work when you have a full script. I didn't have one, so I shot as much as I could before he went, and on his last day, I shot the scene where he cried when he realized Tony was gone. By then, I knew for sure that Tony would be the only person who ended up at the waterfall, and I had to figure out the rest before he reached that point.

Like Borges with his garden of forking paths.
— At one point we talked about having him kill himself and die in Argentina. Then we thought that on his way to Iguazu Falls he would come across a mysterious girl from Hong Kong. So we flew Shirley Kwan from Hong Kong and shot all her scenes with Tony in three weeks. But later on, when I put the film together, I realized something was wrong. With a girl in the film, the theme would turn towards *gender*—how he preferred guys to a woman. But without her, it's in a way unisex. It's about loving someone else, not about gender preference. That's why I took out all her scenes from the film. I actually like those scenes a lot—Chris shot them beautifully—and Shirley was great in her part. After the film release, I put all her scenes as bonus tracks for the special edition DVD of the film.

211

Instead you have the sub-story about Tony and the young guy working at the Chinese restaurant, played by Chang Chen.
— He was only 17 years old then and soon had to serve in the army.
Tony and Leslie are great movie stars and movie actors. Was he good?
— He wasn't as experienced, but he had the energy and freshness for the role. I first noticed him in Edward Yang's *Mahjong* where he plays a playboy. But in person he was actually very shy, so I tried to capture that shyness in the film.

Chang Chen is from Taipei and speaks Mandarin. Tony talks Cantonese. In nearly all your films, people are constantly speaking different languages to one another. In *Chungking Express*, Takeshi Kaneshiro talks to Brigitte Lin in like five of them. Are you making some sort of point with this?
— No, it's very common in a city like Hong Kong where people coming from different parts of the world speak different languages. When I was young, friends of my father talked to us in Mandarin, in Shanghainese, and people understood each other well. In *2046* it's absolutely normal that Zhang Ziyi speaks Mandarin in a Cantonese guest house. All over Asia, there are people

from everywhere and they communicate. On *Happy Together*, Jacky, then our line-producer, couldn't speak Spanish and spoke very little English. But somehow she could communicate well with the Argentinean crew. Of course, Chris soon picked up Spanish. As for the characters played by Tony and Leslie, they were tourists and it's normal that they couldn't speak Spanish, only a few words.

All these languages give you a sense of the fluidity of life.
— Yes, they are texture and add to the verisimilitude of the film.

Back to the film itself. One of *Happy Together*'s major characters is actually Buenos Aires. Was it hard for you to shoot there?
— Unlike Hong Kong where I know almost every street, every corner, even every smell, Buenos Aires is a much bigger city which carries a different energy. Somehow it feels sad. I can understand why, when people go into exile, they end up there. It's a city that's so far away from anywhere and is always melancholic. I spent days and days walking around Buenos Aires because I believed that it was the best way to understand the city. I'd stop at a store and ask, "How much does this cost?" and "What kind of coffee are they serving here?" and "What kind of cigarettes are they smoking?" and "How much is that meat over there?"
   I studied the history of the city and visited most of the gay areas of Buenos Aires. The only place that really attracted my eyes was in La Boca. It was a sailor's town, the port of Argentina. It had the color and energy that I was looking for. It reminded me of Hong Kong. The location manager kept asking me, "What are you looking for?" *Seven Years in Tibet* was also shooting in Argentina then—they basically booked all the best equipment and the prettiest locations. The location manager thought we were looking for something similar, so he was quite shocked when I told him my choice. He said, "You came all the way to Argentina, so why are you shooting in this shabby, dirty little area? Why not choose someplace beautiful?" And I'd say, "Can you show me that alley?" *Laughs*. After the film, very often when I come across people from Argentina, they'd say, "Your film makes our city look very beautiful."

They're right. I'm not sure Chris ever shot more beautifully than he did here. Every image is fantastic. Why, even the colors of the local buses—red, green, and yellow—fit the film's palette.
— Yes, he did a very good job. He is a sailor by nature, so he totally got it.

And for Tony it was some sort of breakout role.
— Tony was popular before the film, but not yet a A-lister. The film got him the Best Actor Award at Hong Kong Film Award. Three years later, he won Best Actor Award at the Cannes Film Festival. It was the highest honor an actor from Hong Kong ever got. From that point on, he always had the top billing in his films.

That was the best I'd seen him up to that point.
— Before the film, Tony could play almost any role as well as anyone could, but in *Happy Together*, he was original. The film was custom-made for him, and Leslie did help a lot by basically playing Carina [Lau, Tony Leung's real life wife]. He told me, "I just copied Carina, so Tony knew what to do." He was very generous.

The personas of both actors are so powerful that it's easy to believe that their characters here are the real them—Tony's the more honorable and decent, Leslie the more amoral. Was it actually that way?
— In fact, they each could be both, depending on the situation.

It was your last film with Leslie who starred in three of your very best films.
— I wish I could have more time with him. Our collaboration had been a good run. Without him, this film wouldn't have been possible.

This seems like a good time to talk about your sense of Leslie in general. People I know have always been curious about him. What did you make of him?
— What impressed me most about Leslie was that since we first met, he always referred to himself as A Legend. "Kar Wai," he'd say, "do you think I am A Legend?" At first I thought it was a joke but then I knew he meant it. He'd say, "Don't call me Leslie, call me The Legend." Laughs. And he was really obsessed with the idea. "I'm going to be A Legend," he would say. "I have to be A Legend." I didn't know that he would go so far as to take his own life.

Why did he want to be a legend?
— He wanted to be remembered. He always told me that his biggest idol was a Japanese actress and singer, Momoe Yama-guchi. She started as a teen idol and was mostly in romantic love stories. She played the Juliet character in her films, and her husband [Tomokazu Miura] was the Romeo. But she was a much bigger star than he was. Then at her peak, she married, retired, and never came back—never made another public appearance. She remains as a housewife and just takes care of her family. For Leslie, that was what he meant by a legend.

He'd say, "I have to quit and retire at my peak. I don't want to see the downside. I don't want to age."

He was already incredibly famous. Why would that matter to him?
— Leslie was not a very secure person. He needed to be loved, he needed attention, he enjoyed applause. He needed to be in the spotlight. He didn't have a hard childhood, but the early stage of his career was very tough. He was always being laughed at or being rejected. He was very unhappy then.

From the outside, he seems so obviously a star that it's hard to believe that people wouldn't see that.
— He was a bit ahead of his time. For the general public, it was, "You're too much." He was over the top. I knew him when he wasn't that popular. He was mostly in TV shows then. Like Maggie, he could be both modern and classic. That's why his performance had a very wide range, from Ashes of Time to Farewell My Concubine.

And you cast him as the Westernized guy in Days of Being Wild.
— He was perfect for the role.

And great at playing amoral.
— He was a romantic. But he was very thoughtful and always caring about other people. That's why we were all so upset that night he committed suicide. At the lowest point of my career, after Days of Being Wild, he was there to support me. Working with him was one of the highlights of my career.

Let me finish up with *Happy Together*. Its Chinese title, *Chun gwong cha* sit, means something like "Spring Light Piercing In." That was Chinese title they'd put on Antonioni's *Blow-Up*. Did you know that at the time?
— Of course I knew. I liked that title even though it was not what the original title meant. It added a touch of sensuality to the film.

Is there a hint of something risque to it?
— There is. It refers to something romantic being exposed. If a woman is taking a shower without closing the curtain and people look inside, that's the term. The term "spring" in Chinese always refers to sensuality or sexuality, so if you spoke of a porno movie you could say it was "a spring movie."

It's funny to me that you took so long writing the film Because when I think of *Happy Together*, I think of the apartment, the waterfall, Leslie in his leather jacket, and Tony's looks of unhappiness. I remember behavior. The line I remember best is one the one Tony says into Chang Chen's tape recorder—and we don't hear it.
— I take that as a compliment. In fact, the best lines are the lines that don't stand out. They are not personal statements, and they must flow from the character.
   You have to understand that I came out of television, which is all about lines and plots. But is cinema is not about lines and plots. It's about behavior. You learn more about a person from the way he behaves than from what he says. Because words can be lies. Tony's character talks like he's a nice guy but he keeps Leslie's passport.

You began our chat by saying that this was a film you were partly making in response to '97. And the movie came out in Hong Kong one month before the handover. Can you explain the politics to me?
— We opened the picture with Leslie saying "Let's start all over again." And during the film, Tony is trying to reach out to his father for reconciliation with his family and eventually the film ends, more or less, with the waterfall. In Chinese, a waterfall is always a symbol of things being united because all waters flow into the sea. I had been asked "What do think about the handover" many times—before, during, and even after the film. *Happy Together* is my answer.

Well, Chris's shot of the waterfall is incredibly beautiful but there's some darkness to it. The whole is so powerful it's slightly sinister.
— I went to the waterfall and was totally overwhelmed. It was so powerful that you felt it was going to suck you in. It's beyond positive or negative. It's an overwhelming convergence. I remember when we put the film together—William was cutting it—I placed this broadcast footage of Deng Xiaoping after the waterfall, and William looked at me and said, "Is it too sensitive?" *Laughs*. I knew what he meant.
   All of a sudden the film carried a political message. Deng was instrumental to the handover of Hong Kong; without him, it might be a very different scenario. We called the film *Happy Together* because at that point none of us knew what was going to happen after the handover. The title was supposed to be a question instead of an answer. But one thing's for sure, the pre-'97 Hong Kong was gone, and that's why we never saw Tony return to Hong Kong. The film ends and we don't know where he goes.

225

#227

229

ﻮ ﻦﻮﻦ

D Q2 leslie5-l せゆ叱ट

00 25

several set.

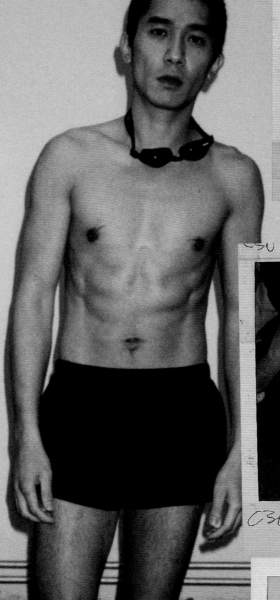

C30 ঢ/曖2 6ते Er passport

B.A. Zero Degree

... in a land of zero degree
with neither east nor west,
has neither day nor night,
which is neither cold nor warm...

A film by KWAN PUN-LEUNG and AMOS LEE

B   Produced by WONG KAR-WAI

C   Featuring: LETICIA YEN (Production Secretary)
      AILI MENG-TEN CHIN (Continuity)
      LAURITA LAM (Translator)
      HSIAO-TAO (Actress)
      Mr Mak (Boss of Chungking Restaurant)

ﷻﻮﺾﻣ-A27C

IT1999 Block

leslie (3) Tropicoz saucer
王 bench   の㊉⑩ leslie 阅车
shirt
Blue pants   Tony 坐ょ長①
Jacket sunglass ⊙⊙

231

B.b. Zero Degree

... in a land of zero degree
with neither east nor west,
has neither day nor night,
which is neither cold nor warm...

A Film by CHAN PUN-LEUNG and AMOS LEE

Produced by WONG KAR-WAI

C   Featuring:LETICIA YEN (Production Secretary)
AILI MENG-YEN CHEN (Continuity)
LAURITA LIN (Translator)
HSIAO YAI (Actress)
Mr MAN (Boss of Central Restaurant)

(C)1999 Block 2 Pictures

Well, we know he doesn't turn up in the America of *My Blueberry Nights*, which you made after *2046*. It was your first English-language film.
— I know you hate it.

I don't hate it. It's just my least favorite. How did you come to make it?
— Ever since *Chungking Express*, there had been offers for me to make an English language film. From time to time my agent or a producer would send me a script: "Do you want to do this?" Most of them weren't very interesting. Whenever I read a script, my first question usually would be, "Who is going to play it?" At some point, a producer asked me if I wanted to make a film with Nicole Kidman. I said yes and a meeting was set up. I met Nicole at the Beverly Hills Hotel and she was very graceful. She understood my process and asked only essential questions. I told her vaguely about the idea—a Russian immigrant in Shanghai after the revolution goes to New York to seek revenge on the Russian aristocrat who murdered her father during the revolution. I needed a title, so I said it would be *The Lady from Shanghai*, which is, of course, a famous movie title. Orson Welles was in a phone booth talking to his producer who asked the title of his next film. He didn't have one at that point, but he saw a pulp novel at a nearby newsstand and borrowed its title—*The Lady from Shanghai*. I did the same thing.

Nicole liked the idea and said, "Yes." With her attached to the picture, we pre-sold the project to Studio Canal with only the working title and a brief outline with only five words: "A dangerous woman in danger." Soon after I went to New York for 6 months doing research on its early Russian immigrants, and spent most of my time at the New York Public Library looking up stories that I could use.

You like researching things.
— Esther always says that making films is only an excuse for me to do the research. *Laughs.* I really enjoy the process. You get paid for learning.

So you worked for six months in New York.
— I also went to Moscow and St. Petersburg. Somehow, the schedule with Nicole never worked out and the project had to be delayed.

Couldn't it be resuscitated? Surely it doesn't have to be Nicole.
— I need the inspiration of a face. Nicole was perfect for the role. After all these years, my experience has been that a script works best when you know who is going to play it while writing it. It's a tailor-made process. To have someone else means the project is back to zero.

Some directors hire a talented screenwriter, cast the best people they can get, shoot the script. Do you envy directors who do that?
— Isn't that what exactly I've been doing? *Laughs.*

Seriously. Do you wish you could do that?
— Yes.

Really? Do you think your films would be as interesting if you did it that way?
— I don't know. It would be different. The only worry is that, even if I had the best script in front of me, a script is only as good as it is. You have to make adjustments during the shooting. Maybe at the end, there's only 30% left from the original.

30% with you maybe, but I can't believe that about everybody. But back to those Blueberry Nights.
— So I was in New York without any idea when Nicole would be available for the film. I was told it could be next year, or the year after. One day, my producing partner asked if I wanted to meet Norah Jones, who had just released her first album. I found her voice very attractive. So we had a drink at the Mercer Hotel and she was very charming. Afterwards I thought, "This is the face I want to make a film with," and asked her manager if she would be interested in doing one. Her answer was she'd never made a film before but why not? So we met again and I showed her my short film— *In the Mood for Love 2001*, which was originally the first chapter of *In the Mood for Love*. I said, "What if this story happens in New York, and the girl is someone like you?" That was how we started the project.

What is it in her face that called to you?
— She has music in her eyes. Before shooting, Darius Khonji [who shot *My Blueberry Nights*] asked, "I want to spend one or two days with the actress because I have to study her face

and do lighting tests." I said, "Forget it, just focus on her eyes." *Laughs*. We pre-sold the film to Studio Canal, and they were worried that she'd never acted before. I said, "It's okay. I've worked with singers and she'll be fine." On our first night, I asked her, "Are you nervous?" And she said, "Yes, I'm nervous," She had been curious about who was going to play her guy, Jeremy. Now, the guy was standing right in front of her, I still remember the first shot she had with him. She said, "I'm with Jude Law?!"

I talked to him shortly after he shot the film. He really liked doing it.
— Jude was extremely charming. He knew it was the first film for Norah and was really helpful. In fact, the film was a challenge for Norah. We were supposed to shoot the film in eight weeks in four different cities across the country, each city for two weeks. Which meant she had a new co-star once every two weeks. So she spent ten days with Natalie Portman, ten days with Rachel Weisz and David Strathairn, and four weeks with Jude Law. Things kept changing. The dynamic was always different. She picked up a certain rhythm with Jude, then had to pick up a very different rhythm with Natalie, and then with Rachel. I was surprised to see how into it she was. Norah didn't see this as a vacation for herself. She worked hard all the way through it.

And making it even harder, this is not a realistic film. You appeared to be shooting the film as different kinds of mythic tropes, if I may use the word.
— My plan was to do a road movie, and each city where we stopped was supposed to be a tribute to an American film that I wish I could have made. I intended to make the film my love letter to American Cinema. So I picked two films that I really liked, *A Streetcar Named Desire* and *The Cincinnati Kid*. I shot the first one in Memphis with Rachel Weisz and David Strathairn, and the second one in Vegas and a town nearby, Ely, Nevada, with Natalie Portman playing a gambler. I even dyed her hair blonde as a tribute to Steve McQueen!

Can I briefly ask you here about your attraction to Tennessee Williams. You have Brigitte Lin doing a bit of Blanche DuBois in *Chungking Express*, and in this one you do a whole riff on him with Rachel Weisz.
— Leslie's pick-up line about the bird without wings in *Days of Being Wild* also comes from his play *Orpheus Descending*. Tennessee Williams is my favorite American playwright. At one point, I even planned to adapt *A Streetcar Named Desire* into Chinese and had Gong Li to play Blanche and Jiang Wen to play Stanley!

I'm slightly surprised by that.
— What I like about Williams is that he is raw. His works can be angry, desperate, but they are never cold. You can feel the heat, the pain, the wisdom. I don't like things crystal clear. I like messy warmth.

Is that why you also like Fassbinder?
— I love Fassbinder. I know you once said you found him cold, but I find him hot and real.

I remember when I was shooting *Days of Being Wild*, the scene of Maggie waiting at the phone both. The shot was on the mid-level of Hong Kong, on a slope, and I asked Patrick [Tam] how he would shoot it. And he said, "I would see it this way. This location is like a Hell to her because she's in a very miserable condition. She's trapped with all these emotions and she's disillusioned and disappointed and hates herself. It's Hell. I would set up a shot like this"—*WKW raises his hand to indicate a camera shooting from above*—to show that she's trapped in an inferno." It was very inspiring. I would never have analyzed the scene like that. The only problem I had was that I didn't agree with his angle. It's the same thing with Edward Yang. I think the way they see people is from the top. They are looking at people like this—*WKW raises his hand in the same way*—and I don't agree with that. I enjoy watching films when we're at the same level as the characters. And I don't enjoy films where I'm looking up at a person, either. I enjoy watching films where we are all equal and we have sympathy with the characters.

Getting back to the North American highway, you really do seem drawn to road movies.
— First of all, on a road movie you don't have to build sets, which with William could take months. *Laughs*. He only needs to dress up things. It works better for him if he doesn't have to start from scratch. And as I said before, a screenplay is a map. Whether it's from one room to another, or from one street to another, or one city to another, or even from one period to another, the difference is only the scale. It is also a map of the emotional ups and downs of the characters. To make a film is like doing a road movie on these "maps."

It's also a *spirit*. It doesn't matter where you start, what matters is where you land. Along the way, there are hundreds of options and you can easily lose track of your orientation. Like a bird, you fly as far as you can until you drop. I've made all my films in that spirit. Compared to my other "road movies," *My Blueberry Nights* was a much shorter trip—we shot the whole film in 12 weeks. Though most of the crew were Americans who worked mainly on Hollywood productions, we made the film in the same spirit as we did in our previous films in Hong Kong. I always reminded my team, "We're not making a Hollywood film here. We are actually shooting a Hong Kong production, only in English."

Was the language difficult for you?
— Yes, it was. It was very frustrating because I couldn't make modifications or line changes as easily as I did in my Chinese language films. It took away my wings. It took away my authority.

Watching the film, one feels that. You've had worse receptions—like when nobody talked to you after *Days of Being Wild*.

But I'm curious, were you startled by the negative reaction to *My Blueberry Nights*?
— I have seen worse. The only thing that surprised me was that most of the time people rejected the film even before they saw it. They would say, "So, you're doing Hollywood films now." And I could sense that for them it seemed like a betrayal because people had seen me as an independent filmmaker who worked outside of the Hollywood system. The interviews would begin, "What was your experience shooting in Hollywood?" or "So you want to be a Hollywood director." Even though I insisted that the film was actually a Hong Kong production made in America, the tone was already set. The film opened Cannes Festival that year and the reception wasn't terrible. People were very polite after the screening, and polite is not the reaction that a filmmaker would want from the audience after his film. It's even worse than angry because at least the film would be controversial if it makes the audience angry. *Laughs*. When I saw your face after the screening with that polite smile, I immediately knew it wasn't working.

Even now I still remember going to you in the Palais after the Cannes screening and telling you what I thought was wrong with it. I always thought it was very impressive of you to listen so calmly. Oliver Stone might've punched me.
— Once you know that something isn't working, you have to ask why. Like Bruce Lee once said about his technique: accepting rejection as it comes is part of the process of gaining acceptance. I don't have the habit of punching people. I just punch myself.

I think that English language critics were especially harsh on it.
— Most of them normally meet my films through subtitles, and as good as those might be, they'd give me the benefit of the doubt. But once it's in their language, it became a different game. When I went to Russia to support *The Grandmaster*, they kept asking me about *Blueberry Nights*. I wondered, "Why are you so interested in this film?" and they said, "It's your most successful film here." *Laughs*. So that's the magic of distance. I told them, "Maybe if I made a film in Russian, you would like it less."

And then there was the problem of the title. Almost everyone I've met thinks that blueberry pie thing was cloyingly cute.
— The funny thing is that I actually hate blueberry pie; I find it too sweet. On our first night of shooting, I asked Norah to choose, from all the pies that we'd prepared, which was her least favorite? She pointed at the blueberry pie. The reason we called the film *My Blueberry Nights* was not for the purpose of being sweet. It was about something the girl wanted to forget.

237

NORTH, SOUTH, EAST AND WEST

I want to talk about two films that came out nearly 20 years apart: your third picture, *Ashes of Time*, in 1994, and your most recent one, *The Grandmaster*. They're both about martial arts. We've already talked about the business reasons for making *Ashes of Time*. What about the artistic ones? Do you actually like martial arts stories?

— Very much. These two films actually represent two different aspects of the genre: *wu shu* and *wuxia*. Films like *The Grandmaster* are usually referred as *wu shu* films, or *kung fu* films; most of them are based on actual historical figures or Chinese martial arts legends. Their action scenes are more realistic and highlight traditional techniques. On the other side are *wuxia* films, which are usually based on novels and fictional characters. Those are purely fantasies.

Like most *wuxia* films, *Ashes of Time* originated from a very popular martial arts novel, *The Eagle Shooting Heroes*, written by Louis Cha. The term "martial arts novel" first appeared about a century ago. The genre reached its peak shortly after, during the first civil war. It was a chaotic time then and people wanted to read about heroes. There was a revival in the '50s, when immigrants flooded into Hong Kong. Among them was Louis Cha, who was born into a prestigious Zhejiang family that had ancestral ties to the Manchu court. He worked for a while as an editor at a local newspaper, had no martial arts in his background, and mainly wrote film reviews. Then a duel between two *kung fu* masters completely changed his life.

What happened?

— It was like a film: A young master was offended by a northern *tai chi* master 30 years his senior, so he challenged him. Despite the age difference, the older master accepted. They announced the match and it became a huge event, because in those days, a challenge like that was a matter of life and death. Since it was illegal in Hong Kong to fight in public, the showdown was held in Macau. Few people were actually allowed to witness the contest, but almost every newspaper covered it. In the end, the fight lasted only two rounds due to injury. And the official result? No winner, no loser, not even a draw! Martial arts became the talk of the town.

Cha's boss saw the opportunity and ordered both him and his colleague Chen Wentong, who would write under the pseudonym Liang Yusheng, to start producing serialized stories for the paper. Their first columns that year were instant hits, driving the paper's circulation way up. The stories were later grouped and published as novels, which led to radio shows and eventually screen adaptations. Over the next 17 years, Cha wrote 15 books which sold millions of copies, of which *The Eagle Shooting Heroes* was the most popular. It's his *The Lord of the Rings*.

And this influenced you to make *Ashes of Time*?

— Martial arts was so popular, it was in every kind of media and surrounded me—even the writer living next door wrote those stories! The big martial arts epics had their time, but that didn't last very long. The success of Bruce Lee's films basically kicked the genre to the side and producers began to make *kung fu* films instead, because they cost much less.

Years later, Tsui Hark's *Swordsman II* came out and the genre became hot again. When Jeff Lau and I decided to make a martial art-epic as our first production, we chose *The Tales of the Eagle Shooting Heroes* because it was the most popular martial arts novel ever. I knew it was going to be very challenging and I took it as a once-in-a-lifetime chance. I thought, "If this is the only martial arts film I ever make, it better have everything I know about the genre. It's going to be my *Encyclopedia of Wuxia*."

Well, the original *Ashes of Time* was very challenging to watch! When it first came out, I found the story baffling. The time jumped around and so did the story—all those characters, all those episodes. But when I saw the reworked version, *Ashes of Time Redux*, a few years ago, it all made sense to me.

— That doesn't surprise me at all—you actually watched the *same* film *twice*. Besides, you were much older the second time around! That makes you a more suitable audience. *Laughs*. Your reaction the first time is also understandable. First of all, it didn't follow the convention of a martial arts film, and without knowing the original novel, it would have been hard to follow the story. And then the characters are similar enough—I only realized it when we screened in Venice that year—that for most of the western audience, even the jury, it was hard telling people apart. Some of them even thought all the male characters were one person and got Maggie confused with other actresses. *Laughs*. They didn't have a clue what was going on.

But in terms of structure, the *Redux* is almost the same as the original except for a minor reordering of some sequences. The biggest difference is actually in sound and music, which always bugged me after our first release. As I mentioned in our earlier talk, we were supposed to release *Ashes of Time* two months after *Chungking Express*. Post-production for *Ashes* became so rushed that most of the sound effects of the film sounded "canned" and because of the budget, Frankie [Chan] had to score it with synthesizers. When I watched the film in Venice, I felt it deserved better. It felt incomplete the way it was and that haunted me for years. In 2008, we revised the edit and re-recorded the whole score in Beijing with an orchestra and Yo-Yo Ma playing cello for the main theme. We released the picture under the title *Ashes of Time Redux*. I finally felt relieved—and audiences felt it made more sense.

Well, you are juggling all these characters—like Brigitte Lin, as a male-female split personality, and battle-loving Jacky Cheung—and also filtering them through the mind of Leslie Cheung's cynical assassin, Ouyang Feng.

— The original novel has even more characters, but of among them all, Ouyang Feng, played by Leslie Cheung, is my favorite. Together with his main rival, Huang Yao shi, played by Tony Leung Kar-fei, they are the most colorful characters in the book. Most of the time, they are referred to as Poisonous West and Malicious East. Both are tragic characters, but in two extremes. West is like fire—he was brought up in the Gobi desert and his tragedy is falling in love with the woman who eventually marries his brother. East is like ice—he is always alone and for unknown reasons remains in exile on a distant island that's full of cherry blossoms.

While East was always Louis Cha's most beloved character, West is the most notorious and the most misinterpreted. In Cha's work, one often finds traces of Shakespeare and Ouyang Feng reminds me of King Lear, while East is basically a sadistic hypocrite who enjoys blinding his pupils and cutting off their limbs. In the book, both characters are already in their seventies, so instead of adapting the book as it was, I took these characters and decided to invent their younger days. I wanted to know what made them so tragic. Why did they wind up like that? By using Ouyang Feng as the narrator, I wanted to share my interpretation of these characters with the audience. I wanted to do justice to West.

So, in a way, you flipped everything—like making Voldemort the hero and Harry Potter the villain.
— It was a bold adaptation. When we released the film, audiences were shocked. It was the most controversial film of the year. Louis Cha wasn't happy with my version. I've never met him, but given the fact that he wouldn't grant us the rights to any of his other books, he couldn't have been amused. *Laughs.*

I can understand that. I can understand why the audience might not like it.
— Yes, of course. They wanted to see the original *The Eagle Shooting Heroes*. But a novel is different from a film. I meant no offense to Louis Cha, but the novel had already been adapted repeatedly into film and TV, so what was the point in making it again exactly as it was? Unlike all the versions that came before us, *Ashes of Time* actually talked about love in the form of a martial arts epic. With the structure of the seasons in a lunar calendar, we told the emotional entanglements of four couples: Ouyang Feng thought he was rejected by the woman that he loved; Huang was rejected by the same woman; the blind swordsman killed himself because his wife betrayed him; and the princess became schizophrenic because the man she loved rejected her. As the story went further, the entanglement was less like a cycle than a deepening spiral. The only exception was the character Hung Chi, who first rejected his wife because he wanted to be the best swordsman and then realized that it was better to be the best swordsman and a good husband at the same time. Only when Ouyang Feng realized at the end that his so-called romantic rejection was just his personal illusion did he finally become free.

And you also added a lot of things. Like that wine that makes people forget—that sounds more like Wong Kar Wai than Louis Cha.
— Yes, the wine is not in the original novel. I invented it. And Maggie's character is only briefly mentioned in the book. She doesn't carry the same weight as in the film where she seems to be the cause of all sorts of troubles. And the character of

Tony [Leung Chiu Wai]...

The swordsman who's going blind...
— He was also something that I invented, too.

As an epic, it's weird in a lot of ways.
— It's my interpretation—in a lot of ways. *Laughs.*

When I think of an epic, I think of Kurosawa getting thousands of extras in color-coded costumes and making them wait around for the perfect cloud formation in order to shoot. Yours isn't that, even if you sometimes echo *Seven Samurai*.
— Your definition of an epic is more about scale, and mine is more about depth. The film begins with the Buddhist Canon, "The flag is still. The wind is calm. It is the heart of man that is in turmoil." The Canon comes from The Sixth Patriarch's Dharma Jewel Platform Sutra. The story of the scripture is about a high monk asking his pupil what he sees on the road. The pupil replies that he sees a flag flying because it is windy that day. The monk answers with this Canon. It means people believe what they want to believe, not what actually is, and this he calls obsession. In the film, each of the characters is trapped by something that obsesses him—lost love, betrayal, combat. The film is about obsession which is a matter of the *heart*. To me, there is nothing more epic that an *odyssey* of hearts.

Watching it today, it looks less like an epic than an experimental film or an LSD trip—the most far out martial arts film I've ever seen. The colors are surreal, the landscape looks like a foreign planet.
— Originally, Jeff and I planned to do two films back to back with the same cast because we could share the same sets. We thought it was cost effective and William started building the first one. My film would be a martial arts epic and his a comedy— a parody of mine. Ever since *Days of Being Wild*, people often parodied my films and audiences found them funny. So Jeff and I thought, why not do it ourselves? Mine was supposed to come out first, but when we looked at the way William was constructing the set—as if it was a place you could actually live in—we decided to make the parody first because the set would take him months to finish! *Laughs.* I wrote the script and Jeff directed. We called it *Eagle Shooting Heroes* and managed to complete it in a month. The film was released, but there was nothing for it to mock because the set for my epic had only just been completed! By then, reforms in China made it possible to shoot on the mainland. That's when we decided to shoot the rest of film there. We thought it would be relatively less expensive. In the original novel, Ouyang Feng is based in the Gobi Desert, so why not go out to the desert and use Mother Nature? "Let's go to Dunhuang!"

The oasis in the Gobi?
— Yes. I thought, "It's all there. There are caves and we won't even have to build a set." But it wasn't that easy. We had to co-produce with a state-controlled studio and recent reforms

247

meant hiring a lot more staff, even if there wasn't anything for them to do. The size of our crew suddenly expanded from 50 to almost 200 by the time we set foot in the Gobi! And by then, we were told that the caves were protected sites—shooting in Dunhuang would be impossible. So we took our crew of 200 and started looking for caves in the desert! *Laughs.*

One day, we arrived in Yulin. It was basically just one street and one guest house. It was already very late and they had nothing to eat, but there was a noodle shop across the street. And even that was so small, there was only one lightbulb, probably the sort of place my brother would have gone when he was in the countryside. The residents told us there was a tourist park two miles away, filled with caves. We went there the next morning and loved it. We told them we would be back in a month.

When we came back four weeks later, the noodle shop had become a small restaurant, and there was a very elegant, good-looking woman running it. We called her the "Carina Lau of Yulin." We wound up spending six months in this town and everybody ate there. Over that time, we watched it eventually grow bigger and bigger. First, it got refrigerators, then air conditioning, then televisions. And they started selling cigarettes, not only local brands, but also American ones the crew was used to. It was our oasis of many shops in one.

At the end of the shoot, when we were saying goodbye, the woman said, "When you guys leave, I'll go back to the hotel." And I said, "Why? Won't you run this restaurant?" And she said, "No, I'm the doctor at the guesthouse."

What?
— Yes, she was their in-house doctor. But when she and her husband knew a film production was coming to town, they invested a bit of money in the noodle shop and turned it into a restaurant. And in only six months, the place was totally different—AC, beer, Coca-Cola, anything you wanted. Our crew's contribution to their business helped prove that Deng Xiaoping's reforms were on the right track. It was at this point that I realized how soon China would become modernized.

Obviously, you found remarkable places to shoot out there.
— It was a far cry from a set in Hong Kong. In the desert, the color is always changing. Morning, afternoon, evening, in the rain—the look is always different. We spent hours in the desert looking for spots to set our cameras. My action choreographer, Sammo Hung, and I would go walking, but no matter where we went it was always the same place. I used that in the film as a line for Ouyang Feng, "You think things will be much different when you get past this peak, but when you get there, it is just the same."

But getting the actors there was terrible. Today, there are direct flights from Hong Kong to Yulin. Back then, it was a nightmare. You had to fly to Xian, then wait until the next day for the next flight—on a classic propeller plane—to Yulin. And there was only one flight each day, with frequent delays and cancellations. There were eight major stars and I was like their travel agent, trying to bring them in. Every morning we'd just wait at the airport, "Are they coming?" "No they're not coming today because of the weather." So we'd go back. And because it was so primitive there and they thought it was safer to fly in together, these stars would only come in groups. All at once, I had all the stars in this small town, but I could only shoot one of their stories at a time. So I split the crew. I had Sammo shoot the action scenes and I told William, "You know Brigitte so well, you deal with her."

Wouldn't these stars, at some level, like doing this? It was a big adventure.
— Later, yes, but not at that point.

Your fight sequences are not normal fight sequences—they're highly stylized.
— When you talk about *wuxia*, it's not about realism. The characters' powers are larger than life. They can knock mountain peaks off just with their hands. It was fun to disregard gravity for a while. We shot the opening sequence and the Brigitte scenes with a lot of wired-shots and explosions. But soon I found that boring. Also, working with the explosives guys in China then was a bit too risky because most of them were actually military servicemen. So we preferred to do the rest of the action scenes without them.

There are two major fight scenes in the film. In one, Jacky Cheung's blade is supposed to be very fast, so I shot it using the same step-printing method from *As Tears Go By* to give you the sense of the knife's speed. In the other, I told Sammo that I wanted a classic Japanese samurai battle, one man against a hundred. Tony's blind swordsman is so tired, physically and emotionally, that for him, it's suicide. I shot that in slow motion so that we feel how very, very heavy his sword has become. This was my approach with all the action. In each case, I wanted to do more than just stimulate the audience with sensation. I wanted the fighting to be an extension of the characters' emotions. It's like what we were saying about love scenes earlier—if you don't find an angle, if you don't reveal an emotion or an idea, it's just boring.

But for a huge part of the audience, the point of martial arts action scenes is to be stimulated with sensation. Your approach is like doing Spider-Man, who everybody knows can swing between buildings, then not showing him swinging.
— If I'm going to do *Spider-Man*, I'll want to see him swing. And I'll devote all my energy to find ways to make that swing seem as interesting and significant as possible. That's exactly what I did in *Ashes of Time*, I tried to make all the action scenes as interesting and significant as possible. You could complain that the film should have more action, but you can't really say the action we had was not interesting. I wanted people to go, "Well, I never thought about it like this."

Is that how they reacted?
— When the film premiered in Hong Kong, I was still in Venice. After the screening, I called and they told me, "People walked out

very quietly. They weren't screaming but they were very quiet."

So they didn't much like it in Hong Kong.
— The difference in reactions was extreme. Some loved it, but the general audience who came wanting a *Wuxia* picture hated it. It did okay at the box-office because of the cast, but the result was far from what we'd expected. A few months later, it became my first film to be released in China and was instantly embraced by the young audience there. Even today, it's still considered a classic in China when you talk about martial arts films.

Why do you think they liked it and the Hong Kong audience didn't?
— The education system in China wasn't as westernized as Hong Kong's. Therefore, generally speaking, the Chinese audience was actually more grounded in traditional arts and literature. Many of them got into the context of the film. They appreciated the adaptation because it was so different from the martial arts pictures that they usually saw. The film earned itself a big following among college students then. Most of them had watched the film more than once, mostly at so-called study rooms, where someone charged a few yuan for a screening of a video off of a tape or disc, which was usually a pirated copy of very bad quality. They enjoyed it so much that some even refused to watch the *Redux* version even though the quality is so much better than the original! They told me they preferred the film as it was because it reminded them of their younger days. That's the power of memory—for them, the flag is still and the wind is calm. And *Ashes of Time* shall always look lousy. *Laughs.*

I'm sure they'd never seen a martial arts film like it. The look of the film is almost wholly original. And it's got all these gorgeous things, like the spinning birdcage in Brigitte Lin's scenes. Was that hard to do?
— In the film, Brigitte had a birdcage with her as a prop, so when she finished her shot, it was just hanging around the set. Light came across it and Chris said, "Hey, that looks nice." So I said, "Let's make it like her entrance. Every time Brigitte comes to Leslie's place, we'll have the shadow of the birdcage to announce her entrance." Chris spent hours doing experiments to learn how to work with this birdcage. And the effect is very Hitchcock. This woman is schizophrenic, and in these scenes, I feel like you can hear the music of Bernard Herrmann.

This is one of those cases where Chris was very creative.
— Painting with light is his talent, but you'd never rely on him to shoot a car chase, an explosion, or an action scene because he doesn't take them seriously—he thinks they're silly. If a car goes by very fast, he'll miss it—"It happened?" If there's an explosion, he'll pan away. If you're shooting an action scene, you'd best not knock on his door.
     Didn't I ever tell you the story about *Ashes of Time*?

No.
— It's the last day of our shoot in the desert, the final scene: We have to burn the set of Leslie's place before dawn and shoot at

daybreak. Because it takes an hour to get to the location and we still have to set up three cameras and the master shot on a crane, we have to leave at 3 a.m. That night, we hold a wrap dinner at the restaurant with the doctor and all the local crew to say goodbye. There's mutton and strong Chinese vodka. It is a very emotional scene.

At 11 p.m., Jacky [Pang] calls and says, "We're in trouble." I go to Chris's room. He's passed out, a totally drunken mess. We have to wake him, wash him, put him in the car by 3, and drive to the set. He's supposed to be the A-camera, but he's sitting slumped over, with the camera pressed against his forehead. I say, "Chris, are you okay?" He says, "I'm okay." And then daylight starts coming up. We get out all the gasoline, Leslie's ready, and one of the cameras is on the crane. And we begin to roll. And then I hear Chris say, "I have to take a shit!" and he rushes into the bushes.

He does it quick and comes back. Then he says, "I'll do C-camera." Camera C was much easier to operate than A, which was to cover Leslie's close-up. So we switch and put him on the crane. But this isn't a modern crane, it's a military crane, controlled by the guy who's on it. So we start burning the set and Leslie starts walking out. The cameras are rolling, but we notice the crane panning toward the fire. "Chris!" I'm yelling, "Chris!!"

It's a disaster. Chris's camera doesn't catch the wide shot because he is too close to the fire. It was already daytime, and we've lost the right light, so the fire won't look so spectacular. I'm extremely pissed and so is Chris—he's mad at himself. We release him from the crane and he just sits there saying, "What happened?" I say, "It's gone. We're fucked. There's no coverage!" And then as the set is still burning, Chris suddenly takes off his clothes, covers himself with water, and grabs a camera. "I have to do some cutaways for you!" He runs in and starts shooting. He just felt so bad, so guilty. "I have to get some shots. There must be something." There he was, half drunk and totally naked in front of the whole crew. *Laughs.* That's Chris.

A lot of directors might have fired him, but you worked with him on several more films.
— I knew he didn't mean it. Like I said before, Chris can always *surprise* you, whether you like it or not. *Laughs.* Chris is family and sometimes your family needs its space.

I'm betting that's true of William [Chang], too—but a different kind of space.
— William is the one who'd created the look for *Swordsman*. And that meant he was the one who had set the trend for the rest of the period martial arts pieces that followed. On *Ashes*

of Time, William decided, "I want to do it differently." He spent weeks, months, creating the fabrics—like Issey Miyake. He said, "In those days, people traveled. They didn't have time to dress up or iron, so everything has to be wrinkled, shabby, and one-tone. And the hair should be long and cover their faces." I still remember the Taiwanese investors complaining about the characters—"They all look the same!" *Laughs*. But in Japan and Korea, people loved it. It became a new model. Suddenly you found many of those martial arts productions for Korea looked like Issey Miyake. Their reference was *Ashes of Time*.

What did you think when William told you his idea for the costumes and hair?
— I said, "Do it." I knew it was risky, but at least the film would look different. I thought those two words, "Let's try."

But you knew your whole company was riding on this film.
— But I also knew that William had a point. We were very ambitious then. We went so far that we even shot some of our stills showing our characters in costume, but with a cigarette or a can of cola in their hands—we intended to use them for our promotional campaign. Our investors freaked out. They thought we were crazy. *Laughs*. Those were our days of being wild.

And for the audience perhaps a bit unsettling. Martial arts pictures are supposed to have heroes. Who's the truest hero in this? Tony? Jacky? Leslie?
— There's no winner. All the characters are under the spell of their time and space. The only thing that remains unchanged is the desert. So they are just passengers. The desert at the end echoes the Canon I mentioned earlier: form itself is emptiness; emptiness itself is form; so, too, are feelings, cognitions, formations, and consciousness.

It's funny about *Ashes of Time*—both versions. In the West, it's almost as if it doesn't really exist as one of your films. But when I talk to Chinese people in places like Singapore, they often say it's one of their favorites. Are you happy with it?
— Some people may find the film experimental, but in fact, *Ashes of Time* was my most accomplished and well-structured picture so far, at least from my perspective. The film actually captured all the things I understand and appreciate about the genre. It really does say, "This is my *Encyclopedia of Wuxia*." Also, it was the first film that I produced and our first production in China. It marked the beginning of my career as a producer/director and kicked off our company's productions for the next 25 years. It proved to us that we could find the balance between making films and filmmaking, and that we could produce those films as creatively as they should be produced.

On a personal level, it also marked the most agonizing moment in my career, as I had to deal with two films at the same time, except now Esther was seven months pregnant. I still remember the night I was at the office working on *Ashes* and Esther called. She felt pain in her belly. I sent her to the hospital and the doctor said she had to stay in bed or we would lose our baby. I was totally devastated. In the following weeks, between going to the hospital to take care of Esther, working post-production for *Ashes* at the office and the sound studio, and doing interviews for the overseas release of *Chungking*, it was like I was a zombie. Ten days before I went to Venice, our son was born. Esther had been in the hospital for almost two months. She was very brave and did exactly what our doctor told her to because she wanted to make sure our child would arrive safely. All through my career, people have called me a master of procrastination. My son's arrival a month early proved them wrong and started a new chapter. In my memory, that autumn in 1994 was the brightest. It capped a great run that was well worth the struggle.

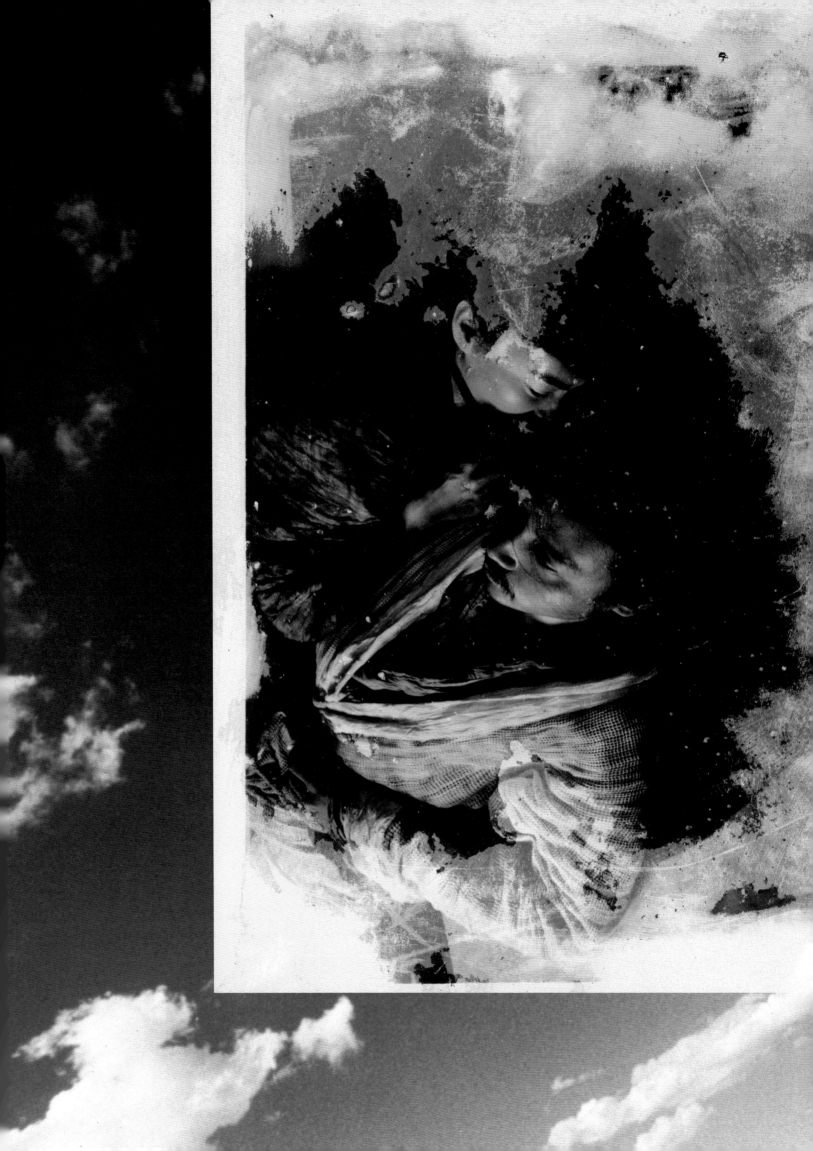

255

257

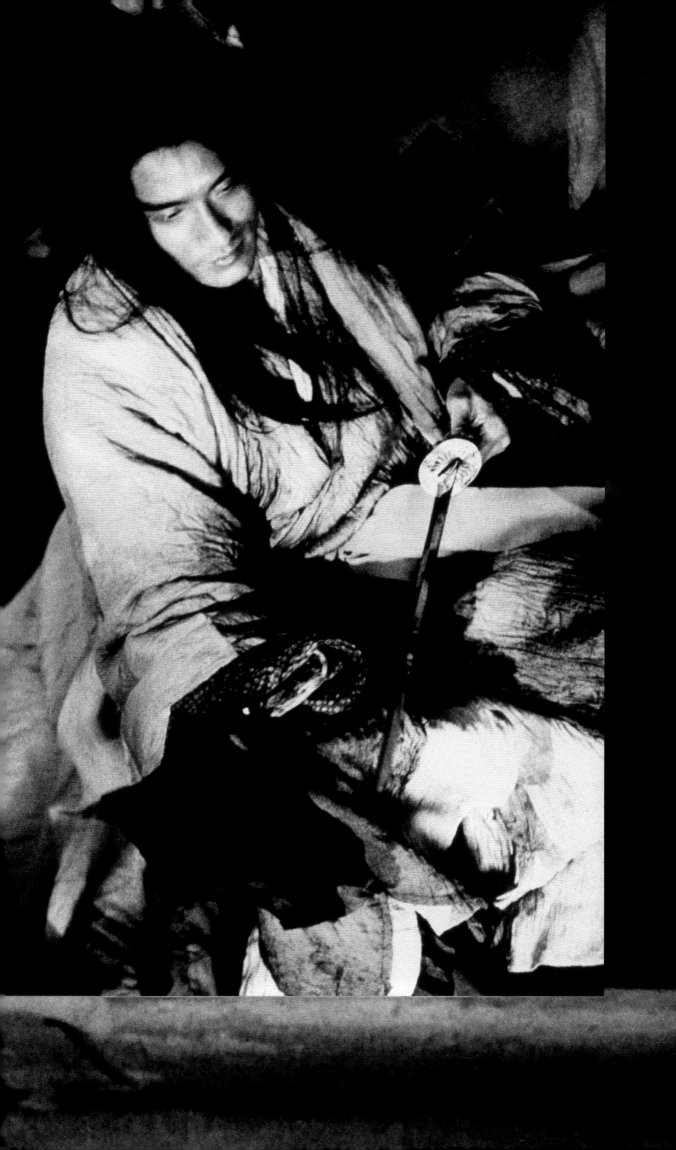

If *Ashes of Time* was an encyclopedia, what does that make *The Grandmaster*?

— I didn't think I would make another martial arts film until I saw Bruce Lee's face on the cover of an Argentinean magazine in 1996. It was during *Happy Together*, while we were shooting Leslie cruising around Constitución railway station. I walked around while Chris set the lights. There were many newspaper stands around, but two of the magazine covers caught my eye: One had the face of Mao, another had Bruce Lee. Mao was as popular as Che in Latin America, so that wasn't unusual, but why Bruce Lee, who had been gone for over 20 years?

I was a big fan of Lee when I was a kid, but I never thought about making a film about him. There had been so many Bruce Lee lookalikes after he passed away that the actual Bruce Lee seemed almost faded from memory. But the magazine cover brought him back to me. Stories about him, either true or false, had been told over and over, yet they never showed him as who he was. Instead of making a film about him, I wanted to make a film about his mentor, the man who created Bruce Lee. And that person was Ip Man.

Before I announced the film, Ip Man was only known to the martial arts world, not to the general public. Since then, of course, several movies have been made about him, but at the time, he was still a mysterious figure. I began doing research and managed to set up a meeting with his eldest son, Ip Chun, when I came back from Argentina. At the end of it, he showed me a Super-8 clip that had only circulated among his father's students.

In the clip, Ip Man was doing forms—the legendary *wing chun* Wooden Man form. And it was shot only three days before he died! According to the son, his father said, "I want to do a demonstration." So they took a camera and shot it. In the film, Ip Man looked very ill and shrunken. He wore only pajama pants and an undershirt and performed the demonstration very slowly. At one point, he stopped. It seemed that he had forgotten something or was in too much pain to carry on. The moment intrigued me and I found it very moving. Why was he trying to record this? What was he trying to prove? Later on, I learned that Bruce Lee had offered him a lot of money to film a demonstration. "I know you are poor," Bruce Lee said, "so I'll give you an apartment if you let me record it." And Ip Man refused. "If I do it for you, I'll have to do it for all my students."

Did you ever find out why he made that recording?

— It was about legacy. That's something very important about martial arts tradition: It has always been about how to pass on the torch. There hadn't been a martial arts film that addressed this point, so I wanted to make it. Originally, I wanted to set the story entirely in Hong Kong and focus on his days here. I knew many martial art masters from the schools around us when I was a kid. Though they were once well-known in China, when they had arrived, they could only teach their art in shabby, converted flats, just as Ip Man did. But to show the full spectrum of this kind of life and the tradition of Chinese martial arts, I felt I had to go beyond the streets of Hong Kong.

To China.

— In the long history of Chinese martial arts, there were many legends, but only a few were regarded as grandmasters. It's also hard to understand the story of Ip Man without knowing his background and the difference between North and South, in terms of culture and martial arts techniques. I first visited his hometown in Foshan and from there I travelled across the country over the next 3 years and met more than 100 masters. I started to realize that the film that I was going to do would be more challenging than telling the story of one man. Instead, it would be about the journey of a grandmaster, what it means and what it takes for a person to become one. That's why I called the film, *The Grandmaster*. And I learned something: "grandmaster" is the recognition you receive years and years after you are gone. And you must have a legacy. So you can't call Bruce Lee a grandmaster because he doesn't have a martial arts legacy, but he was exceptional. Maybe his legacy lives more in cinema, not martial arts.

Because of *The Grandmaster*, I found myself at the other end of the martial arts genre. It was a totally different experience than *Ashes of Time*, a brand new start, my first *wu shu* film.

You tell his story in a way that many in the West found puzzling. It's very oblique and arcane.
— How so?

You leave out so much of what would be in a conventional biopic: Ip Man's relationship to his family, his feelings about what's happening, how he survives historical crises. There are huge historical leaps and no real dramatic arc. Zhang Ziyi's character, Gong Erh, has one but your hero doesn't.
— I couldn't find those incidents in his life and I didn't want to invent them. All the other films about him are basically dramas invented for a movie. And I didn't want to create a superhero and make him do some heroic act. That wasn't the point. I wanted to show Ip Man as he was. His heroism is not about accomplishing an amazing feat. It is about the strength of the spirit, which is at the root of all martial arts.

But you wouldn't have to make him a hero. You could simply show his ordinary life or capture a few years of his life.
— I know what you mean, but then it would be a different approach. Here is this grandmaster. You're thinking, "Ok, he's good. Show us *how* good." But my angle is, "He's good, but what qualifies him to be a grandmaster?" That's why, in the film, we define the three different stages of being a grandmaster through the life of Ip Man: becoming yourself; understanding the challenge of others; and finally, sharing with the world. And that's the stage about legacy. Ip Man opens the film with, "Kung fu: two words. Horizontal. Vertical. Make a mistake, horizontal. Stay standing and you win." At the end of the film, Ziyi's character is horizontal. She cannot share, even though she wants to. Ip Man can and did.

Well, she's much more earthbound. The way Tony [Leung] plays him, he buries his feelings. But she is susceptible to emotion.
— Yes, we had more freedom with her character because—she's fictional. *Laughs.* Gong Er is a composite of many real characters, truly amazing women who defied the limits that society of that period put on them. She has all the qualities, but she doesn't reach the end like Ip Man. He completed the whole path.

Filmmakers often make movies that are disguised versions of their own story. Do you identify with Ip Man?
— No, I didn't have the luxury of an idle youth. *Laughs.* I identify more with Gong Er.

Why?
— Because she was stubborn. She never let go. *Laughs.*

She's also complex. He's almost too pure to be true.
— She was always the underdog. She lived by her own rules even when times were against her

And you think of yourself as an underdog?
— When I was younger, yes. But now it would be very ungrateful for me to say that. I have been lucky enough to have both a home family and a creative one. I can't complain. Ip Man was born into privilege, but by the end of his life, he had nothing except his martial arts.

But for him that's cosmically important. You could almost say he has everything.
— I'm not so sure. If you'd told Ip Man at the end of his life, "You can have all the things in the world, but you can't have martial

arts," I'm not sure he would've turned you down.

In your film he would. He doesn't seem to care about much else. Not even his family. Which leads me to something I've been wanting to discuss—the lack of families in your movies.
— What do you mean?

I mean that you're a very familial guy. You're a happily married man who loves his son. You've called Chris Doyle "family." People say you run your business like a family.
— That makes me a very bad businessman, if I run it like a family. *Laughs*.

But your work has almost no families.
— In *Days of Being Wild*, there's the mother and the son.

But they're grownups—and the mother's given the son away.
— First of all, I seldom have kids in my films because we shoot mostly at night, which is usually not good for them and most of the time it serves only the vanity of their parents—the kids usually hate it. Besides, directing children is tricky. In *The Grandmaster*, we had a short sequence of young Gong Er at different ages, first when she was three and then when she was six, all shot during the day. Working with the six-year-old was delightful, but we weren't as lucky with the other one. The three-year-old could only work for one hour before having to go to the trailer for a nap. Everyone else had to wait quietly for hours in the snow until she was ready again. It wasn't very enjoyable. So I usually avoid including children unless absolutely necessary.

Really, that's a reason?
— Yes. Showing a family without kids is like having a Chinese restaurant that doesn't serve rice. Of course, it's also related to the way I was brought up, very "minimal." I have no idea what life is like with bigger families and their large gatherings. That's not my game. It would take me forever to stage a big gathering if I had to, and eventually it would still look fake. *Laughs*. Some directors like Ozu or Hou Hsiao-hsien are really good at doing it. When you watch Hou's *City of Sadness*, you go, "Wow, he really knows all of them by heart. He even knows stories of the people in the background."

And that would be too hard for you to do?
— Yes, I may understand the characters well, but the dynamics between them when they're together would look wrong. Normally, when we do a street scene, I'm the one rehearsing with the extras—"You do this there and then do that"—or inventing a line or two to keep them occupied, because I already have the full picture of that street in my head. I create all the activity on that street to make it feel real, instead of having the assistant director do it or letting the extras walk by with no purpose. It's exhausting, but I enjoy it.
      Families are different. For instance, I enjoyed shooting the sequence of Gong Er and her father because I knew well the dynamic between them, but I didn't do as well when shooting

the Ip Man household lunch with his wife, kids, relatives, and servants; it didn't turn out as interesting as it should have and I didn't have the faintest idea what to do about it. So I had to cut it out of the picture. I was out of my element. *Laughs*.

Your mention of Ziyi makes me wonder about working with her a second time. It must've been easier.
— It was a remarkable journey for her, with many ups and downs. First, she trained hard every day for six months in the heat of the South. Then in the North, she had four months of shooting nights in minus-30 degree temperatures. And a month of that was fighting. To make things worse, she was going through a personal crisis at the same time. It was a very difficult situation for her. Her career was very fragile then—and delicate for us. People were calling, "Are you really sure you want to use this actress?" There was a lot of pressure on both her and the production, but I said, "It's her."

Well, she's a terrific actress.
— She is also a very tough woman. During the crisis, she was caught among lawsuits, lawyers, paparazzi, agents and her PR team, but she never asked for a day off. Until one morning, Ling Lucas [Zhang's manager] said, "Can you come to Ziyi's room? She's so depressed. She wants to talk to you." And when I went to her room, Ziyi's lips were like this—*WKW makes a duck-face*—from the stress. She looked at me and asked, "I think I would look okay if we cover only the long shots tonight. What do you think?" I had to convince her to take the night off. She was almost unbreakable. *Laughs*. Finally, doctors were sent in and advised rest, so we had to stop shooting for a while.

Why didn't you replace her at that point?
— Because no one could play the part better than her. I wrote the part for her and to an extent based it on her; her spirit during the crisis inspired me. Gong Er is made out of Ziyi and I knew she would be exceptional in the part. I never had to explain her character's emotions. When she read her lines for her final scene, she cried. *The Grandmaster* really helped her because it proved that she is the finest actress of her generation. That's her personal victory.

Why did you set her character so very far North? She's fictional, after all.
— I like the idea of the North, and I had always dreamed of going to Manchuria. It's very different from Shanghai. People are much rougher and the architecture has a Russian and Japanese influence—most of the things are massive. But the people are real. The place is full of history, and because it's so cold, nobody shoots in Manchuria. There are a lot of amazing locations no one has ever put into a movie. It's like a virgin land. Very photogenic. The first scene we did in Manchuria was at this remote temple built 1700 years ago—all the statues are still there. I was stunned by it, but because it's so remote there's no tourism. There's no such thing as a five star hotel, there's no four star hotel, no three star hotel—only an ancient guesthouse

where the entire crew stayed and no one took showers because the only hot water came from one kettle. We spent three days there and in the temple; it was extra cold because the floor is stone. You felt your whole body go *oooooh*. But it was worth it.

Would you rather go somewhere like Manchuria or a great city like, oh, Venice?

— A place like Manchuria. I prefer to be an explorer rather than a tourist; a tourist goes where anyone goes, and an explorer goes where people haven't been. It's always a plus to capture something unique and precious on film, but the exposure may kill it. Ten years after *In the Mood for Love*, the stone wall where Tony spoke his secret is full of graffiti from fans from all over the world. So when we filmed at the temple, I hoped it wouldn't be ruined, but I knew it would become a hot tourist spot. And it did.

Let me bring up a practical point. You're making a film about martial arts geniuses, but neither Tony Leung nor Zhang Ziyi are *kung fu* pros. The other Ip Man films have people who can actually do this stuff.

— Usually action stars can't act, though there are exceptions. Besides, if you want to be true to the character of Ip Man, you have to realize that he didn't look like a fighter. He was an aristocrat who could have been a painter or an actor in Cantonese opera. The last thing he looked like was a fighter. So when I had to decide who was going to play the role, I had to choose: either find a good martial artist and showcase the *kung fu* or take a good actor, focus on the drama, and forget about *kung fu*. I wanted both—to have a great actor like Tony play Ip Man and do all the action himself. That would be an *event*. So why not?

Who found doing it easier—Tony or Ziyi?

— Ziyi, of course. She has a dancer's training, so her body is more flexible and has a better sense of rhythm. Also, her techniques have more dramatic moves and turns. Ip Man did *wing chun*, which is actually very boring because it's so plain and nondescript. It's always one-two-three—and that's it. That made it even harder for Tony because mastering the details in each small motion took more than just time. It was movement he would have to live with!

It's always hard to depict a physical skill.

— When I look at *Raging Bull*, even though DeNiro was not trained as a boxer, he plays a believable one. And it's not just the punching. You need to look like a boxer even when you're not boxing. That's why I needed Tony to go through the training. He and Ziyi had to look, behave, sit, and talk like martial artists. Tony was always very laid back in his previous films. He always sits like this—*WKW slouches down in his chair*. And in real life he's like this—*He slouches even lower*. But he had to learn to be strict and formal. After *The Grandmaster*, he's like this—*WKW sits up ramrod straight*.

If we're at the point of talking about Tony Leung's posture, it's time to ask you about your relationship to him. He's been in

seven of your movies, more than anybody.

— I remember our first meeting. It was in a Japanese restaurant. This was before *Days of Being Wild*. We drank a lot, and Tony had just bought this fancy new racing car, and he said, "I'm going to drop you off." Then he drove so fast we almost had an accident. It was almost like the younger days of Robert Downey, Jr. Tony would always stay up late, get drunk, not show up—but everybody thought he was really talented. He worked with Patrick on a film, and there was a long line of dialogue. Patrick told Tony, "Speak the line as it is written." Tony said, "What do you mean, 'as it is written?' Even the exclamation mark?" And Patrick said, "Yes." There was a lot of drama between them. He was a real headache then. *Laughs*.

But you knew he was talented.

— Yes, he was the most talented of all the newcomers. He was young and hip, and girls were crazy about him. He was very proud of his performances on TV, where he got his fame and where everybody acts with their face. But he didn't realize acting for the big screen was a very different game. His first day on *Days of Being Wild* was in his character's apartment inside the infamous Kowloon walled city. He was supposed to bite into an apple, then say hi to Maggie. The close-up was easy, but the long shot took 32 takes to get right. It was a record for him. He was completely shocked and left without a word after the shoot. Carina told me later that her [then] boyfriend was very upset that I was so harsh on him and he didn't know what I wanted. It hurt his pride and he couldn't sleep that night! *Laughs*. So I invited Tony over to see the day's rushes and showed him the difference in each take. I said, "You have to change your way of acting in feature films. It's a different medium. It's not only about your face. It's about your whole *presence*. You have to act with your whole body."

Did you train him?

— I only refocused him. In fact, the last scene of *Days of Being Wild* was a challenge for him—no lines, no close-ups, only action—it was about the gambler's *presence*. I said, "So you're playing this gambler, right, but do you know what's inside his pockets?" His eyebrows went up. And I laid all these things on the table. "Because he's going out to a poker game, there will be two decks of cards"—which is what I learned from professional gamblers—"and there will be money. Your money will not be just money. It will be in a roll because you are very precise with it. And there will be coins and cigarettes, two packs, because you are going to spend the whole night there. And then there's a comb." "Why a comb?" he asked me. "Because in those days professional gamblers didn't go to clubs. They would go to people's weddings because weddings are always full of people playing mahjong and poker before and after dinner. Professional gamblers would pretend to be a guest, sit down and do their tricks to win money, and then go to the next restaurant. So he has to look very decent." I told Tony, "This man is very meticulous and has to look well-dressed. His fingers are clean."

And then I said, "We'll do all this in one shot as your character's preparation. You have to put all these things in your pocket in

the order you prefer." That way, he had to be aware of his whole body. So then Tony started doing it, and I told him, "No. You have to show me that it's something mechanical, that you do it every day." So he came back and he did it, and I said, "Okay, but *now* you have to do it with the cigarette dangling from your mouth." And he carried it out very nicely. From that point on, in every movie after that, Tony would ask me, "What are in my pockets?"

So when you were doing *In the Mood for Love* —
— He was careful. He asked, "Will I have a pack of cigarettes?" And I said, "No, you're going to have a cigarette case. And you'll have a lighter, not a match." And a fountain pen. Because in those days, writers were careful with their fountain pens, because if you were running out of money and had a really nice one, like a Parker 61, you could give it to the restaurant and say, "I'll come back tomorrow to pay." The pen cost like 30 dollars, enough to buy you dinner in case of emergency.

These physical details are very, very important. Sometimes when it gets hot, most actors will take off their costumes and change into something comfortable. And I will tell them, "Don't do that." An actor should be like Tony when we shot *Grandmaster*'s opening rain scene. He had to wear this cheongsam and, because it was so cold and wet, he had a diving suit inside. But he never sat down. There was six inches of water in the street and he spent the whole night standing there with his hands behind his back. This amazed the actors from China and they asked him, "Why?" "Because," Tony said, "if I take off my clothes it will be trouble to dress me again. And if I sit down, the costume will be wrinkled. And I won't do that." It was very impressive, and he became a model for the other actors.

Tony's really grown into his years.
— Yes, you can easily tell. Like a good whiskey, he's become a more refined version of himself. He has gained a lot of respect from his co-stars. Wang Qingxiang, the actor who plays Zhang Ziyi's father, is a seasoned actor and has done many big films, but when he was in the same scene with Tony, he became very anxious. He said, "I don't understand why, but I feel nervous. I've forgotten all my lines. I don't understand."

And why was that?
— Because everybody thinks Tony is the best actor of his generation. They are dealing with the champ. Usually, he is quite relaxed on set, but the actor next to him would be nervous, no matter how experienced. And yet Tony's never intimidating. He's always helpful and very supportive to his co-stars—one of the nicest guys to work with in the world.

Together, we've made seven films so far. Some have highlighted significant milestones. When we started *In the Mood for Love*, I told him, "In this film, you are going to be a grown-up man, a married man. That's something you've never done before. This is the goodbye to your teen idol days." And this changed him; from that point on, he was transformed into a more established actor. With *The Grandmaster*, I told him, "This time you are at a different stage of your life, and by the end, you will have played

the master in his seventies." Originally we planned to make him look that old with special make-up, but I hated how it looked. So eventually we ended the film in his fifties, on the day when Ip Man founded his martial school in Hong Kong. I still remember that morning when we shot that scene. It was Christmas Day, and there he was, an old Ip Man watching the kids practice. At the end, I told Tony, "Now you are a classic.

The Grandmaster is a movie about legacy. What drives Ip Man is something different than material success. I wondered if your film might be asserting the value of Chinese traditions that are getting lost in its rush to riches. Is that reasonable?
— When I did all those interviews with martial arts masters, usually ended by asking what *kung fu* means, and most of them said, "Time." For them, it's a marriage. If you're going to be good, *kung fu* takes up all your time. These days, it is very hard to focus on one thing only. When somebody says they are going to spend decades doing something, we think that's a turn-off, right? But this is a commitment that people used to be proud of. "I spent half my life making this kind of teapot—and that's it." There was a time when such dedication was admired.

What is even more remarkable about those old masters is how they retained their legacies during the chaos of the New Republic and then after '49, when having these kinds of martial arts families was discouraged by the government..

William Chang sounds a bit like one of those people. He's your most important collaborator—you've been through the wars together. Do you ever argue?
— Never. Even though, in a way, he's even more of a pain in the ass than me. I've worked with other set designers or production designers who can't answer the question, "What is the *point* of this space?" William knows what I mean. He'll ask me, "How are you going to see it?" And I say, "I'm going to see it from here." He instantly gets it. Some people are just architects or interior designers. They create a set that's beautiful, but not shootable—because it's not cinematic. William has the best qualities of a production designer: good eyes, great taste, and he is *cinematic*. He always works to make things happen, to have magic occur at the next corner. Whenever we're on the verge of the impossible, William is the one who says, "Don't worry."

Of course, some of your films had crises because he can be slow.
— I would say we are both perfectionists. The difference is he knows me better than I do, and so his schedule is usually more realistic. I'll say, "We can do it in four weeks," and he'll say, "We can do it in four months." I'll say, "Impossible, we don't have four months."

And still you don't argue?
— That's [producer] Jacky [Pang]'s job. *Laughs.* Then I'll say, "OK. I'll only shoot this corridor and this room. Will this take you a month?" And he will say, "It's possible, but I know you won't shoot only the room and the corridor. I will prepare another

corridor for you." That drives Jacky crazy, and I'll say, "William, no. Just this corridor and this room." He will come back with, "No, I know you will need this staircase." And by the time he's finished, there will be a staircase. *Laughs.*

And will you need it?
— Yes, of course! It's more interesting to have a room and a staircase than just a room. And since it's done, why waste it? The fact is, I can live without the staircase, but he knows I am not going to refuse it when it's there, and the set will look better. He's *very* good at selling his sets! *Laughs.* In *The Grandmaster*, he spent months with his tailors in their workshops, experimenting to get seven levels of black in different fabrics for one scene.

Did you notice they were different when shooting the scene?
— No. He told me only when the film was done. *Laughs.*

I'm curious. Everyone agrees that William is brilliant, and he seems to have all the talents it would take to be a director. Why do you think he hasn't done that?
— You'd have to ask him. I guess he knows directors have to deal with a big box of so many other parts. He prefers things simple.

Like the business part, which you're actually good at.
— You've said before that I'm a "shrewd businessman." I'm not. If I was shrewd, I would have thought up the idea of Evian water and let other people work putting it in bottles.

I mean that you're a shrewd businessman in the way Godard is—you get to keep doing what you want. You're one of the few directors anywhere who not only makes exactly the films he wants to make, but has been able to do it for nearly 30 years. And you still own the rights to 8 of your 10 films.
— Conventional wisdom in this business is, "Take the money and run." If I was a good businessman, I wouldn't own those pictures. Spielberg doesn't own most of his pictures. He lets other people own them and have them make money for him. Besides, running a film company for lots of years doesn't necessarily mean I'm good at business. The guy who owns the bakery down the street may have done for it for even longer, but that doesn't mean he's shrewd. You would say, "He makes good cakes." Why am I different?

I'm not insulting you. I'm saying that in the one of the world's trickiest businesses, you've have the business acumen to keep yourself independent. Most people who make movies like you do, don't own their own movies.
— And they have much happier lives! At least they don't have to pay for maintenance. *Laughs.*

That's a different issue. You're doing what you've chosen to do.
— It took me many years to make these pictures, but to me they're more than just films. I'm the person who knows them best and I want to take good care of them. Keeping them is more spiritual than financial.

Finally, my last question, what are you going to do next?
— I don't know. I have been working almost non-stop since my first film. I want to take a break. I want to spend more time with my family, especially with Esther, as our son is now in college. When I took up the Met exhibition and this book, I thought they were going to be easy, but I soon realized that I was even busier than before! More invitations started to come in: proposals to do retrospectives and awards for lifetime achievement. I guess I have to get myself back to work very soon. *Laughs.*

I never thought this book was going to be easy.

— It's like what Wim Wenders said about his book. Our challenge is "an attempted description of an indescribable career." Personally, I don't like to talk about my films because there was never a good reason to. As they say about jazz, "If you have to ask, you'll never get it." I don't like talking about myself, either. There is even less point in that. Taking almost 30 years of filmmaking and turning it into 300 pages is a scary thought.

I took up this book for only one reason. My son turns 21 this year, leaving his boyhood behind to become a man. For him and for his youth, WKW has meant absence. At first, it was because I wanted to protect him from the spectacle my career has created, but later, he wanted to avoid the attention. Out of all my films, he has only seen *The Grandmaster* and *In the Mood for Love*. When he sees the rest, I hope he can greet them as siblings because, in a way, they all grew up together. And like all siblings, some did well, some did poorly, while a few found glory later on. Perhaps this book will tell him what all these siblings have in common. They were all born of the words one must say in order to do anything bold in life: Yes, let's try.

詠春嫡系旅港師徒合影 一九五二年春月日

PP.80-81
- John Powers (left) in conversation with Wong Kar Wai.

P.82
- Knutsford Terrace, where Wong Kar Wai grew up, has long been known for its lively nightlife.

P.84
- Director Wong Kar Wai.

P.87   Clockwise from top right to left
- Wong Kar Wai, age 11, and his parents.
- Wong's father in Kobe after a typhoon damaged his ship. The crew had to remain there for 2 months during the repairs.
- The Hong Kong entry permit for Wong and his mother.
- Wong's father working as a seaman.
- Wong's mother when she was young in pre-1949 Shanghai.

P.88
- Wong's father outside Bayside nightclub.

P.89   Right to left
- The Beatles' Hong Kong press conference at Bayside nightclub.
- Bayside nightclub, interior.

P.91
- Wong Kar Wai, at 20, holding his first camera—a Nikkormat FT3.

P.92
- Wong's older brother and sister in their youth.

P.95
- An old map of Hong Kong

SIX CONVERSATIONS

CONVERSATION ONE

PP.80-81
- John Powers (left) in conversation with Wong Kar Wai.

P.82
- Knutsford Terrace, where Wong Kar Wai grew up, has long been known for its lively nightlife.

P.84
- Director Wong Kar Wai.

P.87   Clockwise from top right to left
- Wong Kar Wai, age 11, and his parents.
- Wong's father in Kobe after a typhoon damaged his ship. The crew had to remain there for 2 months during the repairs.

P.154
- Wong Kar Wai directing Gong Li on the set of 2046.

P.155
- Film strip from In the Mood for Love 2001 featuring Maggie Cheung.

PP.156-157
- Menu created by Wong for In the Mood for Love.

P.157
- In The Mood For Love: Maggie Cheung's Su Li-zhen out buying wonton.
- In The Mood For Love: An atmospheric 1960's with Tony Leung.
- Su Li-zhen (Maggie Cheung) and Chow Mo-wan (Tony Leung) in In the Mood for Love.

P.159   Clockwise from Top Right
- The many faces of Maggie Cheung from In The Mood For Love. Even in plain fabric, says designer William Chang, "Maggie made everything look gorgeous."
- Wong Kar Wai on the set of In the Mood for Love.
- Wong Kar Wai (middle) directing Maggie Cheung (left) and Tony Leung (right) on location at Goldfinch Restaurant.

P.160
- Silhouette of Chow Mo-wan (Tony Leung) in the street.

P.162
- Chow Mo-wan whispers his secret into a hole at Angkor Wat.

P.163
- In the Mood for Love was the first production to shoot at Angor Wat for many decades.

PP.164-165
- In the Mood for Love: A luminous Maggie Cheung.

PP.166-167
- Maggie Cheung and Tony Leung from In the Mood for Love.

PP.168-169
- Collage of Legs and torsos, Tony Leung and Maggie Cheung from In the Mood for Love.

PP.170-171
- A collage of images from In the Mood for Love with Wong Kar Wai, Tony Leung and Maggie Cheung.

PP.172-173
- A collage of images from In the Mood for Love—many outtakes with Maggie Cheung and Tony Leung

PP.174-175
- A collage of images from In the Mood for Love with Tony Leung and Maggie Cheung.

PP.176-177
- A collage of images from In the Mood for Love with Maggie Cheung and Tony Leung

PP.178-179
- A collage of image from In the Mood for Love with Maggie Cheung and Tony Leung

P.180   Top to Bottom
- From 2046: Tony Leung shows the many faces of Chow Mo-wan.

P.182
- Wong Kar Wai directing Ziyi Zhang in 2046.

P.183
- From 2046: A vulnerable Bai Ling (Ziyi Zhang) on Christmas Eve.

P.184   Top to bottom
- Left: Chang Chen as the smitten apprentice tailor, Zhang, in Eros.
- Right: Out-take from Eros between Zhang (Chang Chen) and Miss Hua (GongLi)
Top to Bottom:
- The long, long, long kiss in 2046 that left Tony Leung amazed with Gong Li.
- Gong Li as a mysterious gambler, also named Su Li-zhen , in 2046.

PP.186-187
- The radiant Su Li-chen as played by Gong Li in 2046.

PP.188-189   Top to bottom
- From 2046, Ziyi Zhang as Bai Ling.
- From 2046, a kiss between Tak (Takuya Kimura) and Android (Faye Wong).

PP.190-191
- A collage of images from 2046 with Faye Wong, Tony Leung, Wang Sum and Gong Li.

PP.192-193
- A collage of images from 2046 with Ziyi Zhang. Tony Leung, Takuya Kimura, Faye Wong and Gong Li.

PP.194-195
- A collage of images from 2046 with Faye Wong, Ziyi Zhang and Tony Leung.

PP.196-197
- A collage of images from 2046 with Ziyi Zhang, Tony Leung, Gong Li and Maggie Cheung.

PP.198-199
- A collage of images from 2046 with Ziyi Zhang, Maggie Cheung, Tony Leung and Faye Wong.

PP.200-201
- Behind- the-scene images from 2046 with Gong Li, Wong Kar Wai. Chris Doyle,
- William Chang, and Tony Leung

PP.202-203
- From Eros, (left) outakes with Gong Li and (right) Gong Li with Chang Chen.

PP.204-205
- A collage of images from Eros with Gong Li and Chang Chen.

CONVERSATION FIVE

P.244
- Wong Kar Wai on the set of The Grandmaster.

P.247   Clockwise from top to bottom:
- Tony Leung as the blind swordsman in Ashes of Time—a character invented by Wong Kar Wai and not found in Louis Cha's original novel.
- From the set of The Eagles Shooting Heroes: happy moments amongst the cast and director
- Maggie Cheung (left) and director Jeff Lau.
- Jacky Cheung (left) and Joey Wang.

P.249   Top to bottom
- Action scenes from Ashes of Time.

P.250
- Brigitte Lin lying on a bed of red chilies in Ashes of Time.

P.251
- The final day of shooting Ashes of Time with Jacky Pang (in red cap on left) making victory sign, production manager Chen Pui Wah, Wong Kar Wai (also in cap), Esther Wong and Leslie Cheung holding sword. Ouyeng Feng's hide out burns in the background.

PP.252-253
- From Ashes of Time: the two faces of Ouyang Feng (Leslie Cheung), Wong's favorite character in Louis Cha's The Eagle Shooting Heroes.

PP.254-255
- From Ashes of Time: Brigitte Lin and Leslie Cheung (in black and white) and Tony Leung Ka Fai as Huang Yaoshi.

PP.256-257
- From Ashes of Time: Tony Leung and Joey Wang.

PP.258-259
- From Ashes of Time: Maggie Cheung and Tony Leung Ka Fai

PP.260-261
- A collage of images from Ashes of Time including polaroid of Brigitte Lin, Maggie Cheung, Leslie Cheung, Jacky Cheung,Tony Leung Ka Fai and Tony Leung and martial arts choreographer Sammo Hung in a chef's hat.

P.263   Top to bottom
- Ziyi Zhang as the beautiful dynamic figher Gong Er in The Grandmaster.
- Tony Leung as Ip Man, the true grandmaster in The Grandmaster.

P.267
- From The Grandmaster: Tony Leung displaying Ip Man's mastery of Wing Chun

P.269   Clockwise
- Production sketches of THE GOLDEN PAVILION by William Chang's team.
- William Chang on the set of The Grandmaster.

PP.270-271
- Wong Kar Wai on the set of The Grandmaster. Inset: holding his infant son, Qing

PP.272-273
- From The Grandmaster, Gong Er's father (Wang Qingxiang) practicing martial arts in the snow

PP.274-275
- A collage of images from The Grandmaster with Ziyi Zhang and Tony Leung.
- The picture of Tony Leung with the other masters that William Chang has dressed in different black fabrics

PP.276 -277
- A collage images from The Grandmaster with Ziyi Zhang (page 276) and Tony Leung (page 277)

PP.278 -279
- Ip Man (Tony Leung) with the two women in his life: his wife, played by Song Hye Kyo (page 278), and Ziyi Zhang as his rival (page 279)

PP.280-281
- A collage of images from The Grandmaster with Ziyi Zhang and Tony Leung

PP.282-283
- A collage of images from The Grandmaster with Tony Leung's street-fightin' Ip Man

PP.284-285
- Behind the scene images of Wong Kar Wai directing from The Grandmaster along with martial arts cheorographer Wo Ping Yuen and cinematographer Philippe Le Sourd

PP.287-289
Family album (clockwise from top middle right):
The Wongs at the 1997 Cannes Film Festival, Wong's first photo of his wife Esther, a family portrait in Argentina, Esther with son, Qing, in Argentina, Esther on location on the set of Ashes of Time, Wong's favorite portrait of his wife

PP.290-291
Family album (from top middle to left):
The Wongs at the 50th Golden Horse Film Awards; a portrait of Esther and son with elephant in Thailand taken by Wing Shya; Qing in 5th grade playing the Portugese adventurer Ponce de Leon in a photo taken by his dad; Qing playing the piano at the Steinway factory in Hamburg, Germany in 2011; the cast and crew of The Grandmaster (from left, producer Jacky Pang, Wong Kar Wai, Esther Wong, William Chang, Ziyi Zhang, Tony Leung, Philippe Le Sourd) at the 63rd Berlin International Film Festival in 2013; Esther Wong, Wong Kar Wai, Tony Leung, Chang Chen in Berlin; the key crew member at the 33rd Hong Kong Film Awards in 2014); Jury President Wong and Mrs. Wong at the 63rd Berlin International Film Festival in 2013

PP.292-293
- A portrait of the Wongs by Philippe Le Sourd taken at the 50th Golden Horse Awards

50s

1958   July
WKW born in Shanghai

60s

1963
WKW arrived in Hong Kong

70s

1978
WKW began his studies in
graphic design at the Hong Kong
Polytechnic

1979
WKW joined TVB as production
trainee

80s

1988
AS TEARS GO BY
Hong Kong release

1989
Married

90s

1990   December
DAYS OF BEING WILD
release in Hong Kong
●

1991
WKW set up Jet Tone Films
●

1994   August
Release of CHUNGKING
EXPRESS in Hong Kong
●

1994   September
WKW attended Venice Film
Festival with ASHES OF TIME
shown in Competition
●

WKW's son was born
●

1995   September
FALLEN ANGELS is released
●

1997   May
HAPPY TOGETHER
shown in Cannes Film Festival
where WKW received
Best Director Award
●

1997   July 1
Hong Kong Hangover
●

00s

2000   May
IN THE MOOD FOR LOVE
shown in Competition at
Cannes Film Festival
●

2004   May
2046 shown in Competition at
Cannes Film Festival
●

2004   August
EROS – THE HAND
shown out of Competition at
Venice Film Festival
●

2006   May
Cannes Film Festival President
of Jury
●

2007   May
MY BLUEBERRY NIGHTS
selected to open Cannes Film
Festival
●

2008   May
ASHES OF TIME REDUX
shown at the Cannes Film
Festival
●

10s

2013   February
THE GRANDMASTER opened
Berlin International
Film Festival And WKW served
as President of the Jury
●

2015   May
Artistic Director of CHINA:
THROUGH THE LOOKING GLASS
at the Metropololoiyian
Museum in New York city
●

ACKNOWLEDGMENTS

The authors wish to thank the following individuals for
agreeing to do interviews for this book:

ESTHER WONG (aka CHAN YE CHENG)
CHRIS DOYLE
JACKY PANG
WILLIAM CHANG SUK PING
TONY LEUNG CHIU-WAI
MATTHEW WEINER
JIMMY NGAI
ZHANG ZIYI

They also wish to thank the following individuals personally:

SANDI TAN
ANNA WINTOUR
VALERIE STEIKER
JON GLUCK
PHYLLIS MYERS
TERRY GROSS
MANOHLA DARGIS
BONNIE NADELL
LING LUCAS
DARREN LEUNG
MICHAEL J WERNER
CHARLOTTE YU
KRISTINE CHAN
SIMON GREEN
WINNIE LAU
JAMIE HO
KWAN PUN LEUNG
for his photo of *Days of Being Wild*
and
CHARLES MIERS / Rizzoli
ELLEN NIDY / Rizzoli
MINNIE WEISZ / Rizzoli

We also want to give our special thanks to

NORMAN WANG

without whom this book would never have been started—
or finished.

First published in the United States of America in 2016 by
Rizzoli International Publications, Inc.
300 Park Avenue South
New York, NY 10010
www.rizzoliusa.com

Photo of old Hong Kong on page 110 courtesy of Sing Tao Daily

Film stills of *As Tears Go By* and *Days of Being Wild* supplied by
Media Asia Film Distribution

Rizzoli Editors: Ellen Nidy and Minnie Weisz
Rizzoli Design Coordinator: Kayleigh Jankowski

2023 2024 2025 / 10 9
ISBN-13: 978-0-8478-4617-7

Library of Congress Control Number: 2015960032

Art Direction and Design: Wing Shya / commonrooom

Printed and bound in China

Distributed to the U.S. trade by Random House